Developing Java™ Entertainment Applets

Developing Java™ Entertainment Applets

· · · · · · · · · · · · · ·

JOHN WITHERS

· · · · · · · · · · · ·

WILEY COMPUTER PUBLISHING

JOHN WILEY & SONS, INC.

New York · Chichester · Weinheim · Brisbane · Singapore · Toronto

Executive Publisher: Katherine Schowalter
Editor: Tim Ryan
Assistant Editor: Pam Sobotka
Associate Managing Editor: Angela Murphy
Text Design & Composition: North Market Street Graphics

Designations used by companies to distinguish their products are often claimed as trademarks. In all instances where John Wiley & Sons, Inc. is aware of a claim, the product names appear in initial capital or ALL CAPITAL LETTERS. Readers, however, should contact the appropriate companies for more complete information regarding trademarks and registration.

Library of Congress Cataloging-in-Publication Data:

Withers, John. 1966–
Developing Java entertainment applets / John Withers.
    p.   cm.
Includes index.
ISBN 0-471-16506-9 (pbk. : alk. paper)
1. Java (Computer program language) I. Title.
    QA76.73.J38W58   1997
    794.8'15133—dc21   96-49129

CONTENTS

ACKNOWLEDGMENTS

Any book is a coordinated effort by a large group of people, and the author tends to hog credit that belongs to lots of other folks.

In just about every acknowledgment page ever written credit goes to the editorial team who helped put the book together. Few people outside of the publishing industry can really appreciate how much of the final product is due to the talent and skill of good editors as opposed to the semicoherent fever rantings the writer first produces. The editorial team for this book, Pam Sobotka and Tim Ryan, should get campaign medals for seeing this book to press in spite of my best efforts to screw it up.

Also due big thanks are R. J. Osborne and Andrew Swann. R.J. did a great job helping with the technical issues of creating and debugging the code for this book. And without Andy and his team from AcidWerks, Chapter 10, among others, would be pretty messed up.

Without Mark Tacchi's Gamelet Toolkit the book would have been much poorer. Mark's excellent work, which he gave to the Web development community for free in a fit of exceptional style and grace, provides a great example of how Java can be used to get the job done.

I also need to thank Universal Access Inc. (check out their Web site at http://blackjack.ua.com/images/sponsors/fox-ad.gif) for the use of the card images that we used to produce the card games in the book.

And, finally, thanks to the friends of Bill W. wherever you may be, but particularly in Huntington, WV. You know what for.

CHAPTER 1
• • • • • •
AN INTRODUCTION TO JAVA

There are probably six programmers left on the planet—possibly some guys doing COBOL maintenance deep in the bowels of mainframe hell—who haven't heard of Java. And depending on who you listen to, Java is everything from the latest fad to the final savior of the human race. Java will eliminate war, pestilence, and hunger in our lifetime! Java just might help us contact extraterrestrial life!

Obviously, the truth is a lot closer to the middle ground. While Java does embody a great idea and holds a great deal of promise, its long term impact and implementation depend on a number of factors. First, what is Java? *Java* is a serious, platform-independent, object-oriented programming language.

• • • • • • • • • • •
The Big Tricks

Java's foremost feature—and why many are hailing it as the greatest single idea since those little twisty things that hold garbage bags together—is its *platform independence.*

Compiled versus Interpreted

Traditionally, there are two ways of dealing with the difficult task of going from written code to running program. The first one we will deal with is interpretation. In an interpreted language a program called an *interpreter* is called to translate each line of your code and execute their instructions. Although the interpreter must always be in memory while your program is running, the system requirements of the interpreter are always going to slow down your program as it runs. In a compiled language, such as the C++ we are familiar with, your lines of instructions are converted using a program called a *compiler* into a binary file that will execute the machine instructions of your code directly on the processor of your machine and others like it. This means that your program runs without the interpreter in memory, and as such is much faster. The downside is that now your code is custom-tailored to run only on the processor type that you compiled it for. To make it run on other machines (called "porting" the code) can be anywhere from a fairly simple task of changing a few compiler switches to a nightmare of changing system calls and trying to figure out differences in architecture memory assignments. Java tries to take the best of both worlds to provide a reasonably fast program execution but get away from the machine dependency of a compiled language. Java does this by compiling a program into bytecodes.

A *bytecode* looks, acts, and smells amazingly like a machine code instruction for a processor, just as you would get in a compiled language. Actually that is exactly what is produced by a Java compile—a set of machine code instructions for a specific processor. However, the particular processor the Java bytecodes control isn't a real, physical chip such as the 80×86 or PowerPC series of chips, but is instead a virtual mock-up of a processor called the Java Virtual Machine (VM). The *Java Virtual Machine* is a simulation of a processor that is compiled for various different platforms. To make that a bit clearer, the VM is a program run on the target computer that pretends to be a processor. The VM looks to Java bytecodes in the same way a processor looks to real compiled code and will execute a compiled Java program.

However, since the Java Virtual Machine can be run on a number of different platforms and compiled Java bytecodes will always run on a VM without a problem, out of the smoke and mirrors of a virtual processor a very cool trick emerges: Java code will run like it is native to any processor that is running a Java VM. This makes Java a strong contender for the heavyweight belt in distributed computing environments where one application is required to bridge multiple platforms.

Although portability is the upside of the Java bytecode/virtual machine setup, the downside is speed. While Java isn't as slow as some of the clunkiest interpreted languages, it isn't exactly a barn burner, either. Expect Java applications to run only one tenth as rapidly as their C++ compiled counterparts, if that fast. While there are some great technologies in the wings that promise to speed Java compiled programs to nearly the speeds of their C++ competitors, those technologies weren't available at the time this book went to press.

Object-Oriented

The other critical point when dealing with Java comes from the fact that Java is one seriously object-oriented programming (OOP) language. With the exception of a few primitive types, *everything* in Java is an object. Programs themselves are just class instances. Every single thing in Java is built up from objects.

What is the point of this? Well, the largest benefit may be that you don't have to make an entire level of implementation decisions. There is no question of *if* you will implement a particular function using procedural or OOP methods; since everything in Java resides in a class or object, you aren't given an option.

At this point, a few programmers reading this book have started screaming: Objects often mean more than a little bit of trouble. Dealing with the heinous memory problems that often result from a slight mistake using objects often offsets the so called "wonders" of object-oriented programming techniques.

Well, as you will see in a few pages, Java has taken care of most of the ugly housekeeping chores that can turn OOP from a prince into a frog. As a matter of fact, Java has taken care from the ground up to be built in such a way as to let you concentrate on what you do best: hacking code. But before we go into some of the interesting features of the language, let's give a quick gander at the genesis of the language so that we can see how it got where it is today.

• • • • • • • • • • • • • • •
The Genesis of Java

Java started out as the control language of the toaster world. Well, maybe not literally, but awfully close.

In its original conception in the early 90s, Java was intended to run control software for consumer electronics. This might seem to be a fairly trivial task, but let us look for a moment at what is required in a toaster control language.

First, any language designed to control consumer electronic widgets needs to be small. Every kilobyte of memory added to a consumer device costs a few more cents. Now if you were just building one widget, that wouldn't be that big a deal. But across a production run of a few hundred thousand widgets, that few cents adds up to a big bonus for the suit in charge of the widget-building division. Hence, you want a small language.

Second, your new language needs to work across a wide range of processors. When the Widget Mk. II comes out, it is probably going to use the newest, fastest, cheapest microprocessor available. With C and C++ (or, real pain, assembler) porting custom code between processors can become a real headache.

Our new language should also be seriously robust. Our widgets exploding due to software malfunctions definitely isn't in the plan.

Enter James Gosling and his Sun team, who in 1990 started working on a new language designed to create software for smart home control. As such, it was expected to work across a wide variety of consumer devices such as phones, TVs, light controllers, and such widgets. Due to the whimsy of software design and corporate maneuvering, this project, as well as the next couple, assigned to the Java team (though in the early stages the project bore other names) ended up as vaporware. However, in the interim the Web phenomenon exploded.

Suddenly, here was a distributed environment running on multiple processors that just cried out for a native programming language to leverage the technology to its fullest. In 1995, Sun and Netscape Communications partnered to include the Java Virtual Machine in the Netscape Navigator browser.

In the short period of time since, Java has rapidly proliferated across the Web, as Websmiths and hackers see the utility of adding the power of Java to their pages and projects.

• • • • • • • • • •
The Features

Now let's take a look at some of the cool features that grow out of Java's roots and its basic orientation as an OOP Virtual Machine Interpreted language.

Distributed Computing

The thing that makes Java so hot right now is that its nature as a distributed language is perfect for use over the World Wide Web (WWW). Because Java code is platform independent (well, in practice it is restricted to machines that will run the Java VM), it can be served up by a server to run on a remote host.

In practice, this results in WWW servers sending *applets*—Java programs designed to be run by the virtual machine built into a Web browser—to individual browsers. This allows complex programs to be run on the host machines and not on the servers. Hence, unlike Common Gateway Interface (CGI) scripting, the work is being done by the surfer and not by the host. This allows more complex data manipulations to be performed for more users without bogging down the host machine.

Robust, Secure Implementation

Java creates a remarkably robust programming environment. There are a number of reasons for this. One is the simplicity of the language, which we will be dealing with in a moment. But another reason for the robust nature of the language lies in the compiled/interpreted system used to create and run Java programs.

When a Java program is initially created, it is run through javac, the Java compiler. At this time, many of the most heinous bugs in the code get routed out. But then Java has the additional step of being run in the Java VM.

The VM has only an isolated section of system memory allocated to it. Therefore, it keeps track to make sure that any problems in the Java code it runs stay inside the memory area allocated to the VM. This means that your code can't overwrite important locations in memory and start doing grievous harm to the underlying system. Just about the worst that can happen is that the VM will get crashed by a bad piece of code. However, the OS and machine underneath the VM won't be affected.

The VM also bestows another important gift—a reasonable degree of security. Because the Java bytecodes are dynamically interpreted by the VM, it has the ability to check the incoming instructions and see if they break any of the security rules posited by the Java specifications. In short, these mean that the Java code can use only the memory area allocated to the VM and the applet can't do any file access on the host machine. Further, the Java applet is limited in receiving information to getting files from the server source of the Java program (i.e., you can access files only on the same site where you hit the Java applet). While some aspects of this security specification tend to limit some of the natural development directions for Java, they provide a reasonable degree of security and the general expectation that when you download a Java applet from the Web, the worst it is going to do is bollix up your VM, which you can then close.

An important thing to remember here—as with all matters of computer security—is that anyone who believes in perfect security in an open networking environment should apply for a job with Santa's programming team. Nevertheless, Sun has been actively seeking ways to crack the security of their VM and has been responsive in rapidly producing updates to Java to close security holes that are discovered.

Multithreading

Java seriously enjoys multithreaded operation. While this statement is rather self-expiatory, we are going to examine it a bit more in-depth, since an amazing number of C++ coders haven't had enough cause to think deeply about multithreading and why it is important to them and their programs.

First, let's briefly examine what a thread is. At its simplest, a *thread* is a linear control sequence. In pseudocode, we might look at a thread as being the following:

```
Do A
Do B
Do C
Do D
```

This is a linear sequence of events requiring that the previous event be accomplished before the next event down the line is executed. This is all well and good in some circles and was pretty much accepted as the Way of things back in the bad old days of procedural programming technique.

However, let's say that we have a complex multiple input environment where we wish to perform some task. Then we start seeing the power of multithreaded programming. For an example, let's create a fictitious data collection and analysis program. We will call it Vinne and Guido's Our Thing Daily Racing Form.

Now, the Daily Racing Form (DRF) program is going to be taking inputs from two sources, the keyboard and an Internet connection, both intermittently providing bets on various horses. The purpose of the program—based on the bets—is to figure the odds on the various horses.

If we were working with a purely procedural language, we would need to keep checking to see if input was coming from the keyboard or from the Net connection and interrupt anything else we are doing to receive that input—an annoying way to have to do things.

By using multiple threads, however, we can create one thread that is taking information from the Net and feeding it to the odds calculation object, another that is taking information from the keyboard and doing the same thing, and a third that is displaying the results from all odds calculations on the monitor. All of this would be happening concurrently.

The problem here is that in C++ we would need to keep manual track of each of these threads: We would have to pretty much manually schedule everything they were going to do. The amount of effort involved would make us wonder why we weren't going to go ahead and just do things in a single-thread sequence, even if it was going to cause the program to stop from time to time to wait on the last operation to get finished.

However, Java was built from the ground up with the idea of multiple threads and handles a great deal of threading on its own behind the scenes. In addition, when you have to take direct control of threads to make sure that actions and data are synchronized between different threads, Java gives you plenty of built-in tools to make the job easy.

Memory Management

The C++ programmer knows a huge amount about the direct manipulation of memory—we have to! We have to explicitly allocate memory when we want to create something; then we have to remember to deallocate it when we are done. Woe to the hapless hacker who forgets to deallocate memory when finished with it, because memory leaks are bad news. This particular mistake is so common that some development kits have tools designed for nothing but spotting memory leaks.

Then we have the other end of the scale: We can release a chunk of memory while there is still a lurking snippet of code that wants to reference it. Instead of returning some kind of grievous error, our call to that chunk of memory returns a random value. This is a bug that we all love to hunt down.

And then there is the whole thing with pointer arithmetic. Although you are accustomed to using pointer arithmetic by now, if you think back to when you were first learning C++ you probably had the only sane reaction to the concept of pointers: a feeling of fear and sickness. This is not to say that pointer arithmetic isn't a powerful tool once you get used to using it, but it is more than a little tortuous and error-prone until it becomes second nature through repeated use.

Well, Java has a few advantages over C++: In the main these come from when it was developed. C started out in the early 70s. Then C++ was built on C's foundation in 1985. That is over 11 years ago since the last major update. Java was finished last year. Everything advances, including language technology.

The other advantage Java has comes from the focus. While C++ is designed to produce the most efficient code possible—but at the expense of the programmer's sanity in some cases—Java takes another approach. Java says that, although high-speed code is a good thing, a programming language that minimizes errors and maximizes programmer productivity is going to be more useful in the long run.

So what does this have to do with memory? Simple—Java takes care of it. All of it. No pointers, no freeing memory. As a matter of fact, Java has no concept of direct memory access. Now this can be a pretty scary concept to the experienced C++ programmer. Visions of dangerously inefficient code start dancing through the head. Although Java code isn't as fast as C++ code by any stretch, the garbage collection routines that free memory and other time savers operate surprisingly well. While your first urge might be to blanch at some of the memory management methodology of Java, my advice is to lay back and relax. After using Java for a while, you will find that its advanced memory management techniques make your coding much more time-effective.

Similarity to C++

When designing a new language, it only makes sense to grab many of the touchstones from the leading development language in the world in order to make the transition easier for experienced programmers. C++ coders will find Java extremely familiar from the start. With just the introduction of a few basic modified concepts, the C++ programmer can start stepping through Java code.

While it can be vaguely disconcerting to learn the little quirks of Java as opposed to C++, the similarity of the languages will have you up and programming in a matter of days rather than the weeks normally required to master the rudiments of a new language.

Heavy Features

In addition to the functionality of a complete object-oriented language, Java is also laden with a wealth of predefined objects to control everything from hash table creation and management to image display and windowing tools. These features, combined with the heavy OOP focus and ease of programming features such as the automated memory management, produce working programs in an unbelievably short time.

All told, Java presents an excellent prototyping language for C++ programmers, whether they are interested in actually producing final programs in Java. Due to the structural similarities to C++, the conversion of Java code to C++ (or vice versa) is a relatively quick and painless process.

Applying Java to the Real World

As with any set of tools, Java has some tasks it is better for than others. Let's take a few moments to look at how the strong and weak points of Java combine to show us where to focus in our studies in this book.

First, we need to remind ourselves of the most salient points from our discussion above: Java is slower than a fully compiled language; Java is easy on the developer; and Java is distributed.

What Java Isn't Really Suited For

Proponents of an individual technology tend to get slightly rabid from time to time in defending their personal choice as the best all-round solution for every computing problem. As Abraham Maslow once said, "When the only tool you have is a hammer, every problem starts to look like a nail." We all know those who are overly rabid about their OS or chosen programming environment or their word processor or some other technological solution they have come to understand, know, and love. The same will be true of Java proponents as time progresses. Some Java aficionados are sure to start pushing the language in situations where it isn't suited, simply because they understand Java better than the alternative technologies.

There are things that Java isn't as well suited for as other options, for example, situations requiring the utmost in performance. Regardless of how advanced the compiler and Java VM become, they are not likely to reach the speed of an optimized, compiled language anytime in the near future. Therefore, applications requiring all the crunch possible out of a given platform are going to find Java a slightly hobbling choice. This tends to make Java a very questionable option for games such as flight simulators and first-person shooters such as Doom. These games require an unreasonable amount of crunch out of the processor to model their 3D worlds, and Java is not well suited to giving that last-clock-tick kind of power.

Developing single-platform, stand-alone solutions is another point where Java probably isn't the best available choice, for instance, developing a game that is intended to run only in Windows 95. It isn't that Java can't do the job, but that other solutions do the job so much better. C++ is much better suited for this kind of application. There are hundreds of available tools and code snippets that work directly with popular C++ packages without porting. In addition, any good commercial C++ compiler implementation comes with a wealth of tools that speed up development time considerably. So for stand-alone, single-platform solutions Java probably should be shelved.

What Java Is Good At

Although Java has its weaknesses, the language also contains a number of strong points. So now that we know what Java isn't good for, let's take a look at what it is excellent at. Multiple-platform concurrent development ranks as one of Java's strongest points. Let's say that you are trying to come up with an application that must run on Macintosh, UNIX, and Wintel platforms. You have three choices: You can develop using an expensive multiple-platform developer; or you can manually port all your code; or you can develop in Java. Multiple-platform development environments are great tools and for many applications they are a flat requirement. Unfortunately, these tools are almost always priced outside of the range of the individual or casual programmer. With hand porting the very distinct possibility of going insane must be figured into any cost/benefit calculations. That leaves Java as an excellent, inexpensive choice for multiple-platform concurrent development.

We mentioned earlier that Java makes an excellent prototyping language. The similarity with C++ makes code developed in Java relatively quick to port to C++ for final implementation, while the extensive included libraries combined with Java's low-error syntax make it quick to write initial test implementations.

We come, then, to where Java really shines and where it gains its fame: distributed computing applications across a multiple-platform environment. When working with a passel of machines connected in a complex networking environment, such as the Web, Java really starts to shine. Here, the benefits of the multiple-platform VM and an integral library of easy-to-use objects for network communication excel. Java isn't just *an* option for general programming on the Web; it is the *only* logical choice.

• • • • • • • • • •
The Future

When we look at the primary, best application of Java right now, it is in the role that Java is being used: the delivery of small applets over the Web. Why isn't this language good for more? Why not write huge distributed applications in it?

The reasons are simple: bandwidth and crunch. We have to have a darned good reason to be programming in Java in the first place due to the speed loss. For those with clock cycles to burn, Java might be a good option for these kinds of applications. But at the moment it can slow things down to the point that it isn't the best option.

However, advances in the Java compiler seem to be one of the priorities of most big software development tool concerns as well as OS developers. Advances in technology such as just-in-time compiling and a good Java-to-C translator promise to speed up the execution time of Java code on individual platforms.

Knowing right now exactly where Java will end up and what applications for which it might become suited and commonly used is almost impossible. However, with the commitment of companies such as Symantec, Borland, Microsoft, and Sun to supporting and extending Java's capabilities, it is a fairly sure bet that Java not only will have some place in the future of computing for the foreseeable future but also might very well fulfill its promise as the native programming language of the Inter- and Intranet environments.

About the Rest of the Book

From here on out we are going to start delving deeply into the details of the twin subjects of this book: game design and Java programming to that end.

The assumption I am making is that you are already an experienced C++ programmer and want to learn to write games in Java. However, I am not assuming that you are an experienced game designer. While it is fairly easy to pick up programming detail from a number of books, it is much harder to understand exactly what goes into creating an excellent game. The elements of a good game design are a mystery to many people (even, trust me, many people who are professional game programmers).

Hence our first task is to make a good overview of game-design issues. We will approach this in two ways. The first is to discuss overall game-design strategies and introduce the various factors that go into making a good game. The second is to use illustrations from both popular games and shareware to show how these game-design issues were or, in some cases, were not implemented.

After we have an understanding of what makes a game good (or at least playable) then we need to learn about Java. So the next section of the book deals with a crash course in how to get from C++ to Java. I firmly believe that the best way to learn a new language is to program in it, so the section on fundamental Java concepts and calls will be short—just enough to get you up and running in the Java environment.

Finally, we will marry Java and game design; learn the finer points of Java programming along with game programming (with a number of chapters on various game-design topics); and along the way, build a few games that will teach how to apply game-design principles and become proficient in Java.

So now let's move on and try to find out what makes a fun game a *fun game*.

CHAPTER 2
· · · · · · · ·
THE PRINCIPLES OF GAME DESIGN

Some people seem to harbor the strange and unusual notion that designing a game is simply a matter of sitting down and programming the puppy. In other words, past the actual coding problems involved, there isn't a whole lot of formal thinking about game design. The hallmark of this process is some programmer saying, "Hey, wouldn't it be neat if I made a strategy game." Then this hapless individual sits down and thinks very roughly about what structure the game is going to take and almost immediately starts thinking of the game-design process as a series of programming problems.

Now, not to undercut programming skills as being paramount to the creation of a good game, the most important part of a game's life—prior to the fun of people playing it—is the earliest design stage where the "Hey, what kind of a game are we going to make?" work is going on. One of the most common mistakes anyone associated with the computer game industry sees is someone (or more often some group) who starts coding a game before thinking about the overarching design issues involved—not the *code*-design issues, but the *game*-design issues.

Why do people do this? Maybe because the majority of the human race isn't as smart as they think they are? Well, I like to give people a little more credit than that and latch onto a much more humane explanation: People can get all kinds of instruction in coding from books and professors and such, but there isn't a whole lot of information floating around out there about how to design a good game. So the process becomes pretty hit-and-miss. People might have played enough games to understand part of what makes a good game. They might have really spent enough time thinking about user interfaces and what, exactly, makes up playability. But in a lot of other cases people are going to code before being fully cognizant about the differences between a good game and a bad game.

What we see as a result are a lot of bad games out there—games that never should have been programmed. If these games were part of someone's personal learning process and only played by them and a few friends, that might not be so bad. But a depressing number of these games end up being shrink-wrapped and fed into the maw of the consumer machine and sold to folks who plunk down their money and end up with a bad game.

"Well, we are talking about Java here, right? I mean, I am not reading this book to make a shrink-wrapped game. I am just going to make this cool little shooter for my Web page." I can hear you saying it now.

Well, there are still a few reasons you should focus on serious game design. If you are putting a game up you are doing it for a reason. Maybe it is to offer something new and exciting to the game-playing public. Maybe it is to try to get your hits up for a small commercial site. Who knows? But there is the old adage that if something is to be done, it is worth being done right: Putting a little game on your Web page is no exception. If you put up a game, wouldn't it be better to put up a good game?

The second consideration might seem small to some people but irksome to others. I see discussions in programming groups hammering Java as not being a real language for development. For various, and sometimes well thought out reasons, there are people who hold this opinion. But frequently I see people pointing out boggy, badly done Java games as their primary examples. This is unfortunate for the whole Java community, because in most cases it is simply an instance of Java being pressed beyond its current best uses. In some others it is just bad game design. The same people could have made similar mistakes in C++ or Object Pascal or Visual Basic or any of a dozen other languages, but since they chose to ignore good game design in Java they end up reflecting badly on the Java community.

So for this and the next chapter we are going to explore what makes a game a *good game,* and how we can think about these issues before we go to work in order to make our games better. Don't think about code at all right now. Put it out of your mind. Don't even think about Java. The following information will serve you in good stead no matter in what language you choose to develop.

The Categories of Games

In order to better think about games, we should look into overall labels we can use to differentiate types of games. While there is no doubt that Mech-Warrior II and Tetris are both games, you can't very well say that they are much alike past that observation. So it behooves us to try to break games down into some rough categories.

The following categories provide a rough starting point to try to see what design issues go into different game types. These categories are very broad, and one game might fall into two or three different categories at once. Don't worry about trying to get a game you know to fall firmly into one category or another; just think of it as multiple inheritance.

Action Games

Action games, often called shooters or twitch games, rely on speedy reflexes and often feature killing things with big guns as a central point of the gaming experience. Most arcade games are action games. Think of Pac Man, Space Invaders, and Galaga. Also most of the console (Nintendo and Sega type) games are of these types. Mario and Sonic games are action games (a bit more about them in a moment).

First-Person Shooters

The first-person shooter counts as a subcategory of the action game. However, in a classic case of the tail wagging the dog, first-person shooters claim such a phenomenal popularity right now that they appear to be a category unto themselves. *First-person shooters* are games that have you looking though the eyes of the protagonist as he navigates around a 3D environment shooting things, normally with a big gun and lots of blood. The names in this category dominate the gaming industry at the moment: Quake, Doom II, Descent, Duke Nuke Em 3D, and Dark Forces are all examples of the first-person shooter.

Fighting Games

Fighting games also compose such a notable segment of the action category they deserve a specific mention. *Fighting games* revolve around the player controlling a viewpoint character who engages in hand-to-hand combat with other characters, often in an exotic martial arts tournament setting. Street Fighter and Mortal Kombat exemplify this type of game. These games mostly heavily rely on strange combinations of controller movements to activate "secret" moves on the part of the characters that provide more lethal techniques. These games are a mainstay of the arcades and have migrated successfully to the consoles. However, they haven't made up a significant sector of the PC market for reasons mainly having to do with hardware restraints.

Side Scrollers

The last major category of action games we will examine is *side scrollers*. These games are marked by the fact that the character is moving though a landscape that is many screens long and moves across the screen from left to right. As the character continues across the screen, more of the environment scrolls into view from the right. These games can be fairly straight action games without much of a combat element, such as the Sonic and Mario titles mentioned above, or they can also involve some elements of the fighter such as almost any of the various superhero console titles put out by Acclaim.

Strategy Games

Strategy games involve taking some kind of a central command situation over the game action. A good rule of thumb for strategy games is if you can see how the game could easily work as a board game (albeit often a devilishly complex one) then you probably have a strategy game. Strategy games focus on a tremendous number of different premises, but some games that are strategy games would include Command and Conquer, Panzer General, Warcraft, and Civilization. A game that straddles the line between strategy and simulation would be SimCity 2000.

A solid branch of the strategy game tree is composed of science fiction empire simulations where the player is placed in command of a space empire vying for control of the galaxy against other races. These games include Masters of Orion, Ascendancy, and Spaceward Ho.

War Games

In the broadest sense, all games dealing with matters of military conflict belong in the war games category. In a more practical sense, *war games* tend to be narrowed down to the strategy games dealing with historical or current conflict, though a very few futuristic games qualify. War games tend to focus on the squad as their smallest movable unit and frequently involve the use of hex grids overlaid on the map to establish distance. War games also include the many naval conflict simulations, such as Harpoon.

Panzer General is probably the most popular war game in recent memory, though a small but steady segment of the gaming market has been churning out these games since the start of computer gaming.

Simulations

Simulations, or *sims,* are a very broad category of games that attempt to accurately model an activity in fine detail. The vast majority of this market are first-person simulations that model the piloting of a vehicle of some type. MechWarrior II, Microsoft Flight Simulator, Wing Commander, and almost every racing game currently on the shelves are games of this type.

Simulations present a very daunting programming job. The majority of them require a good 3D engine as a starting point, but then add on top of that the need to accurately model the characteristics of a vehicle of some type. The most challenging area of simulations are flight sims, which simulate the piloting of an aircraft, most frequently a fighter aircraft. These simulations are rated by users on their realism, so much study of real-world physics and flight capabilities of various airframes is a must.

There are other games, however, that count as simulations that don't deal with driving a vehicle. A perfect example of this would be the SimX series from Maxis. These games model running a city or planet or farm—take your pick. These games are extremely challenging from a player's point of view as you attempt to build a working system out of the various development options open to you.

Sports Games

A *sports game,* rather obviously, attempts to model the playing of a major sport. There are a ton of sports games on the shelves covering football, baseball, hockey, soccer, golf, basketball, and even bowling. The approach of these games can vary tremendously, from the mainly stats-based strategy aspect of a good fantasy baseball game to a first-person simulation of playing hockey. Sports games are hallmarked by their use of real-world sport stats in order to attempt to accurately model the performance of players or teams in the game. However, there are some nonrealistic sports games also, such as BloodBowl.

Adventure Games

In an *adventure game* players take control of a viewpoint character attempting to get through some kind of a story, solving puzzles as they go along to get more information to complete their quest. These games have a long history and range from most of the old Infocom titles such as the early Zork series to very high-tech multimedia extravaganzas such as Phantasmagoria, 11th Guest, and Ripper.

In most adventure games, the actual game logic isn't that big a programming task. The flow of the game is prescribed and follows a simple pattern: If *foo* action is performed by the character then *bar* area or information is opened up. In modern adventure games the most daunting task is the creation of the graphics engine, which tends to involve fully graphical environments hallmarked in most cases by live video shots with professional actors.

Adventure games most frequently tell a story of some sort, and a good off-the-cuff test for an adventure game is that if you think that a game would work well as a book without much effort, you are probably dealing with an adventure game.

Computer Role-Playing Games

Computer role-playing games (CRPGs) have a long and interesting history, having started as pen-and-paper affairs that grew from miniature war gaming. The first role-playing game (though this can be argued) was Dungeons and Dragons (D&D). In D&D the player took on the role of a character in a fantasy universe bearing more than a little similarity to the books of J. R. R. Tolkien. One player would be designated as the Dungeon Master (DM) and would create a game setting using complex rules and mathematical formulas set down in the rule books. Then the other players would take on the role of characters and attempt to move about in this world and generally have fun while developing their characters through combat and exploring and such. Almost any action that can be performed in reality (and many that can't) could be modeled using a combination of common sense, the formulas of the game, and various oddly shaped dice that provided random numbers. A hallmark of these games was amazing flexibility: Since one player was controlling the nature of the world and the game, the players could figure out some way to model almost any activity. Very little stress was put on actually "winning" as such; instead the game's emphasis was placed on developing a real character that acted in an interesting and realistic manner.

Even more than adventure games, role-playing games (RPGs) lend themselves to books. Many books in the real world started out as role-playing experiences for their authors, such as the Wildcards series. With the advent of the computer game, many designers saw the ability to create a role-playing environment in the computer, not only to make a good game, but also to remove the major obstacle to playing RPGs: To play you had to get four to eight people to agree to get together and play the game on a regular basis. And since the game was never "won" as such, the amount of time involved over an entire group was tremendous. It is very common to have the same game that has been going on once a week for two or three years.

The CRPG is hallmarked by a character in a fantasy or, less often, science fictional environment, moving around a world and fighting monsters, gathering gold, and other such activities while developing personal skills. These games are most often set as quest games where the characters are expected to develop their skills and perform a number of quests in order to get some object or accomplish some task that will allow them to kill an evil being that is holding the world in thrall. As the characters' fighting, spell casting, and other skills become more advanced, more difficult monsters and tasks face them.

CRPGs have long been a quiet mainstay of the computer gaming field, some examples of which are the Bard's Tale series, the Ultima series, and the newer Arena series from Bethesda Softworks.

Some people with limited perspective don't make a distinction between the RPG and the CRPG, calling *computer* role-playing games just role-playing games. This is incorrect for a very fundamental reason. With a war game you can fully model the game in the computer, and most of the other types of games we have mentioned can exist only as computer games. However,

RPGs, at the current state of the art, cannot be fully modeled in the computer. The reason is simple: With a real human being running the world and making judgment calls on any action your character might take, a literally limitless array of possibilities for action exists. You can decide to eat. You can decide to paint a picture and see if it is good enough to sell. You can chat up a person you meet in a bar and see what happens. Or you can actually do what the game was designed for and go kill monsters and get gold.

In a CRPG, you can do only the things the game designers thought to let you do. There isn't a CRPG yet that will allow you to paint that picture and try to sell it on the street. However, as software technology improves, some CRPGs are becoming extremely sophisticated and nearing the RPG barrier. Daggerfall: Arena II, from Bethesda Softworks, is a good example of an extremely flexible CRPG with excellent artificial intelligence (AI) characteristics.

Board Games

This category is something of a catchall for those games that don't fit neatly into the other categories. In principle, this category is for those simpler games that model playing an existing board game, such as chess, checkers, or backgammon. We will also shoehorn card games into this category since they are a model of a simple game played in the real world.

Most board game–type programs are relatively simple affairs. They draw on the popularity and easy familiarity of the existing real-world game in order to be interesting. There are, of course, exceptions to this rule. Some of the most sophisticated AI programming ever done has been in the realm of chess programs (Figure 2.1). And a few of the bridge programs available commercially are very well modeled versions of the real game.

Design Considerations

In this section we will take a look at the primary design considerations that should go into your game designs. One thing to remember while looking at these points is that they are a good yardstick. Solid games exist that don't follow one or more of these principles. Very possibly, corners will have to be cut in your design on some of these issues for reasons ranging from the availability of technical tools to time considerations. However, you should

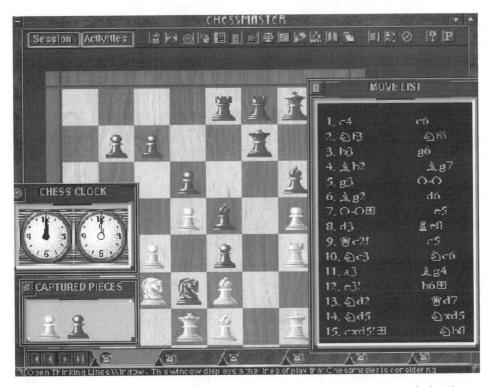

Figure 2.1 The ChessMaster series by Mindscape is one of the best-known chess playing programs on the market and serves as a great example of good AI programming in a game application.

always consider these points; if you need to ignore one or more items at least know you are doing it and why.

Responsive User Interface

When asked about the amount of time spent by the company on various programming tasks in creating the string of award winning shooters that have come out of id software lately, John Carmak commented, "We spent a tremendous amount of time making sure that the interface worked realistically. That when you look one way or the other the game works the same way turning your head does in real life. The interface is everything."

While you can be sure that John spent a huge amount of time having fun programming the graphics engines for id's games, he and John Romero and the other id team members understand probably the most important fact in game design: If the interface isn't properly responsive then nothing else is going to matter. A clunky or inappropriate interface has destroyed many an otherwise good game.

There are a lot of different points that go into the design of a good interface, and what constitutes a good interface is going to change from game to game. There are also interface elements that are a matter of choice. For instance some people have an unreasonable hatred for changing cursor type interface components. The *change cursor interfaces* are those where all the action is controlled by the mouse: When you click one button, it changes the cursor to show a different action is selected; when you push the other button, it performs the action. Other people feel just as strongly in the opposite direction: The changing cursor interface is right up there with Einstein's theory of relativity as one of the greatest discoveries of the twentieth century.

However, there are a number of interface points that we can view as common interface design characteristics.

Make It Clean

The first and probably most important injunction when it comes to interface design is to make it clean. The natural tendency, particularly in games with more complex informational needs, is to want to tell the users everything you can possibly tell them right there on the screen. While as a programmer/designer these information feeds just might seem like the cat's meow to you (and they must, judging by the multitude of people who bollix up a screen with too much data), they will normally intimidate, frustrate, and annoy your users.

In a perfect world we would be able to get away with a screen that was only the playing area. In a first-person shooter this would mean a screen that was nothing but the view, and in a war game, a screen that was nothing but the board. However, this isn't often very feasible. Normally there will be information critical to the player that must be relayed as the game plays out. For instance, in a first-person shooter, knowing how much ammo you have and what health condition you are in is paramount at all times. In many war games there is information about individual troops that needs to be known constantly so you don't send an almost decimated unit out to be chewed up by a superior foe.

However, try to avoid the trap of trying to put all this information up near the center of the playing action. Instead, take a hint from the best-designed games: Keep the minimum of information in the center of the screen and put the remainder down below on a status bar. For various ergonomic and traditional reasons, gamers are almost conditioned to look down to a bar on the bottom of the screen for further information.

Don't Be Too Generous

Second, decide carefully what information your players really *must* know and don't give them more. In general, if you have a lot of different information at your disposal due to the type of game—some sims and war games will have an absolutely rude amount of data they could inflict on a hapless player—then try to add an option to see that information in greater or lesser degrees depending on user selections.

Once in a while you will design a game in which a significant number of players will find having the information in the center of the screen an absolute must. Many sims claim this distinction in the form of heads-up piloting displays. The point of a heads-up display (HUD) is to have all the information you might need overlaid in the center of the screen in a transparent font so that the eyes never need to move their focus. A good example of a game that pretty much requires a HUD is a flight sim. In these games there are a tremendous number of different factors that the pilot must stay aware of at all times, so keeping the eyes centered on the screen is nearly critical.

However, if you are going to put a HUD in a game, or any other displays that run in the main focus area of the game screen, make them optional by player selection. Almost every sim on the market allows you to choose whether to use the HUD, and most allow you to change what information is displayed on the HUD if you do decide to use it.

Other than maximizing the player viewing area, trying to keep on-screen information to the minimum actually required to play the game, and making information feeds optional by player choice, another element of a clean interface is simplifying user input.

In a nutshell, *simplifying user input* means that within a few minutes of game play all the keystrokes required to play the game should become instinctive. If more than 15 minutes passes and a player is still regularly having to refer to a command card or help screen for basic movement information then you can pretty much bet that game is going to get abandoned.

But, you say, "I have this great game that requires the user to be able to perform 230 different actions to control every possible event on their starship." Well, that brings us to two points. Scope and command immediacy.

Scope and the Designer

Scope is one of the most important considerations in your game design. When you are designing a game you must first decide how much of a given world you are going to model.

Every game design has a world. In some simple designs the world is absurdly simple. In the universe of Tetris there is just one reality: Blocks fall from the sky to the ground, every day, all day. However, in some games the world can be quite large, such as in most CRPGs. There the world can span entire continents and alternate dimensions. The bigger the world of your game and the more elements in it, the more complex your programming task, because with big worlds go heavy demands for a serious level of detail.

Level of detail can mean many things, but when we are talking about world size it means the number of different things that can happen to a player and the number of things the player can do to interact with the environment. The bigger the world, the higher the level of detail your player expects. For instance, in a CRPG spanning a continent, if all your player can do is slash at one kind of monster with a sword, and all that will ever be seen is that one type of monster, then your game will get old quick. However, in the small world of Tetris, the simple geometric falling blocks are more than enough challenge.

The size of the world can also be misleading. For instance in Panzer General, one might assume that the size of the world was pretty much the entire planet since battles take place all over. But that logical assumption would be wrong. The world is actually just the battle field, since no matter where you are fighting all you have to deal with is the single battle map presented to you. Hence, Panzer General actually has a fairly limited world.

Your world and the level of detail it demands make up the *scope* of the game. In general, you should try to limit the scope of your projects until you gain a good deal of experience with game-design issues. It is much easier to screw up a large scope game, such as Daggerfall: Arena II or Quake than it is a Tetris or simple card game.

Command Immediacy

The first thing you should do if you start having problems with the number of commands the player is going to have to execute and getting all of them presented properly is to think about lowering your scope. It is pretty darned unlikely that all those commands are actually necessary to give the game good playability. As a matter of fact, you should bet that if you get over 30 or so command functions for the player your game is suffering for it. Your level of detail almost assuredly is too high.

Further, you should compartmentalize even 30 commands. *Compartmentalizing* your command structure is presenting your commands to players in layers related to how often they are actually going to need to use those commands.

First-Tier Commands

In a well-designed game, there are very few commands a player is going to need constantly in order to tool around your world. Tetris has three commands: drop, move, and rotate. Quake has three main commands: fire, slide, and movement (these commands actually use four buttons, but movement can be thought of as one command).

But while Tetris has only those three commands, Quake has a few more: look up/down, jump, run, slide, and change weapon. However, these commands aren't as critical. They can be thought of as second- and third-tier commands. You can tell these are lower-tier commands by the default keyboard layout. The first-tier commands are right under your fingers when you hold them naturally on your keyboard. The other commands require moving your fingers. You will also note, if you are a Quake player, that you can get through the vast majority of the game with just these first-tier commands. This isn't by accident. It is because John Carmack and John Romero and the rest of the id crew have designed about a billion games (most of which you have never heard of and are from well before the time they formed id) and know what they are doing. They understand the concept of tiered-command structure and how important it is to the success of their interface.

Second- and Third-Tier Commands and Selection Keys

There are also some second-tier commands in Quake: Jump, Run, and Slide. You can tell these are second-tier commands again by where they fall on the default keyboard layout. You only need to move your fingers one key to hit them. Again, if you are a Quake player, you will realize that these commands are needed fairly frequently, but not as often as the first-tier commands. The exception can be run depending on the player. Some Quake players live with the run key pressed down. Understanding this, the id crew has implemented a basic game option that provides continuous run, thus eliminating the need for that key for players who like to run continuously. We will be dealing with this more later in the chapter when we talk about customizability.

On the third tier is look up/down. This command set is needed infrequently compared to the first- and second-tier commands, and as such is relegated to the middle of the keyboard.

The final set of commands, the weapon selection keys, are something of a sticking point here and present a real design question. You probably need the weapon selections more often than you need look up and look down. But often you need to make sure that you are selecting the right weapon for the job with no delay. Hence, id has solved this problem with two different ways to select weapons.

One is a toggle through just to get you off of an inappropriate weapon. This key is near your fingers. Then, when you select a specific weapon, you punch one of the number keys, all the way at the top of the keyboard. Given the limits of the keyboard as a computer input device (which is a profound limitation, but outside the scope of this book) the dual weapons selection method is the best bet for the job and splits the weapons selection keys between second- and third-tier command structures.

Other User Actions

While we are looking at Quake (which we shall do some more of in Chapter 3) another important point can be illustrated—many user actions can be handled in the environment of a game and don't require actual commands. This is a good way to offload a frightening command structure from the direct user input of a keyboard or separate commands.

In Quake you can do a few more things than run and shoot and jump, as it would seem from the command list: You can also throw switches and open secret doors. You do this by running into them or shooting them. These can cause somewhat complex changes in your environment but they're done without separate commands. Just as easily, id could have made a special key for opening doors or depressing switches, and some games of this type by less-focused designers have done so. However, by using the commands already in place to effect the environment, id added a range of environmental effects that the user can perform without adding to the actual command structure of the game.

What is the price for this? Well, in the case of many games, Quake included, there is a slight loss of veracity. We will deal with this in greater depth a bit later in the chapter.

We have been focusing for a few pages heavily on Quake, a first-person shooter, but the same issues of command structure apply just as much—and in some cases more—to other types of games. Let's face it, the play paradigm in Quake is fairly simple: See it, shoot it, don't get shot yourself. However, other games demand much more in the way of a user command structure. A strategy game in particular would seem to demand a number of commands that were always on the tips of the fingers. Let's narrow it a bit further and look at only war strategy games.

War Strategy Games

When you are modeling a battle there are a lot of things to take into account and a number of things you want your units to be able to do. A squad can lay down different types of fire, camouflage themselves, dig entrenchments, retreat, or rest and get a little morale back. That is just the short list that is going to be pretty much required to make any stab at a realistic war strategy game. On top of that, the squad is only one type of unit, whereas we are dealing with a number of different types of units in the average field battle, including tanks, artillery, light armored units, antitank guns, possibly special infantry units such as engineers or commando units, naval and air support issues, and a host of other units that we might need to add to our equation depending on the scope of the game.

There is no way we are going to be able to reduce these to the simplicity of a Quake or a Tetris, with just a few simple key commands. But depending on the type of game, we can still make an engaging and easy-to-use command structure.

To take our previous example of a war game, let's look at how two different design houses solved the problem, one with a realistic turn-based war game and another with a real-time futuristic war game.

Panzer General

Our first example is Panzer General from SSI. This game is turn-based. This means you move all your pieces, combat is resolved; the computer moves its pieces and combat is resolved. In some turn-based games the turn order can get much more complex, but in general all you need to understand about turn-based games is that first one side moves, then the other side moves, as in chess.

In Panzer General we see a game without a complex command structure, yet with a wealth of commands. This is accomplished in two ways. The first is to make some obvious moves automatic. For example, when a unit comes to rest for more than a turn in a specific location, it starts entrenching. As each turn goes by without movement, the unit gets more of an entrench-ment bonus against attackers. Now this could easily be a separate command that requires the player to actually waste time selecting it, but it isn't.

How do you tell when a feature of your game should be automatic and when it should be a command? The easiest way is to ask yourself if you can see any circumstances under which you wouldn't want to perform that action. Is there any time you wouldn't want a unit to entrench? Not really. It is a win/win maneuver that provides defensive strength without giving any-thing up. Hence you make it automatic.

Looking back at Quake, we have the running option. Here you have the choice. Many players will want this all the time, and some others for playing-style reasons will not. Hence the option to make it automatic versus a command.

Panzer General also gains in the fact that it is a mouse-controlled game versus a keystroke-controlled game. In practice, it ends up easier to add more nonintrusive command elements to a mouse-controlled game through a combination of having the mouse act on the element in the actual play area to take care of your primary control elements, a side- or bottom bar with icons for your secondary control elements, and using drop-down menus at the top of the screen for tertiary commands.

Panzer General uses the mouse in just this way. The only primary actions of the units in the play area are to move and attack. This is accomplished by clicking on the piece and clicking on an open area or an enemy unit. If the open area is in range then the piece moves. If you move the cursor over an enemy unit and click, your piece will attack if it is in range. However, some

DESIGNERS ARE PLAYERS

During the course of this chapter, and often in later chapters, I am going to be talking about various games on the market (as a matter of a fact, Chapter 3 will be devoted to this). In these discussions, I attempt to confine the examples to popular games or to games that are available in shareware. There are valuable lessons to be learned from much more obscure games such as Elite, Snake by Chuck Summerville, Defenders of the Crown, Boskonian, or the Carriers at War series. However, it cannot be assumed that you are familiar with all of these titles and the myriad of others I would like to reference. Therefore I am trying to stick to popular or shareware games.

However, if you are still getting lost when I talk about the details of Quake, Panzer General, SimCity, or the other examples, it might be a good time for you to put down this book and go out and play some games. If you haven't seen one or two games discussed here, it isn't that big a deal, but if you haven't seen the majority you might have some problems.

The fact is, if I could put everything there is to know about game design in this chapter (and I assure you that I can't, because no matter how much you know, there is an entire book's worth of things you don't know if the topic is as broad as game design), it will do you no good if you don't play games. Game designers are game players. This is how they know what works and what doesn't. Not just from products they have created, but also from the rich storehouse of ideas and techniques developed by other designers.

Plus, on a purely theoretical note, if you don't love games it isn't a good idea to be making them. Like good architecture, game design and programming is a mix of engineering and art. In the best-designed of games you can see a love of gaming and the new world it can create in the work as you play it. This is not to say there aren't companies that don't turn out cookie-cutter games that show no love of the field. But an experienced eye can tell, and within the industry there are some production houses that don't get much respect due to their obvious lack of caring about the art of gaming.

I won't put out a list of games that I think that someone should play in order to get a real feel for the field at its best. However, if you look any time at what the biggest sellers are and try to play at least a few games from every major genre, even if it isn't where you intend to be designing, you will find yourself well served with a deeper understanding of what goes into creating a great game and what might work with your concept.

other elements of the game are controlled through the use of sidebar icons. If you want a unit to rest or to replenish itself, then there are sidebar icons for these functions. Finally, certain sidebar icons lead to menus that allow changing game options.

The penalty you pay for the greater command structure and ease-of-command layering allowed by mouse control is to lose the speed and immediacy of key commands. In most cases, as evidenced by legions of fans devoted to first-person shooters, the keyboard control of a game allows for quicker and more precise reactions in a high-speed game environment. Panzer General, being a turn-based game, doesn't suffer from any delays introduced by the mouse command, but a first-person shooter would. You will note that most first-person shooters and vehicular sims rely on the keyboard and/or a joystick (in the case of realistic flight sims, often an expensive multifunction joystick is a must) for maximum response. This isn't by accident. A mouse tends to be an inherently slower input device than a joystick or keyboard. Some gamers who have a perverse fondness for mouse-only input have made an art of high-speed mouse action, but the vast majority of your players will consider it a clunky interface for a high reaction speed game.

However, there are half measures between keyboard and mouse commands: Our other example, Command and Conquer, makes use of a hybrid design in order to get the easy multiple command structuring of the mouse along with the speed of keyboard commands.

Command and Conquer

In Command and Conquer you take control of various individual combat units as they fight it out in a near future setting. While Panzer General gains the benefits of a slower, turn-based structure, Command and Conquer (C&C) handles basically the same scope in real time. Enemy units are always moving and you have to fight the clock to get established and overcome your opposition.

While C&C doesn't offer quite the same level of realism, and hence doesn't have the need for quite as much command-structure depth as Panzer General, there are still a number of different actions available to each unit. They can move. They can attack another unit. They can patrol an area. They can guard a specific building. And some units can carry other units, requiring a procedure for loading and unloading. These are just a few of the actions available in the game to individual units (there are other, nonunit actions that involve building infrastructure, but we will leave these out of our discussion for right now).

The mouse-control options work basically along the model we discussed earlier for Panzer General. You use the mouse to select a unit then click on a destination for that unit. If the destination click is an enemy unit, then your unit will go attack the enemy. However, if your destination click is an open area of land, your unit will move there. If the destination is a unit capable of carrying the type of unit selected, your troop will go to the carrier unit and get onboard.

These, and a few other purely mouse commands, are all that is actually required to play the game. You can, and many people do, play C&C without learning anything but the very intuitive mouse commands. These mouse commands make up the primary command set.

With just the primary command set, Panzer General and C&C have pretty much solved the command structure problem in the same way. However, with lower-tier commands they start to deviate. Because of the nature of a turn-based game, Panzer General can afford to force the player into taking the extra time to select the proper unit then move the mouse cursor off of that unit in order to select a secondary command from a sidebar icon menu. The same thing isn't true for C&C. Here we have a real-time game and the extra time to select sidebar commands in the heat of battle could critically jeopardize the game's timing and rhythm. Therefore C&C uses keystrokes for secondary commands.

To activate these commands, a unit is selected with the mouse, but then a keystroke activates a specific secondary command for the unit. In this way a unit can be ordered to guard a building or run a specific patrol route as well as a few other options. And this combination of the mouse and the keyboard can still be activated much more quickly than having to use the mouse to hit a unit then track over and select a sidebar command.

C&C also has tertiary commands that deal with building infrastructure and a small sidebar is used to accomplish these functions. However, in almost all cases, building of infrastructure doesn't take the kind of speed priority that moving around actual combat units does, so it can handle the extra time requirements.

C&C probably has slightly more than the 30 command limit mentioned earlier if one were neurotic about counting every possible individual action that could be performed for building infrastructure and moving troops. However, due to a carefully selected mix of intuitive mouse and keystroke commands, the game flows smoothly even in a real-time environment.

Delays versus Nature

Lag in response time from an interface is the sure kiss of death for a game. A large part of the body of game programming technique is devoted simply to making things run faster. The need for speed and optimized programming techniques is paramount in game programming. Very few computer applications outside the research sector put the kinds of processing demands on a computer that games do. Games are the original multimedia application—any successful game today requires the use of good graphics and sound to eat up processor ticks. At the same time, games require a quick response time in a way few applications but streamed simultaneous videoconferencing do. This isn't granddad's database application.

Tool Selection

There are various ways to deal with the potential for processor bog in a game. The first is tool selection. You won't find one shrink-wrapped game written in Visual Basic (if someone out there actually knows of one, E-mail me because I would love to add it to my collection). Visual Basic, as an interpreted language, has serious drawbacks in performance.

Some game programming situations, however, will require the use of certain tools. This might be because the neophyte programmer knows only one tool set, yet wants to get started right away learning game-design principles and practicing techniques. It could be because the programmer doesn't have enough time to do a full development and just wants a good prototype of a running game and needs to use a prototyping language. Or possibly because one set of tools offers some other advantages to offset the potential speed differences.

Tool Speed

It can be assumed that the readers of this book are dealing with the third possibility. You are learning to write games in Java due to the multiplatform and Web delivery options inherent in the Java environment, even though these factors place a few speed limitations on you. It is also possible that you want to prototype games in Java for the ease of programming and are going to port to C++ once you have the interface and logic down, but we will assume the first case since it is the most limiting.

So once a programmer has decided to use slower tools, how do you keep down interface lag? Obviously, you must optimize your code as much as possible. We will be dealing with getting Java to run at its fastest in the programming sections of this book. But another important way to work with delay is to design your game with delay in mind.

How do you do this? Well, first of all, pick the right kind of game for the tools at hand. When you are working in a slightly slower environment, some types of games aren't going to be your best choice for development. Vehicular sims, arcade twitch games, and first-person shooters aren't going to be your best choices for a game design. As a matter of a fact, more advanced versions of these games might be totally untenable.

However, other games suffer much less from delay. Turn-based games and board games don't suffer much from small delays since there isn't a need for high-speed reactions to the events in the game world. Many non-real-time sports games can take the heat. Strategy games on the whole are good to go. And certain CRPGs won't suffer much from some slower execution.

As a rule of thumb, go for turn-based games and avoid anything that requires a first-person real-time view if you are worried about the speed of your tools.

However, another issue about speed is paradoxically having too much of it. When you are finished fully optimizing a game and getting the best possible algorithmic solutions to your video and input requirements, you can be faced with a game that runs too fast in subtle ways that remove some of the veracity of your game. We are going to talk more about veracity later in this chapter, but *veracity* is basically how true your game is to its world and how the small and large elements of the game work in concert to reinforce the reality you are creating.

Player Reaction Time

Human beings work with some delay in their systems. When you perform an action in the real world it takes some time. Humans also have an inherent one tenth of a second delay in their perceptual/reaction loop. It takes fast people one tenth of a second to note and respond to new stimuli. Granted, you can push a button more than ten times in a second if you are really fast, and some fighting games pretty much require this to really come out on top, but to register and respond to something new takes one tenth of a second.

What do these human factors have to do with designing games? Many things. First, you can't make a game that requires faster-than-human reflexes to beat. Again, we will be dealing more with the issue of winnability in a later part of this chapter, but right now we will focus just on the speed issue. It is easily possible to make a game with fast enough code that on a speedy box will run so quickly that there is no way a human can muster the reflexive speed to beat it. Testing the game with a number of players and deciding on speed issues is a major part of the fine-tuning involved in beta testing which we will cover in more depth later. But just keep in mind that some elements of some games are going to have to be fine-tuned as to speed issues to insure that a human has half a chance.

Map scrolling. Speed issues also encompass making sure that things don't happen so fast that they are jarring to players. A good example of this—where a plethora of games have made a mistake in the past—is map scrolling. On a fast box with clean code many games can scroll a map so rapidly there is no delay in the scrolling process at all from a human perspective. To a significant portion of the game-playing human race this is a little jarring. Any event occurring faster than human perceptions betrays the machine underneath your world. When you make map scrolling functions, play with them a bit to make the scrolling process smooth and slow enough to feel comfortable and nonjarring. This is something of a matter of taste, so putting in an option for instantaneous, fast, and slow scrolling isn't out of the question—but you should at least think about the issue.

Using information screens. Another minor point about speed deals with information screens popping up. Again, any action that occurs quicker than human perceptions belies the machine beneath your world. In reality, very little happens so fast that you can't see some precursor to the event, and when something does happen that fast the little lizard part at the back of your brain gets subtly disturbed. The firing of a gun making something seem to instantly explode always gets confused with magic at first among people who have never seen or heard of a gun. Events in nature that happen instantaneously tend to get a mystical and religious significance early in the development of a culture. Take the number of cultures that consider lightning to be the wrath or weapon of the gods as a cue.

Now I am not a professional anthropologist but a game consultant, writer, and designer. Hence some might argue about the significance that I place on instantaneous events in a cultural perspective. But I am on firm ground telling you to avoid events that don't give a gentle warning to the back brain that they are going to occur in a gaming environment. They break the paradigm and disturb the mind in a slight and subtle way.

What does this have to do with information screens? When you are going to pop one up, try to have it take a tenth of a second. Put a light outline up before the screen actually appears and after it goes. This is a very minor detail, but it does make a tiny difference that can be noticed in the mental calmness of a significant number of players, myself included. The game just feels slightly better with a tiny fade in and fade out to information screens as opposed to instantaneously having them appear and disappear in a way that is obviously unnatural and gets that back brain screaming "magic!"

Like everything else in this chapter, these issues about speed are just a yardstick. In some cases you might want instantaneous events to occur for a number of reasons. One is to make use of that subtle disturbance to emphasize danger in a game if it is used sparingly. A fairly common event that comes to mind would be the sudden appearance of cloaked vehicles or ships in a science fiction game or a teleport effect in a science fiction or fantasy environment. If you have minimized the use of instantaneous effects in other segments of your game, the sudden nature of having a cloaked or teleporting enemy suddenly in the player's face will not only be disturbing because of the obvious danger, but also because of the sudden appearance affecting the perceptions of the player.

● ●
Ergonomics and Conventions

When the Apple Macintosh had its debut in 1984, an equally important event occurred almost unnoticed: the creation and release of the Apple Human Interface Guidelines. This standard specified the elements that would be common across all programs on the Mac platform and the features that all Mac programmers would have to agree to implement in a uniform way if they were to get a Macintosh development license.

This was an important turning point in the computing experience. Up to that point, nothing like this existed. There were hardware or operating system–imposed restrictions on programmers, but no computer company cared how the program interfaced with the user. As a result, each new application one tackled was an adventure in learning, since the exact same functions would be handled in entirely different ways in different programs.

Now that the graphical user interface (GUI) of one form or another is pretty much the standard interface for most of the computing universe, we have come to expect that some commands are going to be standard across different applications. The cut and paste keys, for example, are going to work pretty much the same in any Windows application, no matter who built the program or what type of information is being moved.

Games are not yet a mature enough group of applications to have a standardized way of dealing with human interface tasks. There are a couple of reasons for this. The main one is probably that we are still working out new ways to use user input. At this point, very few people believe that we have seen all of the types of games that will come into existence in the industry. Furthermore, nothing has forced the companies to attempt to standardize their input.

However, some conventions are slowly emerging on how to deal with user interfaces. The reason and way they are emerging are very pragmatic: When the biggest game in the industry at any given time implements a feature set in a certain way, there are a legion of players who become reflexively wired to deal with that interface paradigm. If you are making another game of the same type, it might behoove you to take advantage of those prewired reflexes in order to jump-start the acceptance of your game.

First-Person Shooter Convention

The clearest example of this is the first-person shooter. In this category, id decided a few critical things that they almost single-handedly created: They decided that keyboard input would form the primary method of control and then they decided on a keyboard command structure and layout that allowed for speedy control. We have already discussed the tiered-command structure employed by id's newest offering, Quake, and will be looking at this again briefly in Chapter 3.

Because of the phenomenal popularity of id's games, almost all first-person shooters use very close to the same keyboard layout id employs; this is a wise move. Using these standards allows a new player to begin playing the game immediately with a certain set of expectations of control and not have to learn a different layout.

There are a number of different small conventions that have grown up in some game segments. The way the keys on a joystick react tend to have some similarity in their default modes on almost all successful flight simulators.

How do you find out these conventions and take advantage of them? *Play the games.* When you are designing a game, you should play as many games that are similar to your initial concept as possible, look for the common elements, and decide whether you and your players will gain from adopting these conventions.

This isn't to say that you should feel enslaved to make a game with an identical keyboard layout to another design. You could have unique input needs in your game or just have thought of a better way to do things. But give serious consideration to any conventions you find across a range of similar games and make sure that any changes you make are for a good reason and not just to be different.

Customizing Conventions

While keyboard layout is one convention issue that is easy to point at with a clear example, all elements of your game should take conventions into account. Users have come to expect certain customizability options in a game that you had best not be without. We will be dealing with these more when we discuss customization options in more depth, but players expect games to have certain features they have seen in previous titles and start thinking badly of a game without them. For instance, almost every game design programmed in the last few years has an option to turn off the sound, turn off just the effects, or turn off just the music (if the game has no music, then the last two options don't apply). Better-designed games allow you not only to turn off these effects, but also to adjust the volume of all three independently. This had better be a feature of your game if it is going to be commercially viable. Because of the nature of the games you will probably be programming in Java, it is unlikely you will have a music track or be dealing with sound volume, but as I said at the start of the chapter, we should look at all game-design issues and know where our tools and project type are causing us to deviate from good practice.

To learn the numerous little conventions and standard practices that mark a good game you should play as many and as varied a selection of games as possible. I know I keep hammering on this point, but the importance of playing can't be overestimated. And when you play games try to look at them analytically. Think about why they do what they do, particularly when it comes to the user interface. Look for both common points and deviations among games. With games that deviate from the standard set in other games, determine whether anything was gained by the difference.

Keyboard Ergonomics

Ergonomics is the matter of making sure that your interface is natural for the user to use. Unfortunately the keyboard mouse combination that is currently the standard computer input combination is pretty much inherently ergonomically unsound and there is nothing that can be done about this within the scope of our goals of game design. However, we can do our best to make sure that we don't add to the problem.

When you design a keyboard layout (the keyboard layout is the worst offender in a game; there isn't much you can do to make a mouse any better or worse ergonomically), spend a lot of time putting your hands on the keys you most need and making sure they fall under your fingers as naturally as possible when you play. As you put the game through beta testing, examine

In addition to playing every game you can get your hands on, another good practice is to start reading a few of the magazines devoted to the game industry. Look to the reviews. If you judge with a critical eye, you will start to see that some writers have more of a clue of what makes a good game than others. Start seeking out articles by writers who seem to have a good grasp of what, exactly, separates a good game from a bad game. A game reviewer with long experience has played literally over a thousand games, and in some rare cases many thousands of games, over his or her career. You will often find that these writers will talk about how a game that missed the mark could have improved. At these times take careful note and think about looking at these issues in your own designs. For the price of a few subscriptions you can glean important bits of advice for a pittance compared to the thousand-dollar-a-day fees of the best industry consultants (who are frequently these same magazine writers).

carefully how other users take advantage of the commands and if they are having to make any unnatural lunges with their fingers on a very regular basis in order to use a command more frequently than you would. Consider moving a command that many of your users might consider more critical than you do, due to their playing style up a tier or two to get it closer to their natural rest position on the keys.

Although by using the term ergonomics many readers might make the leap that what we are doing this for is to prevent repetitive stress injury in our players, this isn't really our goal (though a well-designed layout might or might not have that secondary benefit). The goal is to ensure that the default layout of the game is as natural as possible. If a significant number of users find the need to always reset the default layout of your game to something more comfortable it will be a point against your product and just another step the user has to take back from the reality of your world.

Veracity and Ancillary Realism

Veracity is how true your world is to itself. When you define the scope of your game you are creating a little universe and your job as a game designer is to draw the user into your universe. One of the highest points of achievement for a designer is to find out that someone has been so drawn into the game that the player looked at the clock and realized that many hours of playing had gone by without ever noticing it.

Many things can draw users out of the universe of your world and make them think about the machine tricks underlying your creation. The biggest offender is bad interface design. Ignoring the veracity of your own creation is a close second and somewhat less excusable mistake. Interface design principles can be easily screwed up by simple ignorance; a game designer simply hasn't played enough games or thought about the subtler design issues before starting. Breaking your veracity is more of a game-design sin. Since you are creating your world, it can't be a matter of ignorance, but just a lack of caring and attention to detail.

Violating the Scope

The most obvious veracity problem, and thus the most easy to avoid, is violating your scope. *Violating your scope* is adding inappropriate game elements that shatter the illusion of reality you are trying to create. For example, if a Mario series game should include a realistically executed WW II infantryman it would seriously destroy the veracity of the game. The world of Mario is filled with mushrooms and gorillas and snails and all sorts of different creatures, but obviously isn't happening in our dimension at all. The sudden intrusion of the out-of-place soldier would in a brief instant shatter the entire universe of the game.

Equally important, you can't insert blatantly fantastic elements into a realistic game. Mario inserted into Panzer General would be equally devastating to the veracity of the reality of the WW II war game.

Be very careful when you are inserting basic elements into your game that they don't smack of too much reality in a fantasy setting, or too much of the fantastic in a reality-based game. But while not as devastating to your veracity as blatantly violating your scope, the smaller, ancillary, elements of your game can add up to either increase or decrease your veracity. In a really great design, every element of your game should add up to help increase the total veracity of your universe.

Sound

One of the biggest points of ancillary realism in a game is the *sound*. The difference that sound can make in a game—and too often people who design smaller games ignore it—is incredible. When we get to the actual programming portion of the book we will be dealing with sound a bit more, but right now let's look at sound in more abstract design terms.

When my partner, R. J. Osbourne, and I were designing and writing the games for this book, we decided that one should be a fairly simple card game. R.J. rapidly turned out the code while I took care of some other related tasks. When he demonstrated it to me, it was obviously lacking some points of veracity. The first that I noticed was the sound—there wasn't any. While having inappropriate sounds would be damaging to the total veracity of the game, not having any sound at all was still bad. Cards make very distinct noises when you do certain things like shuffle them. One of the first things we did in the move from alpha to beta code was to add card sounds. The total veracity of the game was expanded tremendously in a couple of quick lines of code and 20 minutes of recording sound samples with a card deck: not a very high price to pay for the added reality.

Little sound touches like these can really make a big difference in a game. The veracity of Command and Conquer and Warcraft gain tremendously by the simple lines spoken by individual troops to acknowledge commands. The designers could have added a click or beep, a very common way to acknowledge a command, but instead added short sound files specific to the units being moved. The difference this makes in veracity is tremendous. Look at each of the sound effects in your game and make sure they are appropriate for the action being taken. Ask yourself where you could add sound elements to try to make things more realistic.

Another sound issue is music. In general a good rule about music is: Don't—just plain don't do it. The reason is simple: Inappropriate or bad music in a game is much more damaging than no music at all. If you have the resources and specialized knowledge to work good music into your game, then do it. But if you have any questions about your ability to get or judge good, professional custom tracks for your game then don't bother. Long gone are the days when a bit of tinny music synthesized from the Yamaha OPL series chip found on the original SoundBlaster (and a variant is still found there today), or worse, jammed out of the PC speaker with the totally inadequate sound capabilities built into the base PC configuration would actually add to your game.

The best option for music, if you really must use it and aren't a studio musician on the side, is to pay for experienced professionals to create your finished tracks. Otherwise be very leery of adding music to your carefully crafted world.

This is not to say that projects at the right level don't gain tremendously from good music. The soundtracks to Command and Conquer and Fantasy General are excellent and go a long way to helping make the games. The importance of sound wasn't lost on id when they arranged for Trent Reznor and Nine Inch Nails to create the sound effects and music for Quake. However, unless you have the budget and the time to do the music right, just leave it alone. Windows Solitaire and Free Cell don't have gambling music (don't ask me what gambling music is, but I know it when I hear it) in the background because it is outside the range of resources that were devoted to these projects and the designers wisely decided just not to address the issue at all.

Sound is a pretty huge element. But there are a plethora of smaller ancillary concerns that you need to look at to help add veracity to your game. The exact elements you use in a game are going to change depending on the

---

HEY, WHAT ABOUT VIDEO?

The observant reader has noticed by now that we are quite a way through this section and have managed to talk about everything in the world but graphical elements. There are a few reasons for this but the important one is that in a very real sense modern computer games *are* their graphics. You can take away most elements of a computer game and just have a badly designed game. But you take away the graphics and you don't have a game at all. We will be dealing with graphics design at the same time we deal with the majority of graphics programming issues in Chapter 6 where we can give these issues our full attention.

---

design, but let's look at some ancillary elements in a number of different games, and how they were used to add to the veracity of the design.

Ancillary Elements of Veracity

One common element we can look at is the briefing. Most war games and war related sims are broken into separate missions and each of these missions has some sort of a goal: Destroy these enemy units before this much time runs out, or capture these cities. The *briefing* adds ancillary realism to the game. Look at the briefings in Panzer General and Command and Conquer. Both use sound and/or video appropriate to the game type and put the briefing data in terms that add to the veracity of the world. One creates military high-command briefings befitting WW II, and the other uses video clips that really give a feel for the game.

Another game to look at for briefings is MechWarrior II (MWII), by Activision. Here, the game uses the tiniest detail to help add to its veracity. When you are getting briefed for a mission there is a stage at the front of the briefing room. When you click on that screen, a small special graphical effect makes it look like a holographic display is coming to life, fitting the veracity of the futuristic world postulated for MWII. I have heard dozens of gamers comment on this tiny detail and how cool they think it is. There is no detail too small to add veracity to your game.

Probably the ancillary realism heavyweights among recently popular games are Command and Conquer and Quake. In the case of Command and Conquer (C&C) every element in the game has been tailored to make for a believable world. One of the most impressive parts of the game from this point of view is simply the game-install sequence. Instead of being a simple install routine, it uses synthesized sounding voice clips and good graphics to make the install seem a part of the near future world of the game. As opposed to being a boring process, the installation is the first step to drawing you into the C&C universe; good use of video clips from then on keeps you in the world as you continue to play what, at the deepest engine elements, is a fairly simple and even slightly flawed real-time war game. But that isn't where you are: You are commanding your Nod or GDI forces since the veracity of the game is more than enough to cause the vast majority of players to forget about the machine under the universe.

Quake would be my other choice for the most complete veracity winner. Here you have a game with an utterly ludicrous premise—that only bothers to use a couple of paragraphs in its manual to explain how you could have gotten here or why—but it still manages to draw you in. I would be surprised if players don't get their pulse racing and a light sweat at some of the most critical moments in the game.

A large part of the veracity of the game comes from John Carmak's brilliant graphics programming talents and Adrian Carmak's (no relation) equally impressive art capabilities. However, if that was all there was to it, Quake would still have veracity holes. The real clincher with Quake comes from the brilliant use of sound and typography. Even if you aren't playing the version with Nine Inch Nail's background music tracks, the little sound effects details of the game add incredibly to the veracity of the game. Note the tiny details of the use of the sound in the game: how the grenades make a good metallic clang each time they strike the ground when bouncing; how your character starts gasping for air after coming up from being submerged for a long period (but equally important, how he doesn't gasp when only down for a moment). This use of sound is incredibly impressive.

The other big ancillary realism point lies in the information screens. Quake has quite a few option screens and instead of using a standard pop up box, id has made the effort to make their information screens an integral part of their universe. Typography and font creation are complex subjects with many books devoted to them, so we won't deal with them here, but note the custom font used by Quake and how inherently disturbing it is. Running across this font in print you wouldn't have to know what the actual content was to get the impression you were about to tie into some dark and disturbing data.

And, of course, in the game this painful font is laid against a background that matches the background feel of the actual playing areas of the game.

Let's examine briefly some minor veracity points in smaller games that are more like the ones that you are likely to be programming at the start of your design efforts: the card games supplied with Windows 95.

Windows Solitaire

It is common consensus in the game industry that Tetris is the most popular game of all time with something like 45 million installed copies worldwide (if you estimate a count of all the unauthorized hacks of the game). That common consensus, however, is wrong, as I like to point out to other industry experts. The most played game of all time, hands down, is *Windows Solitaire*. Every machine in the world with Windows has it and a ton of boxes with no games installed as such still have a lurking copy of Solitaire.

On first glance there would seem to be no points of ancillary realism in Windows Solitaire. The game has no sound and uses straight Win dialog boxes for option setting. But this knee-jerk response is wrong. There are a few, subtle, points of ancillary realism in the game. First, what is the scope of the game? The scope of Windows Solitaire is to simulate the world of a Vegas or non-Vegas Solitaire game: The world is a card table. The command structures are the simple interface elements required to manipulate and deal with that game.

So how do we increase the veracity of Solitaire? First, we make the card table look like a card table. There are a few options we have to do this, but the easy and perfectly effective way to pull this off is to simply make the background the right shade of green to simulate the felt that covers a card table. Think about that a second. It would have been easier to make the background just a black featureless area and this wouldn't have affected the play mechanics of the game at all. Every element needed to play the game of solitaire could have been hanging there in space.

Go out on the Web and into shareware archives and look for amateur efforts to create simple card games and you will see that a disturbing number of novice designers take just this approach. Look at the difference such a simple thing as the green background makes and you will start to see how a tiny change in your design can affect veracity.

Solitaire also makes veracity points with its deck representation. Think about what you need to represent a deck. Simply putting a card back beside the face-up cards is enough to intimate a deck in a card game. Again, you will see a number of badly designed games that do just that. However, look closely at the Win Solitaire deck and you will note that shadowing the edges of the deck with a couple of lines has created the illusion of a three-dimensional deck of cards. A tiny touch but nonetheless a significant one.

So you see that even in a game of small scope, tiny details can add veracity to your design past the actual mechanics of the game programming. If there were one cardinal principle of game design it would echo one of the tenets of the United States military: attention to detail. There is no detail too small in a game to be considered in light of how it might help the total feeling and reality of your game world.

Customizability

With veracity and interface issues out of the way, we have already covered a huge amount of ground, and many of the points in the rest of this chapter are just going to be going a bit more in depth on points we have already discussed. Customizability is one of these kinds of issues.

Anyone who has been reading closely will note that I have a fond spot in my heart for providing as many options as possible to the user to help customize the gaming experience. This isn't an arbitrary love, but a reflection of a simple reality we have briefly touched on earlier: Gamers have different play styles.

Even in the simplest game you will find that there are myriad ways for different gamers to actually play. For instance, some people will play Decent, by Interplay, with a joystick, others with a keyboard. One of the best Quake players I know keeps both hands on the left side of the keyboard to execute commands. Although it seems cramped and unnatural to me, this odd placement allows him to execute sliding maneuvers while firing more easily and makes the man a truly deadly deathmatch player. Even with the humble Windows Solitaire there are people who are going to want to play the game with Vegas rules and dollar scoring, and others who prefer a less competitive set of rules. Solitaire allows options for both.

The most obvious point of customizability is that your players should have complete freedom to remap any default interface components. Your command structure should be not only completely accessible to the player but also easy to change. Understanding this you might wonder why I placed so much emphasis on designing a command layout. The reason is simple: If you create a good command structure and layout, the vast majority of all players are going to work with your defaults. Having to change the customization keys when playing a copy of the game set up in a new location (a friend's house for example) is a hassle and no one likes having to do it. But on the other hand, the option had better be there. All kinds of gamers exist and some do things differently than the mainstream. In addition, you might think of players who have damage to one hand and are forced to remap the default layout due to inability to use the controls at all in their standard configuration.

Earlier in the chapter we also discussed making information feeds optional, particularly HUDs. When you are designing your informational inputs to the player, try to make as many of them as possible optional. Since there are so many different types of informational requirements for individual games, it would be fruitless to try to categorize them and discuss the feasibility of making them optional and the design techniques for doing so. However, just remember to try to look at any information screen and decide if you can easily add an option to make it go away.

In cases where it is possible, making an information window movable and resizable is a good call. Do this anywhere you can and your players will thank you for it.

Finally, try to set up your information objects in such a way that the user not only can turn on and off a specific windowed feed, but also can configure the type and layout of information within the window itself. A low, high, and medium detail map display would be a good example of this kind of consideration. Look at the different map options available in C&C for a working example of this idea.

Slow and Fast Machines

In a perfect world every game would be playing on a box with the fastest make of general consumer processor available with all the multimedia options currently on the market. Reality is that gamers span all of the possible configurations of old and new computing platforms. You should take this into account when you are designing your game.

Deciding arbitrarily that a gamer must be on a minimum of a P90 with MPEG 1 spec multimedia capabilities is fine if you are an id or an Activision with such an obvious hit title that you know it is going to be selling in the hundreds of thousands of copies and that a significant number of people will upgrade their machines just to play your game (and don't think serious gamers don't upgrade their boxes just for the newest release of a game; I know dozens of people who do this). For the rest of us, the further we can go down the platform spectrum with our game and still have it be playable in some form, the more potential players we can garner. No matter if you want to grow up to create shrink-wrapped commercial games or you are programming games for another reason, having a larger player base is a good goal.

Always consider how to pare down your game to run on the slowest box feasible. That isn't to say that you have to make your game compatible with the last of the aging IBM AT spec boxes out there, but to go as low as is feasible.

The most common way of doing this is to have detail settings on your game that will lower the amount, quality, or resolution of the information given to your players in order to make up for skimpy processor power. Options to cut off all nonessential game elements, such as sound or animations (where animations are optional to your game design), will also help expand your user base and make for more players.

However, when finally spec'ing the game in a brag sheet to your potential playing market, don't spec the game with the bargain basement specs with all options turned down. Figure out the median to make an acceptable gaming experience and spec that. People with slower machines know that they are going to have to deal with some problems for their lack of investment in their platform. When someone picks up a game and it says it runs on a 486DX-25 but it runs only on that platform with the game in a barely playable mode, people tend to become irate.

Difficulty Modes

There is no excuse for a game without start-up options for easy, medium, and hard difficulty. Some simple board games aren't going to be able to apply these options logically, but for almost all games there are going to be ways to make the game harder and easier in the design and algorithmic stages.

We will be dealing with this more in a moment, but know that if you can add difficulty modifiers to your game, you should. These should be selectable from the start of the game and not force an excellent player to play though easy gaming levels to reach the part where the game really becomes challenging. Think about the ability to start with a number of different handicaps in Tetris or at higher-difficulty levels in almost any first-person shooter on the market.

Difficulty is one of the most important elements of a game design. Any game you design should have an acceptable degree of difficulty to make the game challenging but at the same time winnable. Exactly how to instill your game with difficulty is one of those intangibles that takes a lot of thought; there are different difficulty techniques, some simple and some quite sophisticated, that work for different types of games.

However, despite the game-dependent differences in implementing difficulty, there are some design issues that can be noted about difficulty levels.

Too Easy/Too Hard

Difficulty is like Goldilocks and the three bears: Your game can't be too easy and it can't be too hard. It has to be *just right*.

When you are creating your game, you must make sure that it is playable by humans, although making a game too easy is just as bad as making it too hard. People must be challenged by a game, or they won't be playing it for very long. At the same time, with dedication and talent, they must be able to win.

How do you know if your game is too easy or too hard? This is what your beta test is for. What might be an easy or fiendishly difficult game for you might be just the opposite for your beta testers.

It is a common failing among novice game designers to underestimate the talent of some of the more frenetic and devoted of the gaming community. There are some devilishly good players out there. I take great pride in my acumen with games of the various types I specialize in, but I am aware that there are better players out there; I have met some of them and these people can be truly terrifying to watch.

• • • • • • • • • • • •
Good AI Design

When you are building the AI for your design it doesn't matter if you use complex AI techniques or brute-force patterns; there are many common design issues that must be watched for in the design of the AI for your game.

Basically, the rules for AI design echo the rules for difficulty. In most game types, your AI is what is going to make your game difficult or easy. In some types of games it will be feasible to build a practically unbeatable AI. In these cases you will need to weight the AI to make mistakes in order to make your game winnable.

However, a much more vexing problem with AI is when you can't make it strong enough to provide a good challenge. We will be dealing with some of the nuts and bolts of simple AI programming detail and principles later in this book, notwithstanding AI programming is a large and complex discipline. When you can't make an AI sophisticated enough to provide a challenge you have a few options.

The first is to take the time to learn more about AI issues and practice. The AI is the heart of all but the simplest games that don't require AI techniques as such, for example, very basic action games and some rudimentary card games.

It might seem an onerous task to learn everything you can about such a complex field. But a good working understanding of the implementation of state machines, neural nets, and genetic algorithms, just to hit the high points, is worth its weight in gold over the long run. There are very few games out there that couldn't stand to have stronger AI elements, even if they are fairly good games to start with. The AI opposition in Command and Conquer, a great game, isn't anywhere nearly as clever as it could be. The monsters in Quake are impressive from a design standpoint, but obviously don't learn from their mistakes the way an advanced genetic algorithmic implementation could. On the other hand, some games are made or broken by their AI. The excellent AI in Panzer General probably played as big a part as the outstanding interface in making that game a best seller. Daggerfall, by Bethesda Softworks, is a tour de force of advanced AI design, in its use of genetic algorithms, fuzzy logic, and neural nets to make the characters more realistic (see Figure 2.2). Almost any game can gain from more advanced and better-applied AI.

However, if you don't have the time or wherewithal to learn AI technique, then there are still options open to you. The most obvious is to find someone who does, and either hire or cajole the expert into helping you with your game.

If you can't bring an AI guru in on your code, your last remaining option to keep your vision of your world intact is to cheat. This is the method

THE PHASES OF GAME PRODUCTION

When a game is built, there are a few identifiable phases the game goes through from inception of the first dim glimmer of an idea to a finished product. These phases hold true for almost any type of game and are commonly used and understood terms in the industry. No matter if you are producing a shrink-wrapped game or a little Web-page shooter, your game will go, in one form or another, through these phases. The only exception is that the foolhardy who doesn't build a commercial product can skip the beta phase: This is contra-indicated.

DESIGN PHASE

During the *design phase* the elements of the game are thought out and committed to paper. The scope of the game is decided and the individual details required to create the game are roughed out. The product of this phase will be the *design document,* which depending on the team can be a fairly rough outline of the implementation of the game or an intricately detailed list of every single element in the game.

ALPHA PHASE

During the *alpha phase* the basic code structure of the game is programmed, implemented, and refined in the rough. The final product of the alpha phase is the first beta copy of the game.

BETA PHASE

The *beta phase* of game development deals with refining the elements of the game and testing them on a wide variety of players and platforms in order to find lurking bugs, platform dependency problems, and to fine-tune elements such as interface design issues and difficulty levels. The beta phase begins as soon as the alpha phase produces a playable game. There might still be small elements unimplemented or placeholders for art in progress in a beta copy of a game. But the game is playable.

The beta phase is in many ways the most important phase of the game-production process. Many evils in the design and alpha phases can be atoned for in the beta-testing period. Have your beta testers give you detailed reports of what game elements they liked and what game elements they didn't and what they would like to see added, as well as the obvious reports of blatant bugs in the code.

It is necessary to have as large a beta test team as possible. On a commercial project it is not uncommon to have twenty or more beta testers. Some games end up being tested by thousands of users on the Web if the game is compelling enough to hold their interest, and you can make the test known to a wide variety of Net denizens. Often it will be just a few coworkers or friends. No matter how many people are on your test team, make sure you pay attention to their input and try to make room for their likes and dislikes in the game. For every beta tester who doesn't like an element of a game or who wants a specific feature implemented, you can wager there are going to be thousands more who agree when your game goes up or into the box.

When beta testing, don't only take reports from your beta testers, but also watch them play. Many times you will notice them doing something odd or having problems with a function that they don't bother to formally write up because they don't think it is that big a deal. In a perfect game, no one would have any problems with anything. See if you can take care of not only the problems they report, but also the ones they don't.

It is also wise to beta test on as wide an array of platforms as possible. Commercial design and testing houses keep a plethora of differently configured machines for just this reason. However, if you are on a budget, go around to your friend's or coworker's machines and note the different configurations of the boxes and pester the owners to boot and play your game. This will help you tremendously by killing as many platform-dependent bugs as possible before the game goes out the door.

It is not uncommon, in a well-produced game, for the beta testing phase to take longer than the design and alpha phases combined.

GOLD MASTER

The final product of the beta phase is the *gold master*. The gold master is the end of the road. Your game is done. You take a vacation, spend some time with your significant other, whatever it is you need to do to decompress from the madness of active game production.

used in a depressing number of games on the market that could really be enhanced with a better AI (including some games that I still love, but wish could just use more advanced programming techniques).

When you cheat, you simply make the opposition stronger than it should be in order to increase your difficulty. In a war game you can give the AI side more or better units than the player. In a first-person shooter, you can simply increase the number of monsters, the speed of the monsters, the damage the monsters can dish out, or the amount of damage the monsters can take. If you are being really tricky and your AI is not advanced, you can increase combinations of these qualities. You see how this can apply to almost any game type with some obvious exceptions such as some board games. (That is why chess is where some of the hottest AI programming has been accomplished: You can't cheat in chess—the AI just has to be that good. It could be argued that doing brute-force branching on supercomputers is just a high-end way of cheating, but that argument we will leave for another day.)

And, finally, you can often get around AI weakness by changing your scope. The narrower your scope, in most cases, the simpler the programming of your AI is going to be. It is a freshman exercise to build the AI for a tic-tac-toe game due to the extremely limited scope of the game. In a more realistic sense, as a general rule, the fewer the number of elements in your universe and the lower the number of ways they can interact, the smaller the solution space for your AI becomes.

Loopholes

When dealing with any game that is heavily AI-dependent, it is particularly important to heavily beta test your game in order to look for loopholes.

Loopholes are defined as simple actions or groups of actions that allow the user to subvert the proper difficulty or play paradigm of the game. In any type of game it is important to look for loopholes. But in most game designs that don't rely heavily on AI, loopholes tend to fairly jump out during the beta-testing process as somewhat obvious bugs.

However, in heavily AI-dependent games, and particularly those games relying on more advanced self-modifying AI techniques, loopholes can hide amazingly well, waiting for the right player to find the combination to bring them out.

Figure 2.2 Daggerfall, a tour de force of advanced AI design.

You would be astounded at the number of professionally designed and programmed games that I have analyzed that demonstrated blatant, game-destroying loopholes when methodically tested. In war games this is a particular bugaboo but can be a very real danger of all kinds of games. Always be on the lookout for every possible way that your game can be subverted. When using AI make sure that you try to push the game to its limits with as many beta testers as possible to try to shoot down loopholes before they end up in your final product and turn your otherwise excellent game into a junker.

Sense of Accomplishment

Players should always feel a *sense of accomplishment* as they progress through your game. When players get a sense of accomplishment from their game-playing experience it hooks them and keeps them coming back for more. Gaming isn't just an intellectual experience, but an emotional one. You have to tug your players along and keep hooking them to get them to want to keep playing your game and finally beat it.

Myriad techniques exist to provide this sense of accomplishment in your designs. We will examine some of the most important and common.

Increasing Powers

The increasing power hook probably started in proto form with Pac Man and took off from there. Pac Man (in case you happen to be very young or were studying with mystics in Tibet for the last 16 years) is a very simple game that involves the player moving around a simple 2D maze eating dots.

When all of the dots are gone you move on to the next maze. However, complications are introduced in the form of four "ghosts" with cute names that are chasing your noble and steadfast Pac Man around the maze. If they touch him it is a dead little Pac for you. But revenge is available in the form of four "power pills" in each corner of the maze. The power pills are over-sized dots that provide the fine and honorable Pac with the ability to eat ghosts for a limited period of time.

The increasing power hook has gained a huge amount of sophistication since the humble days of the wise and kind Pac Man. There are different flavors of the increasing power hook that have become pretty much expected in various gaming genres. The *increasing power hook* can be defined as adding strength or abilities to a player as the course of the game progresses. Unlike the simple power pills of the sage yet jaunty Pac Man, most implementations of the increasing power hook are expected to stay with a character at least until it is killed. There are temporary power-ups more akin to the power pills, but they don't have the kind of hooking ability of increasing powers that stay around at least until death, giving a real sense of accomplishment to the playing experience. CRPGs probably get the most power out of the increasing power hook. As a character or group of characters controlled by the player continues to play the game they get these hooks in a variety of different ways. The first is that it is expected that as the characters kill more monsters they will gain experience levels that will provide increases in their inherent abilities, such as more advanced spell-casting talents or better sword-fighting skills. These increases and their exact effects depend on the type of character being played. At the same time, all characters gain more ability to take damage as they progress up the level ladder.

In addition to the increase in inherent abilities, CRPGs also provide items that add better skills or new abilities to a character when they possess and use these items. Items and the increasing abilities they represent can be lost, stolen, or destroyed. In some cases items will have only a set number of charges, and after they are run out they become junk. So unlike the inherent abilities, item-derived advantages come and go.

In first-person shooters it is expected that your character will find various weapons and armor items that will increase your ability to take and dish out damage.

There are a number of different ways to implement the increasing power hook in war and other strategy games. Giving more or better units to players as they progress through various battles is pretty much an accepted point. Individual units that have lived through a number of battles can also be given a combat bonus to reflect their seasoned status. You would be surprised how many Panzer General players form deep attachments to particular units that have survived a number of battles and close calls.

In vehicular sims you can give players access to better and more varied vehicles and weapons only after they have "proven" themselves by playing successfully for a while in less capable craft. You can also add piloting and shooting bonuses to the algorithmic structure of the game to make shooting and flying control more accurate as a player rises in rank. However, if you are going to do this make sure your players know it is a feature of the code so they don't become disgruntled with sluggish controls at the start of the game. In addition, avoiding it in realistic flight sims altogether is a good idea, since it degrades the realism of the simulation.

As usual you should play extensively in the genre of your design in order to determine the common ways of implementing increasing power hooks in the type of game you are interested in making. Possibly more than with any other element of commonality in a genre, players will become disgruntled and unruly if the normal ways of increasing their power they have come to love and expect are not present in your implementation.

Goals

You need to provide your players with goals at every opportunity. There should be an *overarching goal* to your design. Examples of overarching goals: Defeat the Axis armies and win WW II; kill the big baddie at the end of the game; destroy all other star empires in the galaxy and take possession of all the planets.

But in addition to overarching goals, you should implement as many *sub-goals* as possible so that your players can get that all-important sense of accomplishment. In a war game it will be to meet the mission requirements for a specific battle. In a first-person shooter it might be just the unstated goal of getting through the level with their skin intact. In a CRPG, subgoals are likely to be called *quests*; there are traditionally a number of varied quests that must be completed in addition to standard monster-killing and exploring to successfully get to the big monster at the end of the game and fight it.

Increasing Difficulty

As your game progresses, the *difficulty* of the game should increase also. Although this is fairly self-evident, it is important to think about as you work on your design.

LEVELS ARE YOUR FRIEND

Levels naturally create a sense of accomplishment and implicit subgoals in your game. Look at Tetris. The only real subgoals in the entire game are just to survive to the next level. I don't judge my Tetris performance as much by the score I achieve as by the level to which I manage to get.

First-person shooters are naturals for levels. You clear out a level of monsters and move on to the next, harder level. That is essentially the whole game in a nutshell.

Most war games implement levels, but they call them *missions* or *battles*. They are still fixed-length engagements and when you are done with one, you get another, harder one.

In most CRPGs, levels are used, but in a much more subtle way. Individual dungeons that need cleaning out naturally constitute levels of the game, and many dungeons are broken down to levels inside themselves, effectively creating sublevels to the game. It is also not uncommon in a CRPG to take characters of a high enough experience and transport them to another continent or dimension, creating yet another layer of leveling.

Implementing some kind of level break in your games constitutes generally good game-design practice. It provides not only a sense of accomplishment, but the level break can also serve as a good jumping off point for a player to save a session and go back to reality for a while, or just take a needed breather.

A game is something akin to a dramatic presentation, a book, or another creative endeavor—it should build to a climax. By building a small increase in difficulty into your game that becomes bigger over time, the climax of your game will be more of a challenge to the player and increase the overall sense of accomplishment. At the point of highest difficulty, your player should be right at the end of the game.

In some games, where there is no end, the difficulty increase will create an end for you. Again, look at Tetris. In the world of Tetris, blocks fall from the sky from the dawn of time till the end of the universe. *End of the game* isn't defined with a preset stopping point or baddie monster beyond which the game is over, but instead the game ends when those blocks fall too fast for your efforts to make a difference.

Bigger Rewards

Hand in hand with increasing difficulty go *bigger rewards.* Whatever hooks you use to keep up a player's sense of accomplishment, they should be increased as the difficulty of the game increases. It starts to feel like a gyp if you get the same number of points for performing a Herculean task as for doing something pretty simple.

More impressive increasing powers and more points need to be given as the game goes on to keep your players happy.

Ranks

A cheap and simple way to give a little sense of accomplishment is to provide ranks with your game. In some cases, *rank* is going to actually make a difference in the abilities of the character; then it is going to become an inherent increasing power hook with a different name. But even if there is nothing in the rank but the name and some sort of designation of the higher rank in the interface (for example, appending Col. to the front of the player's name or referring to them by rank on briefing screens between levels or battles), they can still provide a sense of accomplishment to some players. Making the next rank in line can become a goal irrespective of any other factors.

Points

Providing all but the simplest action games with *points* is almost a cheap way to provide a sense of accomplishment to a player. But from Space Invaders (another Stone Age game, for those of you in the younger crowd) on, points have been with us and a few players will take them seriously. I personally feel that if you have enough other hooks for sense of accomplishment in your game design that points almost inherently betray most worlds. (There are no easy-to-define points as such in real life. Gold, titles, and various kinds of power-ups all have real-world counterparts.) However, points are a hallowed tradition and it takes no more to implement them than wanting to and writing a couple of lines of code to do it.

Hidden Treasures

Various types of *hidden items* in your games provide a real sense of accomplishment to the dedicated players that find them. There are various ways of hiding things: putting them behind secret doors or making them conditional on various undocumented keystroke combinations are popular.

Hidden levels are always a plus in a game that relies heavily on levels. For a very few types of realistic games, hidden levels will damage the veracity of the world, such as a WW II war game. However, making some missions that can be played only if exceptional performance is attained in a given battle serves pretty much the same function.

Only one type of game absolutely demands the existence of hidden components—any game in this genre without these hidden elements will be scorned and shunned by players—and that is the fighting game.

In a *fighting game* it is simply understood that individual characters will have undocumented abilities that are activated by hitting obscure controller combinations. The general name for these abilities are secret moves, so if you are tackling a fighting game you better put in a few of them for each character in your game or suffer the hatred and loathing of all your players.

• • • • • • • •
Summary

In this chapter we have covered some of the most important broad—and in some cases fairly specific—elements that should go into your game designs, regardless of your specific programming tools.

We have learned about the following elements and how they combine to make a good design.

Interface

The *interface* is probably the most important element of a game design and should be clean, feel natural to the user, have a tiered-command structure, be as ergonomically friendly as possible, suffer no evil delays, and minimize the amount of information in the actual playing area.

Ancillary Realism

The small details of your design lend to the overall *veracity* of your world. No detail is too small to be used in promoting the overall feel of the game. Appropriate sound is a critical element to adding veracity to your design, but unless you can get professionally produced music you should just skip it altogether.

Customizability

When you can make anything in your game a user-selected option you should do so. Your game should have the best out-of-the-box default configuration you can possibly come up with, but different users will have different playing styles that will demand different informational input and output options. It is critical that you provide *customizability* for any keyboard commands in particular. If you are using sound in your game, providing as many options for controlling the sound as possible will prevent you from being ridiculed by other game designers and possibly having rude signs taped to your back without your knowledge.

You should also provide as scaled-down a version of your game as is feasible in order to increase your potential player base by making your game playable by people on lower-end platforms.

Difficulty modifiers available from the start of your game all but constitute a requirement. A lack of these options will have dire consequences (see the above comments for leaving out sound options).

Difficulty

There are darned good gamers out there and darned bad ones. Your game needs to walk the line in the middle and scale progressively from a fairly simple difficulty level up to a very hard one, in order to meet the expectations of your players and keep them challenged.

Good AI

Artificial intelligence (AI) is an integral element of many different varieties of game design and you would be well served by studying the subject in as much detail as is feasible for your situation. However, in lieu of good AI programming skills you can cheat by throwing all the obvious factors you can in favor of your computer opponent to artificially provide a good level of difficulty for your players.

Generally, the smaller the scope of your game, the easier it is to implement AI algorithms to deal with your game elements.

AI routines, particularly more sophisticated ones, tend to be a big problem for creating subtle loopholes in your game mechanics. Before releasing your game, though, search out and destroy these loopholes through beta testing.

Game-Production Stages

The commonly accepted stages in the creation of a game are *design phase, alpha testing, beta testing,* and *gold master.*

During the beta stage the working code of the game is tested by as many different people as feasible and changes in the design are implemented to accommodate as wide a range of users and play styles as possible. Grievous errors in both programming code and design can still be cured in this stage without suffering the embarrassment of having your inadequacies as a designer or programmer pointed out by the general public after the release of your game.

Sense of Accomplishment

A *sense of accomplishment,* which can be achieved in your design through many different methods, is what hooks your players and keeps them playing. A few of the various methods of providing your players with a sense of accomplishment include increasing powers, goals, increasing difficulty, bigger rewards, ranks, and various kinds of hidden elements.

• • • • • • • • •
From Here

Now we have a good grounding in what makes a good game design and the bare minimum of a common vocabulary with which to discuss game analysis intelligently. We will continue to cover some game-design issues in the various programming chapters of the book devoted to specific topics.

But right now, with a rough idea of the major elements that separate a good game from a bad game, we will go on to look at a few games and analyze in depth what their designers did to make them work, or in a few cases where the designers missed the ball.

CHAPTER 3
· · · · · · · ·
GAME DESIGN IN ACTION

Seeing various design principles in the abstract is a fine thing, but seeing examples of good game design in action is much better. In this chapter we briefly examine a few different games that particularly illustrate good or bad design elements.

All of these games are available in shareware or demo versions. If you own the registered versions, feel free to reference them during our discussions as opposed to downloading and examining the shareware/demo versions. The elements of design will apply just as well.

If you are particularly familiar with a title, as you probably will be with one or more of the games on this list, then you probably won't have any need to boot the game to follow our discussion. However, if you haven't seen the game, please take the time to get and play the demo. This will pay off later as you see how some of the best designers in the industry pull off their magic tricks and how you can crib off of their long experience.

• • • • • •
Quake

As you can probably tell from the previous chapter, I hold John Carmack, John Romero, and the rest of the id team in very high esteem as game designers. These guys know what makes a compelling game and realize that what you leave out is as important as what you put in for some types of games.

Quake is a *first-person shooter,* the latest in a long award-winning line from id. The first thing you will note on booting the game is the high quality of the 3D graphics engine. It is probably the best in the class of shooters currently out on the market. However, we are not concerned particularly with the graphics engine right now, but the basic design principles of the game.

Let's start from a top-down design view. First of all, the scope of the game is the game map. These maps are filled with various fantastic monsters and the whole play paradigm of the game is pretty much solely concerned with making sure you blow them to kingdom come before they do the same to you. This scope is only marginally connected to any form of reality. The backstory to the game is nowhere near as important as the play paradigm, and Quake has only a couple of brief paragraphs in the manual devoted to how and why you are caught up in the maze and the mayhem.

This matter of backstory is important to note. Some games are going to need more of a backstory than others. In general, the larger the scope of the game, the more of a backstory you will need. The *backstory* is what happened to get your character to the start of the game to make all of this make sense. In most cases you will want to have at least a thin justification for why your players are doing what they are doing. Depending on the game type and your personal preferences, you might need more or less. CRPG players pretty much demand a long and fully fleshed out backstory; action games require only a small justification for the killing about to ensue.

Interface Elements

After the scope, 3D engine, and backstory, we come to the *interface elements.* We have already discussed at length the command structure of the game. However, it might be worth noting again how id decided to make the keyboard the primary input interface. While mouse and joystick support are provided, the vast majority of players seem to prefer the high-speed response of the keyboard.

Note the large playing field dominates the screen and there isn't any information actually in the play area. At some brief instances in the game, short text messages will show up in the main display area briefly, but they will

BACKSTORY BLOOPERS

These days most games at least try to give enough of a thin veil of backstory to justify the carnage the players are committing in many game designs. However, at the start of arcade gaming, this wasn't always the case. A particularly perverse friend of mine once started pointing this out one day walking through an arcade.

The game under discussion was an old arcade classic, Pengo. In Pengo the player takes on the role of a cute little penguin waddling around an ice field. There are critters called snobees also in the ice fields and they are Pengo-unfriendly. The playing field is covered with ice blocks that can be kicked to run across the screen until they hit another ice block. If a snobee happens to be in the line of travel of a moving ice block it will be crushed. Also in the ice fields are diamonds and snobee eggs that will hatch the longer you are on the map. The eggs can be crushed by ramming ice blocks into them.

The goal of the game is to collect as many of the diamonds in the fields as possible. When all of the diamonds on a level are collected, then the player moves on to the next, harder level. Along the way the player will have to kill snobees and crush the eggs before they hatch in order to survive.

There was no backstory to such a cute and obviously fantastic game. However, Chris Haynes (the perverse friend in question) started looking at this game and thought about the circumstances that could bring about the situation we were seeing.

First, there was only one penguin and lots of these snobee critters. Further, there were lots of snobee eggs. It is only logical to assume that we are dead in the heart of the snobee stomping grounds. Further, we are in their mating area, the very kind of place most life on this planet would pretty seriously defend.

All of a sudden, this cute little action game started to turn gruesome. Instead of a cute little penguin, our lead character started looking a lot more like an evil being trying to wipe out the snobee race. And the only apparent goal was to get the money represented by the diamonds. Because of a little bit of thinking and the lack of a backstory, we went from having a lead character who was a heroic, cute, embattled little penguin facing tremendous odds to playing a treasure-robbing, genocidal, aquatic waterfowl bent on the destruction of the possibly peace-loving snobee race. The little guy was crushing their eggs for crying out loud!

Backstory is your friend.

rapidly disappear so that you aren't distracted from concentrating on the gaming experience.

Options even turn off the information bar on the bottom of the screen in order to give players total concentration on their game.

Options

Quake is absurdly rife with options. First there are the options on the option screen (see Figure 3.1), where some of the most common optional switches most players might want to use are located. But beyond that, by pressing the "~" key, a player can access the command-line control console that supports roughly 150 different options for the hard-core Quaker, lists of which are widely available on Quake sites on the Net.

Even though there is a serious load of options, this isn't to say it is totally perfect. For instance, some players might like to be able to customize the order and types of information on the information bar at the bottom of the screen, a feature that isn't supported (or if it is, I haven't found it in the plethora of console options).

Despite this one minor gripe, one might be wise to take a page from the id book and think about the fact that if these guys thought it was a good idea to offer their players over 150 different game-customization options, you might want to take the time to add as many as you can reasonably think of to your designs.

Veracity

Quake is just chock-full of *veracity*. Practically brimming over with it. Okay, most of us aren't going to be able to get Nine Inch Nails to do our sound effects and have the talents of Adrian Carmack to give the game a uniformly distressing artistic look, but we should aspire to these things. The sound and art elements combine brilliantly here to make a world of uniform pain.

The typography of the game as an important factor has already been mentioned, but let's look at some even more subtle details. Go in the game and start spinning around to the left and the right. Note that you move slightly faster in the middle of a spin and that there are a few frames added at the end after you have left off the keys (it is almost imperceptible on a fast machine)

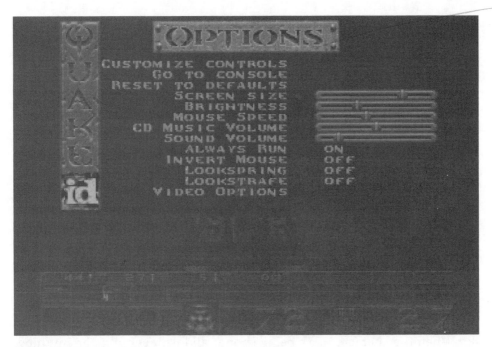

Figure 3.1 Quake options screen.

to have you slowing slightly at the end. This isn't as evident when only turning 90 degrees, but if you start spinning a couple of continuous 360s the effect becomes more pronounced. Your first reflex will probably be to attribute this to the way the 3D rendering happens to work, if you notice it at all. However, when talking with John Carmack about the Doom II engine I found out that this effect is deliberate. If you think about the real world and spinning or looking rapidly left and right, you move slightly more rapidly in the middle of the action as a rule than at the start or the end of it.

Tiny details like this are why these guys are driving Ferraris and the rest of us aren't.

However, I will tempt fate by throwing a veracity stone at Quake: the way you open doors by shooting and then running into them. The shooting part doesn't bother me. While this is dumb in the real world, it works in Quake and cuts down on the number of options for which you need specific commands. However, running into the doors is the problem. People don't do this, in Quake or anywhere else. While there are situations where cops will hammer a door with their shoulder to make a busting entry, this isn't the only way of doing it. Watch videos dealing with trained people doing this and depending on the situation they use their off hand to open the door so they aren't in and being shot at before they can determine where their problem areas are. A detailed discussion of advanced fire-team tactics is beyond the scope of this book, but the point is that I don't feel that always ramming a door to open it is realistic.

How could this have been solved? Easily. The code has to check for the player running into a door anyway. How much harder would it have been to add a couple of frames of a hand coming from the bottom of the screen to push on it? No real time difference—you could make it very rapid, but at least the suggestion would add an infinitesimal amount of veracity. Then again, this is such a minor point, and many gamers might disagree.

If you wanted to add another cool feature, you could have reloading happening at random intervals when the character is moving around with the shotgun selected and isn't actively in combat. It would seem that a simple check could be performed to see if something is shooting at the character. When the character isn't being shot at and isn't shooting at anything, sometimes a vanishingly short sequence of frames could show one hand loading the shotgun and a clicking sound come out as the shells are being jacked in. It would instantly stop if you fired and wouldn't add any appreciable time to your firing on a monster. This would only be for show, and not have any actual effect on game mechanics, but would add a cool little bit of veracity. An effect akin to this was in the Doom II engine but didn't make it into Quake.

Sense of Accomplishment

Almost every sense of accomplishment hook is in Quake in some form or another. The increasing power hook is there with power-ups. Hidden elements abound. A good scaled increasing difficulty and level breakdown provide a feeling of having pulled something off after every level.

The use of hidden elements, in particular, is rather clever in Quake, since at the end of the level they tell you how many secret areas there were in the level and how many you found. This provides incentive to run levels over to try to find that last lurking secret area, and gives you a real kick when you get them all the first time.

What Isn't There

What isn't in Quake is almost as important as what is. Some programmers leveled some snide criticism at Doom for being a bit on the simplistic side, from an implementation point of view, and John Carmack commented that he could have implemented all kinds of different things and really made a monster out of the game with the kitchen sink thrown in. It isn't that he can't do the code or the designs, it is that he purposely keeps the play paradigm as simple as possible. In his words, "We want it to be visceral."

As a result there isn't much to do in Quake but shoot things. There are puzzles, sure, but of a very simple type having to do with thrown switches and figuring out how to get to some areas of the maps. There could be a lot more to this game. You could have real character development in the forms of levels and many more actions than the basic move—shoot and figure out what to shoot—that are available (see Figure 3.2).

If you think about it, all the elements are in the engine to easily turn out a CRPG with just a few changes. However, id knows its niche; the creation of

Figure 3.2   Quake play shot.

first-person shooter action games. Nothing in a recent id game takes away from the run-and-gun play mechanics that they have become rich and famous perfecting.

This matter of making sure you understand your niche and not trying to add to your scope unnecessarily is an important lesson to learn. You can add a million other cool things to a game design at any point. Any designer who can't think of a ton of things to add at any given time isn't trying very hard. But will it help the game? That is the critical question.

Kitchen Sink Scope Follies

Not keeping very careful reign on your scope and play-mechanic issues can lead to real pain. The following story is true in all the particulars (and is famous and the butt of many jokes in the industry), but I am going to change the names involved to protect anonymity.

Six years ago, a very talented AI programmer we will call David Bright decided that games he saw on the shelves could really gain from well-used AI programming techniques. To this end he started coding a game we will call StarRunner 2100. A year later he was pretty much putting a wrap on the code but realized that his graphics programming ability wasn't up to his AI talents. The game had the AI elements he wanted, but the visual look wasn't anywhere near the industry standards of the time. So he contacted a graphics coder, got some graphics code, and started over with his engine from scratch to improve the game's visual look.

Another year passed and with the code in beta, David realized that there were some new things he could do to speed the game up. He tore it apart again to optimize his work. A year goes by and the game is again going into beta. David at this point realizes that there are a ton of cool features he can add to the game. Back to the drawing board.

The game company David was originally producing the game for has gone belly up during this time. David ends up mortgaging his house, getting personal loans from everyone he knows, and extending his credit to the limit in order to continue work on the game. A year goes by and David is back to beta, but there are just these little things that need some work. So the game starts getting torn down again.

Now David had some really impressive code in this game. He had reason to be proud. The level of detail involved with this game destroyed anything on the shelves by an order of magnitude. To give one brief example of the detail of game, let's say you got into a space battle in your StarRunner and shot at another ship and missed. The game would figure out if there was anything in the path of your shot. Let's say there was an asteroid field and your shot had the power to knock an asteroid out of its orbital path. The game would then calculate the future path of the asteroid. So maybe a year later in game time the asteroid would ram a populated planet. The game would then determine exactly what on the planet was hit. If a factory region happened to be struck, the game would take the resultant economic effects into account. So totally across the galaxy by this time, and with no real memory of the battle that caused it, you would see the price of foo rise by a tenth of a percent because of one misplaced shot: Everything in the game was this fanatically detailed.

Another game company buys and drops the work. The guy at the company who signed the contract was fired immediately. David and his game already have a reputation in the industry of seeming like a good idea but being impossible in reality.

Finally the game came to rest with a young company with more money than smarts who purchased the contract on it without knowing the history. They now regret it. Scheduled to release almost a year ago as of this printing, it is questionable if it will release at all. Their beta testers will admit privately that the game is unplayable. There are six pages of keyboard command combinations that must be learned in order to try to play the game and according to people in the company no one but David can actually play the thing.

There are some other alternatively amusing or sad side notes to the as yet unfinished saga of StarRunner, but the key thing to get out of all this is to *set your design standards and stick to them.* You will never release the perfect game. There are always more features you can add or better technology that might have come along since you started your project, but this leads to an insane cycle of trying to create the perfect game of the type, an unattainable goal.

• • • • • • • • •
Descent II

With *Descent* we have one of the large and ever growing group of games that are referred to in the industry as *doom clones,* another term for first-person shooters. But Descent shows that just because you decide to use the play mechanics from another game and use their general scope, you can still make enough changes that you are creating an original game you can be proud of.

To make the game unique, the Descent team decided to put your character into a small spaceship as opposed to running on foot. This added a level of three-dimensionality that isn't present in most other shooters (see Figures 3.3 and 3.4). Up and down are real movement options as opposed to having to wait on elevators or jump. Further, the maps are much more elaborate in some ways than most of the maps in Quake due to this real movement along the vertical axis.

Most of the major design considerations of Descent are the same as those for Quake, but let's look at a few telling differences to see what makes this game unique.

Interface Considerations

First, although Descent essentially has the standard keyboard layout for a first-person shooter, the keyboard isn't going to be the primary input device for most players. Instead, since this game marries some of the elements of a flight sim with the first-person shooter, a joystick is going to be preferred by most people. Advanced joysticks are supported in the game, and it is fairly hard for most of us to really get into the game without one.

Figure 3.3 Cockpit Display 1.

Figure 3.4   Cockpit Display 2.

By default, there is also a bit more clutter in the playing area than in Quake. This might not be too clever, but you start getting into an issue of veracity versus interface design. If you are in a small ship, there would be a windshield of some sort. Further, options give you the ability to change to the traditional setup of the status bar across the bottom—the preferred design method.

Veracity Issues

Most of the veracity issues in Descent are about the same as in Quake. The designers learned (some would say stole, but I think that as long as you make significant changes there is nothing wrong with taking elements of good designs) from id and made sure they had good integration of all elements, including the use of good custom typography.

The designers of Descent also got a boon in the form of the status and damage display information. The reason is simple: In real life a guy running around doesn't have a status bar he is looking at all the time to figure out what he is carrying and how he feels. However, in a ship you do have these things. So Descent gets an instant boost by presenting this information in a way that seems somewhat more natural and realistic.

The music and sound effects are good for the purpose and work with the game, even if they don't hit the high points set by some other games.

Even though we hit on backstory early when we were discussing Quake, it is technically a veracity element. The backstory for Descent II is much more detailed than that of Quake and in the CD version of the game includes a long movie that sets the scene well. There is also a minor detail, but one that will matter to some people: You aren't killing living beings. The problems are all *robots*. While the real difference is none in terms of the game play, for a minority segment of the player base, the difference is significant in terms of philosophy.

However, the game does take a small veracity hit in some ways because of the games that have come before it, such as Doom II. While the backstory explains why you are indoors in a maze in this ship, it just feels odd to be dealing with doors and such while flying around in a ship. On the whole, the mazes look like any other first-person shooter maze environment, even though the hallways and smaller rooms make you start to wonder why things would look like this in a place built for ships and self-propelled robots. The sense of scale also gets confused from time to time in some situations and you can start thinking long and hard about exactly how big your ship is in relation to things around you.

While minor, these points do detract slightly from the gaming experience. In Doom II and Quake, most players will never pause during game play and start thinking about the game mechanics as such. Most Descent players, however, have done this at one time or another.

Sense of Accomplishment

Descent II shares with Quake all of the same basic sense of accomplishment hooks, but some of the power-ups are cooler, given that they are ship-controlled weapons as opposed to handheld weapons. In particular, the guided missiles are incredibly cool and bring great joy to those who learn to use them well.

Learning from Descent II

What do we learn from Descent? First, you can steal a lot of the elements from a game you admire. As long as you make substantial changes, your new design is still a unique product that deserves consideration in its own right. Second, your backstory can help you with some of your veracity issues. The basic premise of Descent is a bit goofy in some ways, but the backstory explains this stuff well.

Command and Conquer

With Quake and Descent II we are done examining first-person shooters. *Command and Conquer* (C&C) represents another category, a *real-time war game.*

Interface Elements

The informational needs of the war game are different from the informational needs of first-person shooters. In general, there is much more data to contend with. However, C&C sidesteps many of the informational requirements by deciding to avoid heavy realism.

C&C doesn't include a lot of the standard war-game model elements. There is no obvious morale which can cause units constantly under fire to break and refuse to follow orders. There isn't the idea of seasoned troops that become better with more experience. There are no supply or rest issues with individual troops. Your little guys pretty much fight when and where you tell them and you only end up with problems when they take too much damage and die.

This focus of scope to the lower-realism level removes the need for many informational inputs to keep close track of the status of your troops. All you really need to know about your units in C&C is what type they are, where they are, and how much damage they have taken. As such, C&C manages to simplify its interface considerably. All you need to deal with is the building command sidebar, your map (when you have one), and your individual troops.

We have already discussed the good use of the mouse and keyboard command interface with this game. Play around with it a bit and see how much you can do with fine control of your individual units when you want to play with the keyboard commands, and yet at the same time the speed you can get with using the mouse.

Veracity

Again we see how a good design team has all elements adding to the game's veracity. The use of sound when you activate a troop unit and all of the graphics integrate well and there are no out-of-place elements to take you out of the game and make you start wondering about the machine underneath.

AI

AI is an integral part of a war game, more so than with many other game types. The AI for C&C is barely adequate for the job: The machine opposition doesn't use the resources at its disposal well at all. You will rapidly discover that with a few simple techniques there ceases to be any real chance that you are going to lose in a given battle, but that you are just trying to solve the problem of how to best use the AI's blind spots against it.

This huge mistake makes the game stop being a war game and turns it into a puzzle game on most of the maps. We will examine another clear-cut example of bad AI design later in the chapter, although the AI weakness in C&C is large enough to be instructive. For many types of games the AI techniques would be more than adequate. C&C has as much AI as the two first-person shooters we have already looked at, for example. But while less than astounding AI is okay for that type of game, it is a killer in a war game.

Learning from C&C

C&C illustrates a few major points we want to keep in mind. First of all, by limiting the realism of our scope we can create a game that might not be realistic but can make up for it in *playability.* Second, AI is more important in some games than in others, and war games are particular sticklers for a good AI. The fairly minor imperfections in the AI of C&C leave the game playable, but change the focus and remove the challenge from the game at many points.

Allied General

Allied General (AG) presents a realistic war game to C&C's less-realistic scope. Here the player is using real troop-unit types to attempt to re-create historical situations. Yet, as with C&C and all of the examples in this chapter so far, it handles the interface elements of the game so well that no onerous demands are placed on the player.

Interface Concertinos

We have dealt with the Panzer/Allied General (they share the same interface elements) play interface elements in the previous chapter. But play around with the interface briefly and get a feel for how easy it is to control the individual units. If you have dealt with any realistic war games in the past, you will see immediately how elegant the Allied General interface is. The actual issuing of commands doesn't take the player out of the game. (See Figure 3.5.)

Also look at how much information that AG is keeping track of, such as morale and unit strengths, but at the same time how little of that information is thrust at you in the playing field. Instead the information is easily available by examining the unit, but doesn't intrude when you don't need it. (See Figure 3.6.)

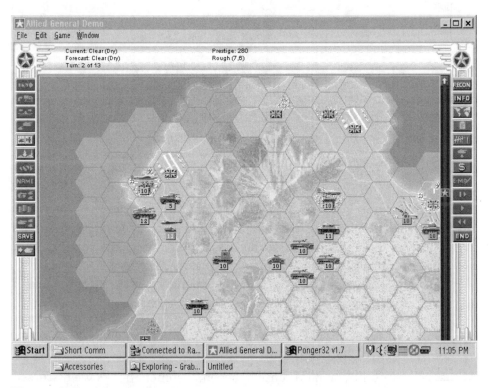

Figure 3.5 Main screen.

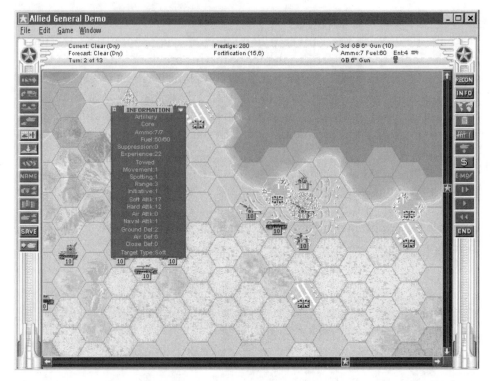

Figure 3.6   Unit status screen.

AI

The AI of this game is more than strong enough to handle the tasks put before it. Play with the game a bit and see how difficult it is to easily carve up your opposition. The AI knows to attack your weak units with strong units of a type that are most effective in putting pain to them. It also knows to support its own units with artillery and other units that can make it exceedingly difficult to attack enemy unit clusters effectively.

A quick tip: The key to the game, in my experience, is the effective use of air power, where the AI is not quite as strong at defense.

Sense of Accomplishment

AG uses many of the standard sense of accomplishment hooks we discussed in Chapter 2; however, pay close attention to the way you build your own forces. As the full version of the game continues, you end up with strong personal feelings for units you have promoted up the ranks and have survived over the long haul. Persistent and promotable units are a good way to add a sense of accomplishment hook to a war game.

The Incredible Machine

So far we have been dealing with games of destruction. However, there are games that are fun, playable, and have nothing to do with killing other things. *The Incredible Machine* (TIM) is one of my favorite games of all time and is so elegant it seems simple, but really gives a huge amount of challenge. (See Figure 3.7.)

TIM also introduces us to another category of game that I didn't discuss in Chapter 2 because it is small, but incredibly diverse: the puzzle game. *Puzzle*

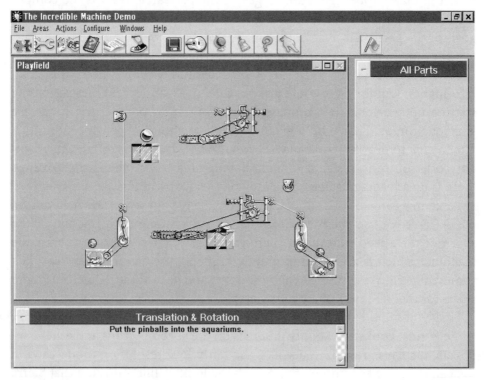

Figure 3.7 A built machine.

games are those games where, fairly obviously, the player is trying to solve a puzzle. While many games involve puzzles of some sort, games that would actually fall in this category are those games that don't seem to fit in any of the others. It is something of a case of "I will know it when I see it" thinking. There aren't that many pure play puzzle games out there, but when you run across one you will pretty much immediately realize it.

Interface Elements

TIM has only two first-tier interface input requirements: select and move an object into position. There is also the need to start a machine to test it, which along with customizing objects form the second-tier interface input options. On the third tier are game-control elements. As far as the output in the interface, TIM 3 doesn't do as well as it could, and seems to be getting slightly worse in some ways since its earliest incarnation. Note that the screen is split into four major zones. First and largest is the play area. Next is the component menu. Below these is a goal-information area that tells you what the goals of the particular puzzle are. Finally you have the menu and speed button bar running across the top of the screen. (See Figure 3.8.)

What do we really need here? We definitely don't need the goal-information window. We could just put that up as a brief text message at the start of a puzzle and then provide a menu option to pop it back up in case someone forgot. That would give us a total of about 20 percent more total screen area to devote to our playing field. And while you can turn this window off, you can't resize the main playing area to use the extra space, so there is no advantage gained to removing the goal window.

Next, in a game of this simplicity, do we really gain with the speed button bars? Can't we use the menu commands, which take up a fraction of the space of the speed buttons, to perform most of these tasks? To start the machine, which is a fairly important command, we can integrate a switch somewhere into one of the other windows and gain about 10 percent more space for that all-important playing area.

Finally, it would appear that Sierra has decided that their market for this game is kids. Look at the goofy graphics on the speed buttons and other supporting displays. Take into account the fairly low resolution mode used in the game that gives it more of a comic book look. While I am sure that Sierra

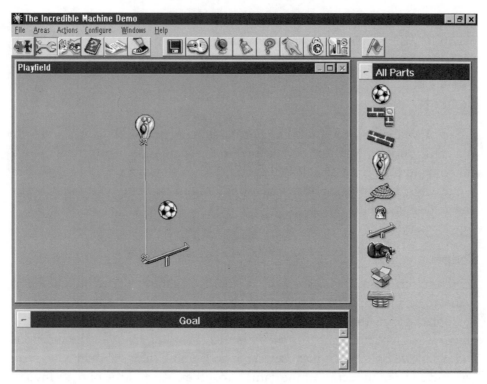

Figure 3.8 Some individual elements on the screen.

has run demographics to figure out where its market lies, I know a vast number of adults who play this game and these graphics don't exactly scream out "adult."

Learning from TIM

In TIM we see one of those true sparks of genius: The game is totally original. The major thing to learn from this game is that your designs don't have to be complicated in order to provide many challenges and options for game play. Also, we learn here not to be afraid to run out onto new ground. Working with TIM we can see that a good enough concept doesn't need to fit into one of the most popular categories and can break new ground.

However, in spite of the great qualities that TIM embodies, we might want to consider it also as an example of badly thought out interface design in some ways. Twenty to 30 percent more of the screen could have been devoted to the playing area without working too hard at it.

••••••
Scorch

In *Scorch* we depart from examining professionally produced games and look at a game done by a single programmer in his spare time. Unfortunately, we are going to poke a lot of holes in Scorch: Although it is a pretty fun game in some ways, it betrays its nonprofessional origins in some pretty ugly ways on the design level.

Scope

Scorch suffers from serious scope problems. The game can't decide whether it wants to be a multiplayer game or a single-player game. There are many of the weapons options that are totally useless from a practical sense in the single-player version of the game, yet they are there. Further, many of the weapons and defensive options are just useless, period. These things should have been winnowed from the scope of the game altogether. Most of the options involving dirt are good examples. Another example is the tanks, which add movement to the scope of an artillery game. However, the way tanks are implemented in this game makes it a useless option for all practical purposes when playing on anything but a totally flat field and too much extra effort to bother with from the point of view of the player. The movement options should have been removed from the scope of the game, or fully embraced and the game turned into a two-dimensional tank game. (See Figures 3.9 and 3.10.)

The easiest way to revamp this design and still keep it somewhat intact would be to split the game into two distinct sections: the single-player and multiplayer games. The single-player version would have a drastically reduced set of command options and the multiplayer game would implement all of the single-player options, but also add in the other options which might provide some subtle fun when playing against one or more human opponents.

In either version, some of the less-useful equipment options and movement should be removed. You can tell playing the game that every idea the programmer had about how to add to the game has gotten stuck in the release code and not been pared down by a vigorous beta test.

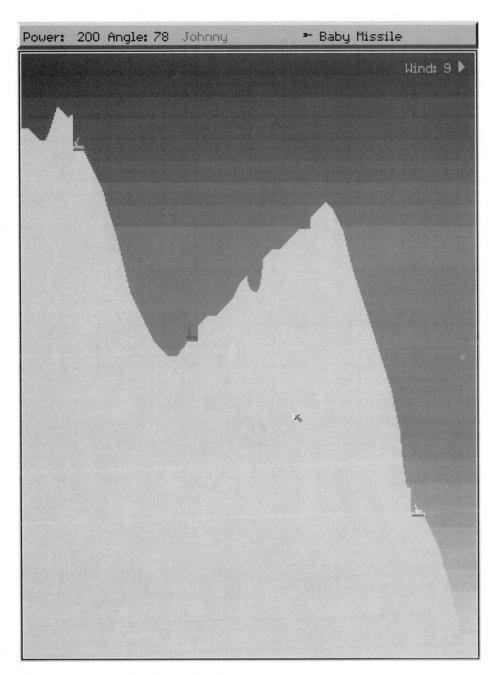

Figure 3.9 Scorch playing field.

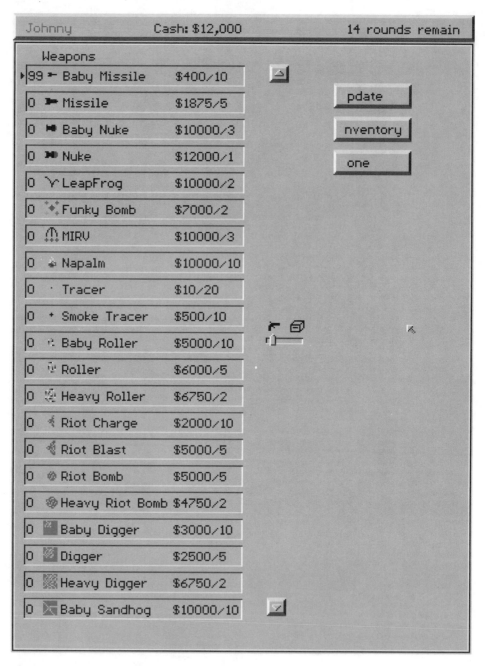

Figure 3.10   Weapons buying screen.

Interface Elements

Scorch primarily uses only three first-tier input commands: fire, change firing angle, and change shot power. On the second tier is change weapon. All of these commands work fine and are executed from the keyboard. Unfortunately, the third-tier commands are muddled and can be performed from the keyboard or from mouse control, but belie both scope and programming tool problems. It is hard to get back to keyboard control from using the mouse to change some of the plethora of third-tier commands, on the tool side. And there are just too many fairly useless options on the scope side to clutter things up.

Many functions such as parachute and shield deployment should have been made automatic from the start, and while there is an option to make them automatic with the purchase of extra equipment, this provides more of a playing complication than it is worth.

AI

The AI in this game is the weakest point. It is obvious that the designer was more interested in head-to-head play than in the AI play and has neglected making his AIs fully capable of dealing with all the eventualities of the engine. The AIs are all right when you keep the game on the fully default environment settings; one AI, the pool shark, deals with one environment option well (bouncing walls) but when you start using the plethora of wall options available to you, the AIs start having a fit and can't seem to mount effective opposition. Either the AI needs to be stronger or the environment options need to be curtailed when working in single-player mode.

Loopholes

The game also suffers from a game-mechanics problem of fairly huge proportions. If you get ahead right off the bat, that is it for the game. If you can acquire shields and make sure you have more of them than your opponents, it is just a matter of playing the game out for something to do.

Options

This game is a counterexample to the injunction to add as many options as possible to your designs. Don't design options that your programming skills can't cash. This game has myriad options for setting up the game, but they destroy the abilities of the AIs to properly play. When you are putting in options, make sure that they work with all the elements of the game. If you can't get them to work, then take them out—it's just that simple.

Also, there are tons of options for weapons and equipment that really don't do all that much for the game. The total list of things you can do in this game could be dropped by about half and no one would miss it but the designer.

Beta Testing

It might seem from the hammering we have been giving it that this game is grossly inferior. This isn't really the case. The game is a good idea and has many cool points to recommend it. I and many of my associates have a soft spot in our hearts for this game and keep booting up new revisions of it even with all its flaws. There are no warts on this game that a really good beta test couldn't cure. If anything but the most cursory beta test was given to this code, I would seriously be surprised. The beta test should be one of the most rigorously conducted phases of your work on a game, and if it is done properly and with attention to detail, the vast majority of the flaws that can creep into your code from the design and alpha phases can be routed out. But you can't hold onto bad options just because you have already implemented the code and are proud of yourself, as might be the case with this game.

That is what you should take away from your inspection of this game: The effort you put into your beta test will make or break your game. The beta test for Scorch didn't pass muster. Hopefully in later revisions this game will get fixed, because it isn't a bad design through and through; there are just enough basic mistakes to take the edge off what could have been a pretty killer, modest-level game.

Nethack

Nethack is another game that isn't produced professionally, so it shows a couple of minor warts; but this game shows many great elements of a modest group effort that isn't outside the scope of a few individuals working part time to complete a game.

History

Nethack is part of a group of games referred to as Rogue-like games. Rogue was a game developed years ago on the UNIX platform and used text-based graphic elements to produce a fairly modest little CRPG. Text characters were laid out in a grid and each character represented an element in the game. This provided a form of graphic interface that would be stable and displayable across multiple-platform types. Other games that used this type of interface were most of the early Star Trek games that date back to the beginnings of the personal computer (Altair's are *cool*).

Though Rogue gained a great deal of underground popularity on UNIX boxes, the game was copyrighted by the company that distributed it with their systems. Therefore, in the grand tradition of UNIX hacking, a number of different programmers started creating games that used most of Rogue's interface elements and command structure. These were *Rogue-like* games.

Roughly a dozen different flavors of Rogue-likes have evolved over the years, but one of the most popular is Nethack. The name *Nethack* comes from the fact that the designers of the game aren't in one location but collaborate over the Internet. The hack part comes from the game being heavily based on code from an earlier Rogue-like of that name.

In the last revision, Nethack has left behind the character-based interface (though it is still supported) to create a game that uses a graphic interface. The graphics interface is simple, essentially a one-for-one replacement of text characters with a small array of graphics tiles. However, it is good enough to get the job done.

Nethack is a major force of discussions in the Rogue-like games newsgroups as well as having a few Web pages devoted to it. Most serious gamers with a UNIX background have played Nethack at one time or another and there are executables available for a wide variety of UNIX platforms as well as for Intel boxes. The source code is also available for programmers to pick up techniques used in the game as well as to find out specific information about that monster or trap that is causing you undue angst.

Interface

The interface for Nethack is pretty good on the output side. Almost the entire screen is devoted to the playing area except for a tiny status bar area at the bottom of the screen. The graphics are simplistic, but they get the job done. This is an important point to note: There is a huge amount of stress placed on graphics in current game designs. This isn't inappropriate, as engaging graphics drive game sales. However, when you are producing a product with a small team and you aren't going for a shrink-wrapped game, it often isn't feasible to use the latest in ray casting and texture-mapping technology for your game.

The important thing with graphics for modest game designs is that they are attractive and get the job done. Tetris didn't have complex graphics. The Incredible Machine doesn't pull all of the graphics tricks it could to make the game a real graphics powerhouse. This is because these games don't require cutting-edge graphics to get their point across. Scorch, the other nonprofessional game in this survey, doesn't have the kind of graphics power it could, but it gets the job done, and there is no black spot against it for graphics performance.

If you have the resources and talent, put every graphic trick you can think of in your designs. Just remember there is no dishonor in simple graphics for a modest game as long as they convey the information the user needs in an appropriate manner.

On the input side, this game is patently inferior. Nethack is keyboard only and has about a billion little commands for everything you can think of. There is no keyboard remapping available. On the first tier, with simple movement and attack combos everything is fine. Trying to do anything more complex, however, leads to a mishmash of ALT and shifted characters that have even the most experienced players occasionally referring to the on-line help to try to figure out what the heck they need to key in to get the job done right now.

Part of this can be attributed to the type of game. CRPGs, of which this is about the barest-bones example worthy of the title, demand a lot more possible actions than most other types of games in order to give them veracity. (We discussed this in Chapter 2.) So Nethack is expected to have more commands than many other games.

Another portion of the problem can be attributed to the keyboard-only interface. With a mouse-driven or hybrid mouse/keyboard combination, these commands could have been made a lot simpler. But a lot of the problem is just plain bad input-interface-design characteristics. Or, to be more accurate, no input-interface design at all. It is obvious that things have just been tacked on to key combinations as features crept into the game without any real thought about interface-design characteristics.

Now you might have thought that all that incessant droning I was doing in Chapter 2 about the importance of interface-design characteristics was pretty obvious and boring, but note that the only two nonprofessional game designs we are looking at (and the majority of the class) suffer from interface problems. Thinking about user interfaces from the start of the design stage of the product is a must if your game is going to work and play well with users.

How could we clean up Nethack on the interface front? There are a number of things we could do. First, we could remove many of the options from the scope of the game. However, let's assume that we want them all (that is questionable, but this is a CRPG, and the more user actions the better). Better yet, we could menu out some of the options.

We could accomplish this in this way: If there is an object in the room, you can stand on it and then hit a standard key. That key will bring up a menu of all the options you can perform with that object. This would be good to decide at sinks and fountains if you are going to drink from them or dip an object into them—and equally good for sitting on thrones and suchlike. If there is only one option for that particular thing (such as going up or down a set of stairs) then the action will automatically be performed when you press the magic key.

Next we could set up some options for the player inventory better and allow players to select an item from their inventory and automatically have actions applicable to that item taken (drink for potions, don or take off armor, and so on). Nethack kind of does this now, but you still have to deal with a plethora of different commands and then select the object. By bringing up an item-selection menu and doing things the other way around, we lower the number of total key commands we need.

A total overhaul of the user input interface in this way is needed. Due to the organic nature of the game development and programming process in Nethack, it is easy to understand why the development team hasn't taken too many sweeping and drastic steps over the years. If we could build a game like this unfettered by what has gone before, we could drastically improve the design of the interface elements.

Scope

The scope of Nethack is pretty focused: The world is the dungeon. It would appear to be just the map of a specific level, but since you can move between levels, and aren't locked out of one when you have completed the last one, the whole dungeon is your world.

However, you could very easily enhance this exact same game and add a city and multiple dungeons to it without any significant additional effort. This would help with veracity and give more options for play variety. Omega is one Rogue-like game that attempts this, though the only working code I have gotten for the game is hopelessly bollixed up.

The Nethack development team has decided not to do this for reasons that remain their own. However, it would improve the game tremendously and make it quite a bit more realistic to have a slightly larger scope as long as the command interface was improved to compensate for any added options.

Sense of Accomplishment

CRPGs, by their nature, are rife with sense of accomplishment hooks. Just about every type of hook we discussed in Chapter 2 gets thrown into a CRPG: You have items, intrinsic power development, increasing difficulty, and levels. There is also hidden stuff (though not all that much in Nethack, comparatively) and you get puzzles to figure out (again, not that many actual puzzles in Nethack).

If you are developing a CRPG, you probably don't need to think all that strongly about adding and developing your sense of accomplishment hooks. They are going to grow organically out of your gameworld.

Options

For all intents and purposes, a compiled game of Nethack has no real options. There are a couple of very simple switches that allow you to run over something and automatically pick it up or leave it unless specifically commanded to pick it up, but in general there just aren't any options. There are a couple of reasons for this: The first is that Nethack isn't that vigorously designed; the other reason, though, is the way it is developed and distributed.

While Nethack executables are compiled and distributed, this isn't really the primary transmission format of the game. Being primarily a UNIX game, it is expected that a majority of users are going to download the source code and compile it on their machines manually. As a result, at compile time, users can change various sections of the code to customize Nethack to their preferences—a very clunky way to do things, but not all that uncommon in the UNIX hacker community (actually, more common than distributing executables in many cases).

Although there are some more options to the game, you just can't get at them from inside the design. No matter what the reasoning, this wouldn't be the way of things in a well-executed design.

Procedural versus Object

In the bad old days of programming we had The Old Way (TOW), where programming was procedural. C is TOW. C++ is, theoretically, Object-Oriented Programming (although the number of programmers who basically use a few objects in a slipshod manner and write most of their code TOW in C++ is amazing).

We are going to be building our designs from the ground up in OOP. In this particular book that is because the focus is on a language that allows you to use only OOP methods. However, if you take away the game-design principles you have learned here (and I have done my best to make sure that these sections on game-design principles are generic enough that you can transport them to any programming environment), and move to another language with them, you really are going to need to stick with good OOP practice.

Why? Because you can implement a design so much better. Nethack provides a good example.

Let's go back to our major complaint with the game: a totally fried command structure. Our quickest solution to this is to add a few automatically displaying menus when you attempt to perform an action or deal with an item.

I like to think that the Nethack development team are bright enough people that one or more of them has probably thought of this somewhere along the way. So why haven't they implemented this or another solution to the nasty interface problem? Most likely because it would be such a major hassle.

Think for a moment about what it would take to implement the kind of interface considerations we are talking about in procedural code. You would basically have to rewrite the whole game from the ground up with your menu items hard-coded in. Pain, fear, and loathing ensue at the mere thought of it.

However, when we are working in objects, things get much simpler. We just add methods to our item objects that tell us what we are allowed to do with them and what conditions must be met for these actions to be accomplished. Then a few quick lines give us the menu framework and the game is fixed from the interface point of view.

With some other games, it is impossible to imagine programming them procedurally. If someone reading this can send me a game demonstrating the basic play elements of The Incredible Machine programmed procedurally, I will FedEx them a cookie.

As an added side benefit, OOP makes the beta test a lot easier. Wholesale modifications of game mechanics are much more easily implemented using a good OOP design than with a procedural design. In the coming chapters we will be spending a lot of time not only programming OOP games, but also discussing the decision processes we used to reach the structures and implementations we end up with. You will see that thinking in OOP from the ground up makes your game more robust, causes option adding to be a simpler process, and speeds your beta time considerably.

If, for some strange reason, you are one of those last few programming holdouts who think that OOP is an okay idea for where you really need it, but stick to as much procedural technique as you can get away with, I hope you will walk away from this book understanding that for games programming, full OOP implementations from the ground up are really the only viable option, no matter if you are using Java or some other development environment.

Learning from Nethack

Nethack demonstrates a few basic-design points that are particularly good for the reason that you are more likely to be programming a game like Nethack than a game like Quake. First, Nethack uses graphics appropriate to a small-scale programming effort and there is nothing wrong with that. Personally, I might have done a little to spruce up the visual presentation, but you do what you can with the resources available. As long as your game transmits the information the player needs in a visually pleasing manner, you have accomplished your goals on a modest effort game.

Second, you get a ton of sense of accomplishment right away when you decide you are going to make a CRPG, and you don't have to go much out of your way to do it.

Finally, and since we have just hammered this in I won't go on at length about it here, games that are written with OOP thinking from the ground up get a big bonus and are easier to modify to meet changing design requirements.

Learning from This Chapter

There are only 7 games we have analyzed and from each one we have been able to find good principles to guide us in our own efforts. We could just as easily go on to 20 or 30 games and find something important to take away with us as designers from each one.

Learning to play as many games as possible and look at them analytically is the mark of a game designer. If you walk into id software you are just as likely to find them playing another current game as developing or testing their own latest effort. This is true of all the best design houses. Whether bad or good, you can always take away an example from someone else's efforts. Also here we have seen that you don't have to be a big design house to make a decent game. Both of the more modest efforts we have looked at happen to have pretty large flaws at their hearts, but these aren't, as we have seen, major problems from a programming point of view. The problems stem from ignorance of good game-design principles and methodology. You won't have to make these mistakes in your efforts, since we have spent so much time hammering on basic game-design issues.

If you take nothing else away from this chapter and the last chapter, remember that the vast majority of all mistakes made in games, professional or amateur, are not mistakes of programming. They are *mistakes of basic design.* Learning *design principles,* whether from this book or from figuring them out on your own, is the most important single thing you can do to make sure that your games will be playable and fun for your users: That is the real point of all game-design and programming efforts.

Next Up

In the next chapter we are going to get into the nuts and bolts of Java coding, where we will dally for a couple of chapters, learning where Java deviates from C++ and how to code an applet. So now that you have a good idea of how to design a good game, let's figure out how to implement one in Java.

CHAPTER 4
• • • • • • •
JAVA FUNDAMENTALS

Java looks amazingly like C++. So much so, in fact, that in many cases a good C++ programmer can follow the general flow of Java code without actually knowing the language. As we saw in the first chapter, this similarity to C++ was intentionally placed into Java to make it easier for C++ programmers to learn.

But while there is much similarity, there are more than enough points of differentiation to make Java totally unique. And the close relationship of the two languages can lead to many points of confusion as the C++ programmer falls into using C++ syntax with Java and getting severely unexpected results.

In this section, I am going to step you through the basics of the construction of the Java language. There are two fundamental parts to learning Java. The first is to learn the basics of the syntax of the language and the use of the various keywords. The second, and by far more complex for the C++ programmer, is to learn the details of the various prebuilt packages that come with Java and their uses in constructing your own games. This section will deal with the first of these jobs, teaching the syntax and other language basics.

Here you will learn how to deal with the compiler, the difference between building an application and an applet, data types, conditionals and loops, creation and use of methods and object, packages and interfaces, and throws and exceptions.

In most cases we will simply be skimming the areas where C++ and Java are the same. We will be going into detail only in those areas where Java deviates from basic C++ practice.

Setting Up the Package and Use of the Compiler

The first step to programming in Java is to get a copy of the *Java Development Kit* (JDK) from Sun. The newest revision of the JDK as of this writing is 1.0.2 and all the code in this book is designed to work with the 1.0.2 package. This package is available in different platform versions at http://www.javasoft. com/. Follow the instructions there to get the version of the JDK for your machine.

At the time this book is being written, only the Solaris and Win95 versions of the JDK are available from Sun. The setup for both of these platforms is basically the same.

The Win95 version of the JDK archive will be transported in a self-extracting .EXE file. Simply place the JDK in the directory where you want it to unpack and run the .EXE. This will explode the files and subdirectories that make up the JDK distribution. The Solaris version is packed in a gzipped distribution file. Again, place this in the directory where you wish the JDK files and subdirectories exploded and unpack the distribution.

In both cases, you will need to change your PATH environment variable to point at the Java bin directory. If you don't know how to change the PATH

It is important to note that there is no way we can cover every nuance of the Java language here. That would require a book far larger than this one devoted to just that single topic. However, we can give you the fundamentals as well as some of the more advanced concepts as they apply to creating good games. But this book alone is no replacement for the language manuals. The two main manuals you should be concerned with are the *API documentation* and the *Java Language specification* (not to be confused with the Virtual Machine specification). Both of these are available under the documents section at http://www.javasoft.com.

environment variable for your platform then, trust me, you really aren't ready for this book. On a UNIX machine call this environment variable CLASSPATH.

• • • • • • • • • •
Hello World

Tradition rather demands the creation of a Hello World application at the start of any programming book. So here is the traditional Hello World written in Java.

```
1: // HelloWorld.java
2: // A Java implementation of the traditional Hello world
      program
3: import java.lang.*;
4: class HelloWorld {
5:    public static void main (String args[]) {
6:        System.out.println("Hello World");
7:    }
8:}
```

Although our Hello World program is a pretty simple piece of code, it does illustrate a number of Java points and principles and shows us a few of the ways that Java deviates from C and some of the ways it is basically the same.

Let's break down what we are seeing line by line.

Line 3 presents us with an import statement. The *import statement* is roughly analogous to C's #include directive. The import statement brings in external classes or class libraries our program is going to require to run. Class libraries are called *packages* in Java. The example in Line 3 brings in the most fundamental package in Java, the java.lang.* base package. This package includes basic io and language-definition functions for Java and is required by all Java programs in order to run. Since all Java programs require java.lang, this package is automatically included in all programs. Therefore, you will never need to actually use an import like the one in Line 3, but it has been placed in this program for demonstration purposes.

In Line 4 we are creating a *class definition* for our Hello World class. Remember that almost everything we are going to do in Java will deal with *classes* and *objects*. Hence, instead of defining a function to print our string, we are working with a class. This isn't a minor distinction, but one of the permeating features of the Java language.

In Line 4 we are also given a whirlwind tour of many of Java's *reserved keywords* for dealing with methods, the static, public, and void keywords, all of which make an appearance here. You will be getting a list with exact definitions of all of the reserved method keywords in a moment, but static makes this a class method, public makes the method accessible to outside objects and void means (as it does in C++) that the method doesn't return a value.

More important, on this line we also see the method of passing command line arguments into a main method. Here we run into a significant difference in the way Java and C++ accomplish the same task.

In C++ we would be passed two different variables, an int and a pointer to an array of character strings. The int would indicate the number of command line arguments that had been passed, and the array would hold the actual arguments. In Java, we deal with only one variable, an *array of objects,* named by convention args[] or argv[]. Java contains a number of built-in methods to deal with and parse the information in this array. We will go into that later when we deal with Data Management.

Next in the program, on Line 6 we invoke the *println method* with a single argument of the string literal we desire for output, "Hello World". Note that this is a method call to an object stored in the out variable of the System class. This shows that method calls are identical to the dot notation used in C++.

We can also see from the placement of braces in this example that the use of blocks is pretty much the same in Java as it is in C++.

Compiling Our Program

Now that we have written our code, it is time to compile it. *Javac* is used to compile Java code into bytecode files usable by the *JVM.* The source code files are saved using the following format <name>.java. These files are then compiled into class files that will share the same name but have the .class extension. The class files are bytecodes executable by the JVM. Java source files should be named the same as the class they define.

To use the Java compiler, we execute the following statement from the command line:

```
javac HelloWorld.java
```

This will cause javac to compile our HelloWorld program. This will result in a file called HelloWorld.class which contains the bytecode image interpretable by the JVM. In order to run this program we must invoke the JVM and tell it to run our HelloWorld.class file. This is done by using the following command line:

```
java HelloWorld
```

The result of running this class is the expected Hello World! message, as shown in Figure 4.1.

Language Fundamentals

The following pages represent the building blocks of the Java language, the basic types, the expression operators, and the fundamental control-flow statements. Java supports basic variable types, also called primitive types (see Tables 4.1 and 4.2).

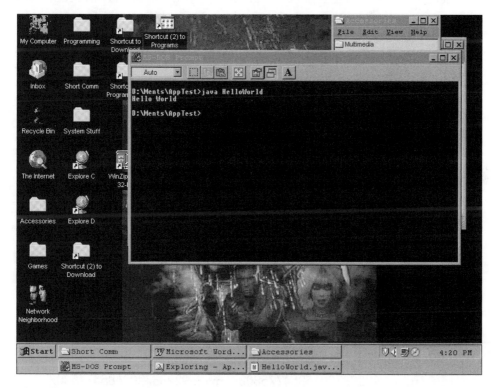

Figure 4.1   Hello World output.

Table 4.1   Variable Types

boolean	This is a true and false value. There is no conversion to other types. The keywords true and false may be used to fill a boolean variable. By default, a boolean value is false.
char	A character holds a 16-bit Unicode value from \u0000 to \uFFFF. By default, a character value is \u0000.

Assigning a primitive type is accomplished with the assignment operator =. The following section of code will assign the number 54 to the integer variable OldInt:

```
Int OldInt = 7;
```

The *primitive types* are the only things in Java that aren't objects. For reasons of speed they are built into the language structure itself. However, if you need to get the functionality of an object, you can use Java's predefined object wrappers to convert a basic type into an equivalent object type.

The *wrapper object* for each type is the same as the basic type, but the first letter of the type is capitalized. So the following code will convert an int basic type called OldInt to an object:

```
Integer theObjectInt = new Integer (OldInt);
```

Table 4.2   Numeric Types

byte	8-bit signed numeric value min: −128 max: 128
short	16-bit signed numeric value min: −32768 max: 32767
int	32-bit signed numeric value min: −2147483648 max: 2147483647
float	32-bit floating point min: ±3.40282347E+38 max: ±1.40239846E−45
double	64-bit floating point min: ±1.79769313486231570E+308 max: ±4.94065645841246544E−324
long	64-bit signed numeric value min: −9223372036854775808 max: 9223372036854775807

The default value of the integral types is 0. The default value of the floating point types is 0.0.

Booleans

The *boolean type* holds the logical values true and false. Unlike C, these values may not be treated as integers. They also may not be cast to or from other types.

Valid Variable Names

Java variable, class, and array names may start with a letter, underscore, or dollar sign. They can't start with a number, but may use numbers after the first character. Many symbols are reserved operators in Java, so it is best just to steer clear of them in naming.

You may also use valid Unicode characters in your naming. Note that Java variable names are *case sensitive*.

Type Casting

Casting is the process of converting a value or variable from one type to another. For instance, you may wish to store a float value in an integer variable when you no longer care about the decimal dust involved. Java will perform simple casts such as this automatically, but a slew of compiler warnings will result, warning you of the dire consequences of losing precision. Instead of going with implicit casting (just throwing your variables into whatever type is handy and hoping the compiler generates the right results), explicit casting is a good idea.

To perform an *explicit cast,* use the following syntax:

```
type castingToVariable = (type) castingFromVariable;
or, in an example:
float foo = 10.55;
int bar = (int)a;
```

This places a value of 10.55 into the float variable foo and then casts that value into the int type variable bar, which will have a value of 10 due to loss of the decimal information in the cast process.

Escape Sequences

Java supports the same basic *escape sequences* as C (see Table 4.3).

Table 4.3 Escape Codes

\b	backspace	\\	backslash
\f	formfeed	\?	question mark
\n	newline	\'	single quote
\r	carriage return	\"	double quote
\t	horizontal tab	\000	octal number
\v	vertical tab	\xdd	hex number (where d is a hex digit)

However, in addition to these escape sequences, Java also supports Unicode characters with the following literal \uddd, where d is a valid Unicode character call.

Unicode

Java supports the Unicode character set defined by the Unicode Consortium. In a nutshell, *Unicode* is a 16-bit character coding format that supports a huge number of characters (over 30K). This allows for a nice, standard way to deal with characters from various different languages.

The reality of the situation is that the vast majority of the programmers reading this book are going to have no need for the Unicode specification extensions and are going to be working with the basic ASCII Latin 1 characters with which the English computer-using world is familiar.

But Unicode escape use has an important difference from the use of the familiar escape sequences shown above: Any use of a Unicode escape is treated as the actual character, no matter where it appears in your code. You can use Unicode escape characters in your variable names. Also note that Unicode escapes are processed before other escapes.

Expressions

Expressions and *operators* in Java are the same as C. The only significant difference is the inability in Java to create compound expressions using the comma operator as in C. The exception to this is that Java does allow the comma operator in the initialization and continuation section of loops.

Tables 4.4 and 4.5 show the Java operators and their precedence, respectively.

Table 4.4 Expressions and Operators

Arithmetic			
+	addition	/	division
−	subtraction	%	modulus
*	multiplication		

Assignment			
x += y	x = x + y	x *= y	x = x * y
x −= y	x = x − y	x /= y	x = x / y

Bitwise			
&	AND	<<=	x = x << y
|	OR	>>=	x = x >> y
^	XOR	>>>=	x = x >>> y
<<	left shift	x &= y	x = x & y
>>	right shift	x |= y	x = x | y
>>>	zero fill right shift	x ^= y	x = x ^ y
−	complement		

Logical			
&&	and	^	xor
||	or	!x	not X

Note on logical operators: The & and | used singly are also valid operators for the 'and' and 'or' operators, respectively. However, when the single character versions are used both sides of the expression under test are evaluated no matter what the result of the first test on the left side. With && and || the evaluation stops if the left side of the expression doesn't meet the operator

Table 4.5 Operator Precedence

.[] ()	&
++ −− ! − instanceof	^
new (type)expression	|
*/%	&&
+−	||
<<>> >>>	¿:
<>	all assignments
== !=	

condition. The single version of the operators is conventionally used only for bitwise operations.

Comments

Java uses three different *comment types:* Java supports the basic C comment /* *open comment* operator and */ *close comment* operator. Everything between an open and close comment will be considered a comment. The C++ comment operator // is also supported. When // is used, that line is commented out.

Java also has its own comment, the *doc comment*. The doc comment starts with /** and continues until it sees */. The doc comment allows you to use the javadoc program distributed with the JDK to automatically generate documentation for your programs.

Control Flow Statements

The worker bees of your code are the control flow statements that allow your program to modify execution based on external or computed conditions. The Java conditionals will all be familiar to the C++ coder.

Block Statements

A *block* is a group of statements surrounded by {}. A block will go anywhere a single statement will go and the new block creates a new local scope for the statements inside it. This means that you can declare and use local variables inside a block and those variables will cease to exist after the block is finished executing.

```
If . . .else
```

The *if* conditional is primarily identical to its C++ counterpart.

```
if (<condition>) <statement to execute if true>;
```

for example,

```
if (foo>bar) foo = foo - 1;
```

The execution statement may be a block of lines. Optionally, the *else* keyword can provide the execution of an alternate statement if the test is false:

```
if (foo>bar) {
        foo = foo -1;
```

```
        System.out.println("Well scope out that huge
    foo");}
else System.out.println("The foo is no longer hogging");
```

Note that *if* conditionals must return a *boolean* value, and cannot return an *int*.

The Conditional Operator

Java supports the conditional operator. The *conditional operator* is an expression that returns a value from a conditional test.

```
test ? trueresult : falseresult
```

Test must be an expression that returns a *true* or a *false:* If the test is true, then *trueresult* is returned; if the test is false, then *falseresult* is returned.

In the following example, if foo is bigger than one, then the variable larger is set to true; if foo is one or smaller, larger is set to false.

```
boolean larger = foo > 1 ? true : false;
```

Switch Conditional

The *switch conditional* allows the testing of a variable against multiple values. The switch statement is basically identical to its C counterpart and works as follows:

```
switch (test) {
    case firstTest:
        firstResult;
    break;
    case secondTest:
        secondResult;
    break;
    case thirdTest:
        thirdResult;
    break;
    default: fallthroughResult;
```

If one of the case tests makes the cut, then the result before the following break is executed. However, if none of the case tests makes it, then an optional *default* line can be added, as in the above example, that will then execute.

The switch is limited by the fact that it will only deal with *byte, char, short,* or *int* types for the test. Don't try anything else—it won't work. People will ridicule you. Further, the only test permitted is one of equality.

Javadoc generates somewhat complete, automatic documentation for your programs laid out nicely in HTML format. You will see examples of java-doc documentation throughout this book. Further, the single most important piece of documentation about Java—the API documentation—is also a javadoc product.

In order to use javadoc, you must use the /** open */ close to comments meant to be used inside the documentation. These comments must also come right before variable, class, or method definitions. Look inside some of the Java source in documented programs from the support site to get a good idea of where to place javadoc comments in order to produce good docs.

Along with the basic commenting, javadoc also recognizes a number of special tags that allow you to further add to the documentation. The list of special tags and their uses is below:

`@see classname`   Creates a "See Also:" hyperlink to the specified class. Used for variables, classes, and methods.

`@see full-classname`   Same as above with the full classname.

`@see full-classname#method-name`   Creates a "See Also:" hyperlink to the specified method of the specified class. Used for variables, classes, and methods.

`@version version`   Adds a "Version:" line containing the version. Used only before a class definition.

```
switch (oper) {
    case '+':
        addargs(arg1,arg2);
        break;
    case '*':
        multiargs(arg1,arg2);
        break;
    case '-':
        subargs(arg1,arg2);
        break;
    case '/':
        divargs(arg1,arg2);
        break;
    default: System.out.println ("You just didn't op
right, now did you?");
```

For Loop

The *for loop* format is as follows:

`@author author` Adds an "Author:" entry with the name of the author. Used only before a class definition.

`@param parameter-name description` Adds the parameter and its description to the Parameters section of the method entry. Used before method definitions.

`@return description` Adds a "Returns:" section containing the description text to the method entry. Used before method definitions.

`@exception full-classname description` Adds a "Throws:" entry containing the class name of the exception and the description. Used before method definitions.

On the whole, games are beasts of strange coding ideas. In order to do something neat and interesting—to make things *cool*—game programmers often get into all sorts of interesting tricks and techniques. But in a fully OOP environment, this can make things very difficult to figure out.

Dealing with all of the different objects and figuring out what does which to whom when can be a nightmare. The moral of this screed? *Document!* With this easy documentation generator built into Java, now is the time to seek amnesty for your old, nondocumenting ways and become a document good egg. Trust me, it makes you feel better and maybe even improves your chances of getting into the positive afterlife of your specific spiritual belief system.

```
for (initialization; test; increment) {
    stuff to be done
}
```

where *initialization* is the declaration of the control variable for the loop. This variable, if initialized and created here, is local only to this loop. Note that this is a deviation from C. *Test* must be a boolean test, and *increment* can be any expression or function call.

```
for(i = 0; i < 100; i++)
    System.out.println(i);
```

While Loop

The *while loop* repeats a block until the test condition is true.

```
while(test) {
    stuff to do }
```

The condition is a boolean expression. In the case of a false test result, the while loop will never be executed. To guarantee a single execution use the do loop structure.

Do Loop

The *do loop* executes a statement or block until a test condition becomes false. The structure of the do loop is as follows:

```
do {
    stuff to do;
} while (test);
```

The test, just as with the while loop, is a boolean test. However, unlike the while loop, since the test is executed at the end of the loop, fallthrough ensures that at least one iteration of the loop will be accomplished.

Break and Continue

The *break* keyword will exit a loop. *Continue* increments a loop, or just starts over, depending on whether a for loop or a while loop is being executed. Both of these keywords can be used in conjunction with a labeled loop. To label a loop, you place a label followed by a colon right before the first line of the loop. For example:

```
loop1:
    do {
        x++;
        System.out.println(x);
        if (x == 100) break do;
    }
```

When the break to a labeled loop is called it will pass program execution to the first line past the labeled loop. In the case of a continue, it will reexecute the loop from the top.

Further, you can break or continue to any statement of loop within a method definition, not just the enclosing loop. This allows break and continue to mimic some of the functionality of a goto statement. If you are a big fan of the venerable spaghetti coding technique, you might want to shed a tear, because this is as close as you are going to get to a goto or label jump in Java.

•••••••
Objects

The basic unit of programming in Java is the *object*. For all intents and purposes, there will be no code outside of objects in your programming. While this seems a little forced, once you get used to it, the object orientation of Java makes most of your programming tasks easier and almost forces reusability of code.

Classes

The *class* is the pattern for your object instances. Note here the very important point that the syntax is slightly different from C++ class creation and the modifier keywords you can use with a class don't mean exactly the same thing as some of their C++ counterparts.

The *class* is made up of three parts: (1) the class definition line itself; (2) the methods that are going to be common to all instances of the class; and (3) the fields that are going to be common to all instances of the class.

The syntax for creating a class is:

```
Modifiers class className [extends superClass] [Implements
                                         interfaces]{
[methods and varibles for your class]
}
```

The *className* is the name of the class you are going to be creating. The *superClass* is the class from which your new class is going to be a descendant. We will explain interfaces later, but here are the modifer keywords and the effect they have on your class:

abstract	Contains only methods without implementations.
final	Cannot be subclassed.
public	The methods and fields of the class can be used by code outside of the class package.
private	The methods and fields of the class are accessible only to code within the same file.
<none>	The class will be accessible to all other classes in the same package.

synchronizable   This is for the control of threads. A synchronizable class instance can be made into arguments.

Methods

Method syntax for Java and C++ are closer to being in synch. The following syntax defines a method:

```
Modifiers ReturnType methodname (varlist) {
    [Stuff to do]
}
```

The *ReturnType* is the type of the value being returned. This can be a primitive type, a classname, or the keyword void for a method that returns nothing. In order to return a variable, the method must use the keyword return at some point followed by the variable value to return. The *methodname* is the name of the method following the general Java naming conventions. The *varlist* is a list of the values being passed to the method. These become local to the method being called. The format of the list is:

```
(type variable, type variable . . .)
```

The following modifiers are available for methods:

public	Other methods outside the class may access this method.
protected	Only subclasses can access this method.
private	Only methods in the same class can access this method.
<none>	Only methods in the same package can access this method.
final	This method cannot be overridden.
static	All instances of the class share this method and invoke this method with the <Class>.method.

Final and Static

The final and static keywords are used to denote constants and class variables, respectively. The *final keyword* creates a constant that cannot be changed in your code. The *static keyword* makes a variable a class variable that will be the same throughout all instances of a particular class. And, of course, a final static variable will be a class constant. This gives you an effect roughly akin to the use of the C++ const.

Method Examples

The following code fragment provides a very simplistic example of method use:

```java
public class Shark {
        boolean hungry=true;

        boolean IsSharkHungry() {
            if (hungry) {
                System.out.println("The shark is
                                    hungry.");
            }
            else {
                System.out.println("The shark is not
                                    hungry.");
            }
            return hungry;
        }

        void FeedShark(boolean satiated) {
            hungry = satiated;
        }
```

We can get a lot of mileage out of this tiny bit of code. First we define a class variable called hungry. This class variable will be visible to all of the methods in this class. Next we define the IsSharkHungry method. This method is going to be returning a boolean value when it is called. The only thing the method does is determine the value of hungry and call a method from the System package that will print the status of the shark's stomach to the screen. Then it returns the value of hungry to the method that called IsSharkHungry.

Note the use of the keyword return to send back the return value to the calling method. This is the same as C++. This method would be called without passing a value to it. It determines everything it needs to know from the value of the class variable hungry.

The FeedShark method, on the other hand, must have a boolean value passed to it from the calling method. This value will be placed in the method variable satiated. Then FeedShark will load the value passed to it from the calling method into the class variable hungry where it will be available to IsSharkHungry the next time it is called.

We can see here that scope works the same as we are used to from C++. The class variable hungry is available to all the methods in the class. However, the method variable satiated is only available in the FeedShark method and thus the need to move that passed value into the hungry class variable where the other methods in the class (in this case only IsSharkHungry) can access it.

If we wanted to we could also define a class final and static boolean variable called Fed which would have a value of true. We could then use this as a constant during our shark-feeding procedures.

Discussing References

In Java, everything but the primitive types is passed by *reference* only. There are no reference and dereference operations. Java takes care of all referencing operations automatically and removes the ability to perform direct memory manipulation from the programmer. The major effect of this on the C programmer is the sudden banning of pointer arithmetic. While this might be disturbing at first, it results in two basic advantages: elimination of the myriad of bugs associated with pointer mistakes and increased security.

This use of only references with objects raises a number of points, not the least of which is the method used to create objects.

Creating Objects

Creating the variable for an object doesn't create the object itself. Instead, it creates a variable to hold a reference to the object. To *create* (or *instantiate*) an object you must use the new keyword, which is roughly analogous to the same keyword in C++. The syntax of object creation is shown below.

```
variable = new classname();
```

A common technique in both C++ and Java is to create your class-level global variables at the top of the file and instantiate them in the class constructor. The class constructor is a method in the class definition that has the same name as the class. For example, if we wanted to create a class BadGuy that creates a ShotGun object as a weapon, we could do this:

```
public class BadGuy {
    private ShotGun MyGun;

    // Following is the constructor
    BadGuy() {
        MyGun = new ShotGun();
    }

// Other methods of BadGuy can use the MyGun object.
}
```

```
public class ShotGun {
    private int rounds;
    private int range;
    private int damage;
}
```

Here we have created two classes: the BadGuy and his trusty weapon, the ShotGun. BadGuy is instantiated after creating a variable to hold the BadGuy object is created as in the following snippet:

```
BadGuy Enemy;
Enemy = new BadGuy ();
```

This code would cause the constructor for BadGuy to be called and that constructor would create a gun for our new enemy. The gun, an instance of the ShotGun class, would have variables to hold the rounds, range, and damage of the weapon.

However, we can also add alternate constructors based on the arguments passed when instantiating BadGuy. Java will use the *constructor* that most closely matches the type and number of arguments being passed to it. Let's re-create BadGuy so that he can be armed or unarmed when we call him.

```
public class BadGuy {
    private ShotGun MyGun;

    // Following is the constructor
    BadGuy() {
        MyGun = new ShotGun();
    }

    BadGuy(boolean armed) {
        if (armed) {
            MyGun = new ShotGun();
            }
    }
}
```

In this example we now have two constructors for BadGuy. If we just create a BadGuy with no arguments, he is going to be armed by default. However, if we call a BadGuy with a boolean argument, that boolean value will be placed in the method variable armed and used to determine whether to create BadGuy with a ShotGun in the MyGun reference or to leave that object reference null for a possible arming of BadGuy in the future.

You might wonder how Java decides to use the constructor that "most closely matches" the variables passed to it. This point also comes up in implicit type casting. How does Java decide what basic type is close to another basic type?

There is a lookup table built into the language that provides a reference value to each type. The most closely matching reference value will determine which constructor or implicit cast Java will use. For an exact breakdown of the casting process, look in the Java Language specification. You may create as many constructors for a class as you wish with as long an argument list as you wish.

Subclassing

Inheritance works the same as it does in C++, so we will not dwell on it at length here. However, there is one important distinction: Java does not allow multiple inheritance. You may have only one parent class for any of your child classes. This is a trade-off between the power involved in multiple inheritance and the potential for serious mistakes that is the other side of that power. As we discussed in Chapter 1, Java always errs on the side of programmer sanity in toss-up cases of implementation; however, Java does implement two different features that take the sting out of the loss of multiple inheritance, *Interfaces* and *Packages*.

Instanceof

The *instanceof operator* will return true if the object on the lefthand side is an instance of the class on the righthand side. Using this operator you can determine if a class is an instance or a subclass of another class. For example:

```
if (MyGuy instanceof BadGuy) { ... }
```

In this case, if the object MyGuy is an instance of BadGuy or one of its subclasses, then the value returned is true and any code between the braces would execute. If MyGuy were a null value (the reference hadn't been assigned an object yet), then the value would be false. If MyGuy isn't an instance of BadGuy or one of its subclasses then the value returned would be false.

Interfaces

While you cannot have multiple inheritance in Java, you can have Interface implementation in your classes. An *interface* is a set of methods that contain no implementation code. In order to use any of the methods defined in an interface, your class must override the methods from the interface with an implementable method.

Interfaces are defined with the following syntax:

```
interface interfaceName [extends interface_Name]{
    [variable list]
    [method stubs]
}
```

The following example will provide us with an interface to work with.

```
interface Shooter {
    int damage = 5;
    void takeDamage (int hits);
    void lowerAmmo (int shots);
}
```

Here we have defined an interface that might be handy for implementing some features of a game with objects that take and dish out damage. Although not explicitly stated, the variable in this example is a final and static variable and the methods are abstract. These are implicit in the interface definition.

Now we can implement a class using this interface using the implements keyword that we defined in the class definition syntax earlier. When we do that, however, we are going to have to provide an implementation for all of the methods in the Shooter interface or our new class will be abstract. We might decide to do this, and then implement the last bits of the Shooter interface in a subclass. The subclass would then be capable of being instantiated. Remember that until all of the methods in an interface are implemented in your class tree, you cannot instantiate an object that has an interface. You may subclass interfaces from other interfaces and they will inherit the values and methods of the parent interface.

Before moving on to Packages, you should be aware that you can use the instanceof operator to determine if an object implements an interface or not. Therefore you can know if the object will have an implementation of a method in the interface.

Packages

A *Package* is a construct that groups related classes and allows other objects in the same package preferential data access. Unless a modifier keyword is used, methods and variables in classes in the same package are able to access each other. In addition, a package groups together a bunch of classes allowing them to be imported into another class as a group. This creates handy function libraries. The main concern you are going to have with packages in most cases is using the standard classes provided with Java.

You can use the classes in a package in two ways. The first is to use the fully qualified classname of the class you are calling on. For example, we could instantiate a randomizer object using the java.util package with the following fragment:

```
long ourSeed = 100;
java.util.Random randomGen = new java.util.Random(long ourSeed);
```

This would provide us with a Random object that would make it possible for us to create random numbers using the object as defined in the java.util package.

However, you can shorten this process by importing the entire java.util package into your program before you start and then you can use not only the Random object, but also all of the other nifty stuff in there in an abbreviated manner.

The import keyword syntax is:

```
import package.class;
```

where package is the full package name and class is the full classname. Now our code above can be called as if the Random class was local to our file:

```
long ourSeed = 100;
Random randomGen = new Random(long ourSeed);
```

We can also import all of a class wholesale by using a * to denote the classname. So the command:

```
import java.util.*;
```

would import all of the classes in the java.util package including the Random object as well as the Date object, Stack object, and lots of other handy stuff.

You will need to familiarize yourself with the classes in Java's included packages. This information is in the Java API documentation available for download at javasoft.com which I asked you to get earlier. If you blew this off, go back and do it now, because we aren't going to explain the calls we make to those packages in this book. The API documentation alone makes for 500 pages of documentation and we don't have the space to reprint it here.

You can make your own package simply by placing a line at the very start of your class file that defines what package your new class is a part of. The syntax is as follows:

```
package newPackageName;
```

where *newPackageName* is the name of your new package. However, you need to understand a little of how Java packages are pulled into the compiler to actually make this work.

Package names aren't arbitrary; they are actually path commands telling the compiler where to find the compiled classes in the package. The compiler will look for a directory with the same name as your package name in one of the directories in your path. For instance, if you create a package called java.lang.mystuff, the compiler is going to look for the java directory (which it will find or you haven't added it to your path statement and aren't going to get much luck getting anything to compile on your machine). Then it will look for a subdirectory called *lang* and another called *mystuff*. Then it will pull whatever class you have specified out of mystuff and add it to your program.

Somewhere along the way of dealing with Java and packages you are going to run into references in the documentation to CLASSPATH, and if you are on a Win95 machine you are going to get screwed up by this. You can spend a lot of time messing with the compiler and trying to get this to work right. If you are on a Win95 box just do the following: Make sure the Java bin directory is in your path and make sure that all of your packages run off of this directory or another directory that is in your path environment variable. So when you create your own package, make sure that all of the compiled class files are in a directory that matches the package name.

• • • • • • • • •
From Here

In this chapter you have learned the bare rudiments of where Java deviates from C++. You should have enough grounding at least to be able to follow Java code on the reading and have a rough idea of what it is doing.

In Chapter 5, we go into the details of actually making the language work, by discussing the finer points of exception handling, threading, more complex data structures, and how to make applets function.

CHAPTER 5

• • • • • • •

MORE ADVANCED TECHNIQUES

In Chapter 4 we covered the bare fundamentals of the Java language and mainly concentrated on those areas where the deviation from C++ concepts was relatively minor.

However, in this chapter we are going to move on to the sectors of the language where the deviation from C++ is more pronounced. Some of these features are significantly different from their C++ counterparts and some elements, such as applets, don't have any C++ counterpart at all.

First we will look at *Data Manipulation,* which due to the packages included in the basic Java distribution is generally much easier than, though different from, C++ data manipulation. Then we will examine Java's exceptionally robust error-handling methods and equally powerful thread-management techniques. Finally, we will examine what is required to create an applet.

Data Manipulation

Java is fairly strong in the data management sector due to the advantage of having strong built-in libraries, in the form of the basic packages, that are sure to be available to every implementation of the JVM, no matter where it lives. This makes even the more advanced data-handling functions a reliable part of the language spec itself, as opposed to being implemented through different third-party support libraries, such as is the case with C++.

Arrays

Arrays are fully implemented under Java; however, you have no pointer arithmetic to manipulate them with. Considering this sweeping difference, the implementation of arrays under Java remains remarkably unchanged as compared to C++. You use a two-step process to create a working array. First, you define your array and then create an initialized instance of it. The new keyword creates the array and zero-sets variables.

Creating an array variable uses the following syntax:

```
TypeofArray ArrayName[]
```

where *TypeofArray* is the class or basic type the array is designed to hold and the *ArrayName* is the name of the Array. As an option, you can move the brackets to sit after the TypeofArray and the syntax will still work. Some Java programmers prefer this method as they feel it more correctly illustrates the real relationship involved. I prefer the C++ syntax, but we will be mixing both of them up in the rest of the book to get you used to tracing through code that uses either style.

To actually instantiate this variable as an array, you must use the following syntax:

```
new TypeofArray[elements]
```

where *TypeofArray* is the class or basic type the array will be holding and *elements* is an integer indicating the size of the array.

These actions are most frequently performed on a single line where they look like:

```
TypeofArray ArrayName[] = new TypeofArray[elements]
```

When an array of objects is created, the objects in the array slots aren't instantiated. However, an array of basic types is immediately ready for use and numbers are set to 0, Strings are set to null, and booleans are false. For example, to create a series of 52 integers, 0 through 51, we could use the following code fragment:

```
int[] Cards;
Cards = new int[52];
```

Of course, both steps can be taken care of in one line:

```
int[] Cards = new int[52];
```

Arrays of basic data types and Strings can be created with defined values instead of zeroed by putting the initialization values in braces after the variable definition.

```
String[] Vehicle = {"Automobile", "Plane", "Boat", "Train", "In-line skates"};
float [] Caliber = {0.177, 0.22, 0.38, 0.44, 0.45};
```

To create an array of some object type other than String, you must create both the array of the class and initialize each object member of the array. For example:

```
DemoClass[] DCA = new DemoClass[ArraySize]; // Create the array of objects
for(I=0; I<ArraySize; I++) { // Initialize each object in the array
     DCA[I]=new DemoClass(); // This instantiates each member of the array
}
```

Accessing an array under Java is nearly identical to the syntax used in C. Place the index between square brackets directly after the array label.

```
if (size[1]=='S') { … }
++InterationCounter[c];
```

Vectors

Vectors are a specialized class designed to manage groups of objects. Nonobjects must be wrapped inside an object to be used by a vector. In an array, you must predict the size of the array prior to using it—not so with a vector. A vector object also inherits many methods which make it easy to access and query about the objects it contains. Consider the following example (see Figure 5.1):

```
// VecTest is a simple test of the Java Vector.

import java.util.*;

//We will create two tiny classes, good guys and bad guys.
class BadGuy {
   boolean armed;
   int ammo;
```

ARRAYS OF DOOM . . .

As an experienced C++ programmer, you get a lot of an edge working with Java. You already have a grasp of object theory, and the fact that many of the commands in Java are modeled on C and C++ make understanding the flow of Java code fairly easy. However, once in a while the similarities between Java and C or C++ (actually, in most ways Java is much closer to C than C++) causes a problem as the hapless programmer tries to deal with Java code as C++ code. Nowhere is this more prevalent than with references and pointers.

As you are learning Java, say the following phrase to yourself over and over before you go to sleep at night: There are no such things as pointers. . . . There are no such things as pointers. . . .

Most C++ coders will get cocky about this. "Oh, man, I know that already; he told me a chapter ago. How dumb does this guy think I am?" Well, I don't think you are dumb, but I think that you might not understand the full implications of the lack of pointers. Where this is going to trip you up is in arrays. Arrays in Java aren't like arrays in C++. As a matter of fact, an array isn't really an array at all. It isn't so much a feature of the language as it is an artifact of the language. *Arrays in Java are objects in Java.* These array objects happen to be customized to hold other objects or basic types.

In C++ arrays are a part of the language. You use an array to carve out a chunk of memory with objects instantiated in it, and then you use pointers to get to those objects. In Java, the array object is instantiated with slots to hold a number of references to objects. "Hey, he said references. References to objects are pointers." No, they aren't; there are no such things as pointers. And this is where things get messed up for a C++ coder. Watch the following bit closely.

```
BadGuy BadGuyArray[]= new BadGuy[5];
```

What happened here? Well, we created an array, called BadGuyArray, to hold a group of BadGuy objects, which we are assuming are defined elsewhere. Now the C++ coder is going to start working with this array right now. The unlucky individual in question is going to start getting a slew of compiler errors when running javac over it.

Why? Because all we have done in the line is instantiate an object of the array type that is ready to hold BadGuy objects. There aren't any references to BadGuy objects in the array: We need to put these in manually. There are two ways to do this. The first is to instantiate our BadGuys external to the array and put them into the array by hand.

```
BadGuy FirstDude = new BadGuy();
BadGuy SecondDude = new BadGuy();
BadGuy ThirdDude = new BadGuy();
BadGuy FourthDude = new BadGuy();
BadGuy FifthDude = new BadGuy();
BadGuyArray[1] = FirstDude;
BadGuyArray[2] = SecondDude;
BadGuyArray[3] = ThirdDude;
BadGuyArray[4] = FourthDude;
BadGuyArray[5] = FifthDude;
```

Well, that would do it. And the sad thing is that I have seen a boodle of Java code written just this way by C++ coders who didn't quite get the hang of Java arrays.

However, we don't need to do the above. Not only is it inelegant, it is also out of the question when we are dealing with larger arrays. A 200-member array done this way would take an hour of typing just to instantiate the members and put them in the array.

Instead, we can create the members in place as follows:

```
for (int i = 0; i < 5; i++) {
    BadGuyArray[i]= new BadGuy();
    }
```

This would instantiate new BadGuys in all of our array slots. These BadGuys could then be accessed as array members in the way familiar to C++ coders.

So the thing to remember when dealing with Java and arrays of objects: You have to instantiate the array itself, then you have to instantiate the members. You can do this external to the array and put the members in the array, or you can instantiate the members in place.

However, when you are creating arrays of simple types, you don't have to worry about any of this. With simple types, Java instantiates the members automatically, allowing you to assign values to them for manipulation right away.

Remember, every night till you get it: "There are no pointers. . . . There are no pointers. . . ."

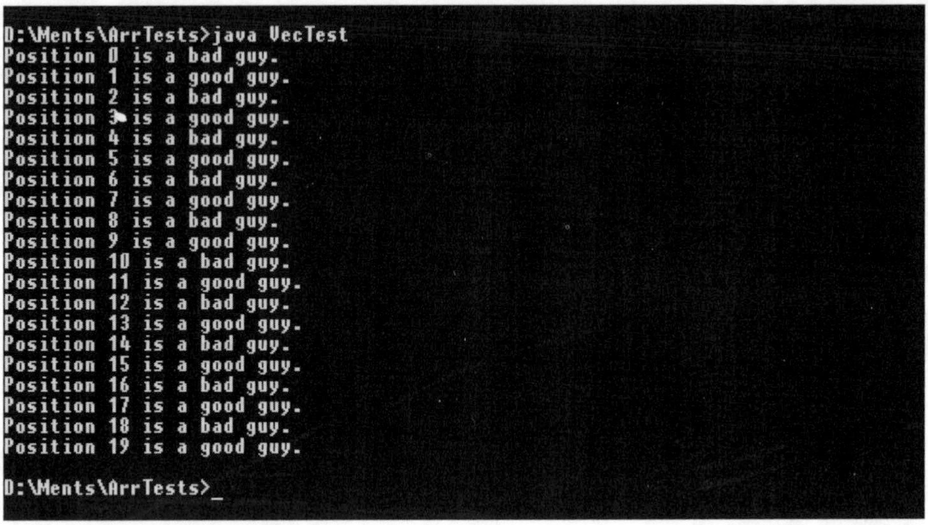

```
D:\Ments\ArrTests>java VecTest
Position 0 is a bad guy.
Position 1 is a good guy.
Position 2 is a bad guy.
Position 3 is a good guy.
Position 4 is a bad guy.
Position 5 is a good guy.
Position 6 is a bad guy.
Position 7 is a good guy.
Position 8 is a bad guy.
Position 9 is a good guy.
Position 10 is a bad guy.
Position 11 is a good guy.
Position 12 is a bad guy.
Position 13 is a good guy.
Position 14 is a bad guy.
Position 15 is a good guy.
Position 16 is a bad guy.
Position 17 is a good guy.
Position 18 is a bad guy.
Position 19 is a good guy.

D:\Ments\ArrTests>_
```

Figure 5.1   Output of VecTest.

```java
    int hitPoints;
    int speed;
    }

class GoodGuy {
    boolean armed;
    int ammo;
    int hitPoints;
    int speed;
    boolean cop;
    }

public class VecTest {

    public static void main(String args[]) {

    Vector AllGuys = new Vector();

    //now we have a new vector, time to add something to it.

    for (int i =0; i < 10; i++) {
        BadGuy addingBadGuy = new BadGuy();
        GoodGuy addingGoodGuy = new GoodGuy();
        AllGuys.addElement(addingBadGuy);
        AllGuys.addElement(addingGoodGuy);
        }

        /* We have now added ten bad guys and ten good guys to
    our array using the addElement method inherent to the
    Vector class. Now we should make sure things worked the
    way we think they did. */
```

```
for (int i = 0; i < 20; i++) {
    if (AllGuys.elementAt(i) instanceof GoodGuy) {
    System.out.println ("Position" + i +
                        "is a good guy.");
    }
    if (AllGuys.elementAt(i) instanceof BadGuy) {
    System.out.println ("Position" + i +
                        "is a bad guy.");
    }
    }
}
}
```

You will note that in this example we have instantiated a vector and then just added objects to it. The way you add objects to a vector is using the .addElement method of the vector class. There are lots of other nifty methods in the Vector class for dealing with the objects in vectors. You should stop now and read the various methods that Java has provided with the Vector class to make dealing with the objects in a vector's array simple.

Note that we never told the vector how big it was going to be. That is the strongest point of the vector: When you aren't sure how many objects you are going to be dealing with, you can still use a vector and it will resize its internal array to cope with as much as you can throw at it.

If you were looking closely at the above example, you will probably be saying, "Wow, it takes any kind of object! With the array you have to tell it what class it is going to be holding. This is great!" Well, it is great, but it isn't a particular quality of the Vector class: We can do this with a normal array.

If an operation can be performed on a superclass, you can substitute a subclass in its place. What you are seeing with Vector's accepting any and all objects is a result of that fact. The Vector class implements an array of type Object. Since all classes in Java are implicitly descendants of the Object, when you create an array of objects you can put any object in the array.

This is not to say this isn't a handy trick, and one you will see used in some of our later examples, but it is a quality of arrays, and not just a quality of vectors. However, if you do this, you will still have to wrap basic types in an object wrapper as they aren't descended from the Object class.

Strings

Strings are not arrays of type char as they are under C. They are full objects. As objects, they come complete with a set of methods which make them

---

WRAPPERS

A couple of times in the text we have mentioned wrappers. *Wrappers* in Java are classes created to add object functionality to the basic types. There are object wrappers for each of Java's basic types. The name of these classes are the same as the basic type, but they are initial capped: booleans are Booleans, ints are Integers, and so on. You will find these wrapper classes located in the java.lang package; therefore, you don't have to import them, as they will be available to any Java program.

Look over the documentation for these classes: You will end up finding them of great use. If you want to do much extensive work with vectors you will at one time or another pretty much be required to wrap something at some point.

---

very easy to manipulate. You can still treat them as if they are null-terminated arrays, but they contain a much broader standard interface.

Commonly used String-class methods:

int length();	Return the length of a string
char charAt(int position);	Return the character at a position
String substring(int index);	Return a substring beginning with index
String substring(int f, int t);	Return a string between index f to t
int indexOf('char');	Return the index of first occurrence of char in String
int indexOf("String");	Return the index of first occurrence of a substring in String
String toUpperCase();	Return a string where all letters are uppercased
equals("String");	Compare one String object to another String object

Java strings allow a subset of the printf()-like string manipulation syntax. A limitation is that they do not work while painting text to a java.awt graphic screen.

\b	Backspace
\d	Octal
\f	Form feed
\n	Newline
\r	Carriage return
\t	Tab
\u	Unicode character
\x	Hexadecimal notation
\"	Print a quote character
\'	Print a single quote
\\	Print a backslash

While overloading of operators is not allowed in Java, the + and += operators have been designed to handle concatenation of strings. It is perfectly legal to say the following:

```
String Song = "Over the river and through the woods" +
" to grandmother's house we go!";
String JDK = "Java";
JDK += " Development Kit";
```

A limitation String has it that its contents, once defined, are constant. If you want to manipulate the contents of the string, you need to use a similar class called *StringBuffer.* A StringBuffer object easily converts to a string and must be converted to a string object to use String's methods. A StringBuffer's size is handled internally. To the programmer, there is no need to do memory management or predict the size of the string which will be contained in the buffer. Both the String and StringBuffer classes are in the java.lang package.

Another point you want to note about dealing with strings is slightly counterintuitive with the rest of the language—spanning a string across two lines is bad mojo. A return can't be inserted between the quotes in a string or else the compiler gacks. Almost everywhere else in Java your spacing or lines will be ignored by the compiler, but not inside the quotes in a string.

This isn't that big a deal, since you can concatenate across two lines with the + operator as we did in the String Song example above. The result will be read as one line, but it is something to keep in mind. For this book, for example, to put some of the code in the text we have had to concatenate across two lines to fit the book's trim size when in our actual example code to the compiler everything was on one line. (You may feel free to put it back that way if you are typing the examples as we go along. The only reason for most of the breaks is typographical and has little to do with the running of the code.)

Exceptions

Sometimes things don't always go as expected in an applet or application. An applet which you have designed may work fine in your perfect world, but die a horrible death when put in the indelicate hands of a user who does all kinds of crazy things with your code. Wouldn't it be great if you could tell a method to just "try" to do something and see whether it fails? Instead of having to couch every line of code with conditionals to handle errors, what if we could just block whole sections of code that might run into trouble? "Try this, if it fails—die peacefully." In Java, this dream has come true. Certainly not the first language to handle exceptions, Java has implemented it very well.

When Java encounters an error, it throws an exception. *Exceptions* are objects that can be used by your error handling routines in order for you to create graceful procedures to handle nastiness that can arise in your code. The production of an exception object is called throwing it; using it in a conditional recovery sequence is called catching the exception.

Note that exceptions and errors aren't the same thing. An exception is an object that is thrown when an error condition occurs. Although 99 percent of the time you are going to be treating these artifacts as if they are the errors themselves (i.e., creating recovery procedures), you can also throw an exception object manually in order to trigger testing conditions for either debug or kludge testing of a prototype. In some cases, as with some I/O operations, your routines will be throwing exceptions in order to signal common conditions such as End Of File.

The basic syntax for setting up an exception handler uses two new commands: *try* and *catch*. The syntax is as follows:

```
try {
    /*the stuff you are going to do that might cause an
    exception.*/
    }
catch (ExceptionName e) {
```

```
    /*Stuff to do if the code in the try block throws an exception
of the type named in the ExceptionName object in the catch
statement */
    }
catch (ExceptionNameTwo e2) {
    /*Stuff to do if the code in the try blocks throws the
    exception named in ExceptionNameTwo */
    }
finally {
    /* The code in this block will be executed no matter if an
    exception is caught or not. This is exit code for your
    handler that is going to need to get performed in any event.
    */
```

Should you wish to manually throw an exception you can do so with the following syntax:

```
Throw new ExceptionYouWantToThrow();
```

Let's build on our previous examples to create some quick code that demonstrates exception handling.

```
// ExceptTest is a simple demonstration of Java Exception //handling

//We will create our bad guys.
class BadGuy {
    boolean armed;
    int ammo;
    int hitPoints;
    int speed;
    }
public class ExceptTest {

    public static void main(String args[]) {

    BadGuy BadGuys[] = new BadGuy [5];
        for (int i = 0; i < 6; i++) {
        try {
        BadGuys[i] = new BadGuy();
        }
        catch (ArrayIndexOutOfBoundsException e) {
        System.out.println("No more room at the inn. . .");
        }
        finally {
        System.out.println("Cycle " + i + " complete.");
        }
        }
    }
}
```

In *ExceptTest* we have created a class called BadGuy and then created a five-slot array called BadGuys to hold our BadGuy objects. Finally, we purposely ran over our array-index boundary in order to create an error condition that will throw an exception (see Figure 5.2).

We have placed the code that is going to produce the error inside a try block. This causes the thrown exception to get caught by the nearest handler that will deal with it and is within the scope of the try/catch block. Since we have only one catch statement—and we have optimized it to catch just the type of exception we know we are going to be throwing—the block inside the catch statement will execute as soon as we try to put a sixth BadGuy in our array.

However, on each iteration of the for loop that contains our exception handling code, the finally block will execute, telling us which iteration of the loop we are on. The use to which we have put the try/catch/finally statements here is fairly obvious. Even so, there are a couple of questions that arise from this code.

Exception Types

Where did that ArrayIndexOutOfBoundsException object that I put in as the argument to catch come from? Well, the JVM generated that for me and threw it up for the first catch statement that came along that could handle it. However, the more important thing is how I knew to look for that specific exception.

```
D:\Ments\ArrTests>java ExceptTest
Cycle 0 complete.
Cycle 1 complete.
Cycle 2 complete.
Cycle 3 complete.
Cycle 4 complete.
No more room at the inn. . .
Cycle 5 complete.

D:\Ments\ArrTests>
```

Figure 5.2 Output from ExceptTest.

If you look through the API documentation you will find that each package and class shows what exceptions and errors they throw. Look at the java.lang package listing and you will see a long list of exceptions that can be thrown by various evil deeds that can occur with elements in that package. Also note that there is a distinction between *error objects* and *exception objects*. In real life there is no remarkable difference between the two. Both are objects thrown when some kind of an error condition is reported by the JVM. However, they have been split into different classes to give an indication to the programmer what to do about them. As a general rule, error objects represent major world-rending JVM pain that we shouldn't try to catch or deal with. This stuff is probably going to crash the JVM and bring our project to a screeching halt before we can do anything about it anyway.

However, the exception objects are things that aren't necessarily going to bring the world crashing down about our shoulders; they will generally be caused by our coding something not too bright into our programs. In the case of the Runtime Errors in java.lang, we can catch these errors if we want to, or we can let them go by and bollix up our code—it's a matter of choice. In some few cases, such as end of file exceptions and so on, exceptions will be an integral part of our control flow process.

You should familiarize yourself with all of the exceptions that can be thrown by the java.lang package. These little guys are going to be in everything you code since these exceptions are defined in the base package of the language.

Forced Catching

With the exceptions in java.lang you have some leeway as to whether you are going to decide to catch an exception or not. Runtime exceptions don't have to be caught if you don't want to do so. However, that isn't the case with the rest of the thrown errors in other packages. If you use a method that can throw an exception, Java is going to play cop and force you to set up an error handler in order to catch that exception before you are going to be allowed to successfully compile your code.

How do you know if there is an exception you are going to have to catch? By looking at the method definition in the API docs. Any method that can throw an exception will have the keyword *throws* followed by the exception object it can throw appended to the end of the definition right after the argument block. If you see this, it means that you are going to have to deal with that exception somehow, or Java is going to get petulant with you. If you don't want to deal with the error-handling code at the level you are at when you call the method that is going to throw an exception, you can pass the exception along by implementing the throws keyword in your method and pass the problem up the line. This isn't a bad idea in some cases, where you might want to just have a very large exception-handling block on as high an implementation level as possible in order to centralize your exception-related code. However, at some point in your implementation you must handle all exceptions brought up with the throws keyword in any method in your program.

This is getting a little deep on theory and short on practice at this point, so let's do another quick example that shows how all this works and should clarify how you have to handle thrown errors.

```
/* ExceptTest2: A slightly more robust example of exception handling
*/
/* A new version of BadGuy with some evil exception throwing methods in it */

class BadGuy {

    void EvilDoingMethod() throws NullPointerException {
       System.out.println("I am doing something evil. . .");
       throw new NullPointerException();
    }

    void VileMethod() throws ArithmeticException {
       System.out.println("I am doing something vile. . .");
       throw new ArithmeticException();
    }
}

public class ExceptTest2 {

    /* WorkingWithEvil is going to decide not to deal with the
    exception thown by EvilDoingMethod, and is just going to pass
it on with the throws keyword */

    static void WorkingWithEvil(BadGuy BadGuy1) throws
                            NullPointerException {
    System.out.println("I am passing on something evil. . .");
    BadGuy1.EvilDoingMethod();
    }

    /* WorkingWithVile, however, will take care of the exceptions
thrown by VileMethod right here so there is no need to throw the
exception up the line */

    static void WorkingWithVile(BadGuy BadGuy1) {
      try {
          BadGuy1.VileMethod();
      }
```

```
catch (ArithmeticException e) {
    System.out.println("I have removed the vile" +
                    "influence.");
}
}

public static void main(String args[]) {

BadGuy BadGuy1 = new BadGuy();

/* Because WorkingWithVile has already handled the exception,
we don't need to worry about trapping it here when we call
WorkingWithVile */

WorkingWithVile(BadGuy1);

/* However, WorkingWithEvil still has an unresolved exception
throw associated with it, so we have to put it in an error handler
if our code is going to compile */

try {
    WorkingWithEvil(BadGuy1);
}
catch (NullPointerException e) {
    System.out.println("I have vanquished the evil.");
}
}
}
```

Here we have created two different methods in BadGuy that are throwing out exceptions. One method in ExceptTest2 deals with an exception-throwing method from BadGuy right away. However, the other passes on the exception to the next method up the stack using the throws keyword itself to get out of dealing with the exception right then (see Figure 5.3).

Finally, in dealing with exceptions, you can create your own brand-new exceptions by subclassing the Exception class in java.lang.

Threads

In general, a computer follows a set of instructions *in order,* as we illustrated in the first chapter of this book with a chart that showed a sequential program flow as:

```
Do A
Do B
Do C
Do D
```

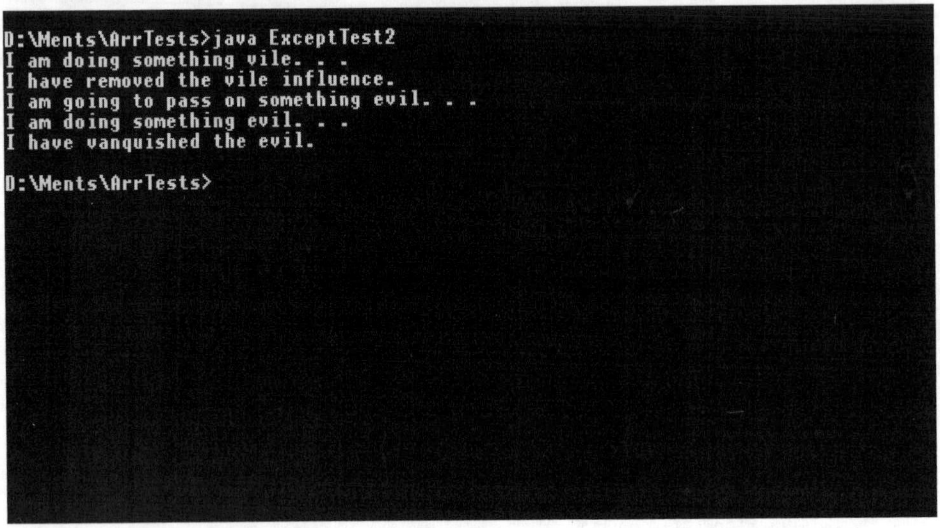

```
D:\Ments\ArrTests>java ExceptTest2
I am doing something vile. . .
I have removed the vile influence.
I am going to pass on something evil. . .
I am doing something evil. . .
I have vanquished the evil.

D:\Ments\ArrTests>
```

Figure 5.3 Output from ExceptTest2.

A line of sequential instructions operating in order is a *thread*. With newer OSs and programming languages like Java, it is possible to have more than one thread working on your computer at once. Let's say we have another thread made up of the following:

```
Do 1
Do 2
Do 3
Do 4
Do 5
```

When both of these threads are running concurrently in your machine, the processor will switch back and forth between the two of them rapidly and keep all of their information in order for them. In this way, the two threads can each execute more or less at the same time, and neither one really understands that it isn't the only thing running on the processor. The new flow looks something like:

```
Do A
Do 1
Do B
Do 2
Do C
Do 3
```

```
Do D
Do 4
Do 5
```

Everything is going on concurrently. If both of these threads are accessing some of the same data (which in Java they will be) they can be performing actions based off of each other's work as the flow of execution is going along. For example, one thread can be searching for keyboard input or mouse commands while another is drawing the screen. This makes life much simpler in some ways for controlling program flow, especially if you can start and stop these threads at will and make them wait for events happening in other threads before continuing their own efforts.

Note that the concurrence of the two threads is actually just an illusion produced by a fast processor and task switching. While each thread thinks it is the only game on the processor, in real life, the processor is switching back and forth between a number of different threads of execution at any given time. On some multiprocessor machines these threads might actually be running on different processors, but in most cases a thread is only going to have delusions of grandeur.

In Java thread switching is accomplished by creating a queue and putting the various threads in it. The thread at the head of the line is given time on the processor until it cedes the processor to the next thread in line. Sometimes it will do this because it is done with its job and go off into the great night of released memory; in most cases, though, it will just be getting out of the way for a set period of time or until it gets some kind of signal to jump in and go at the processor again.

Another way that the processor can be ceded by the currently controlling thread is being forcibly thrown off the processor by a thread with a higher priority. Threads have a priority value in Java and when a high priority thread enters the queue it will jump ahead of all threads with a lower priority. Thread priority is a really good way to screw yourself up, so for a moment we will postpone our discussion of thread priority until we really have to have it.

The thread queue is basically an easy thing to understand: It works (on threads of equal priority) on a first-come-first-served basis and when a thread cedes its position in the queue it goes back to the end and waits its next turn.

Thread States

A thread is always in one of five possible states: newborn, runnable, running, blocked, or dead.

1. A *newborn thread* has been instantiated but hasn't been added to the queue. To put the thread in the queue use the start( ) method.

2. A *runnable thread* is in the queue and scheduled for processor time when all the other threads ahead of it get done with their little electronic communion with the silicon god.

3. A *running thread* is currently in control of the processor. This thread will keep control until it decides to be polite and step aside or a higher-priority thread boots it back to the end of the queue.

4. A *blocked thread* is blocked from getting in the queue and being runnable. A blocked thread is waiting on something to occur until it will reenter the queue.

5. A *dead thread* is either done with its work or gets iced by another thread. A dead thread gets killed and goes off to thread heaven.

Creating Threads

There are two ways to create threads of your own: You can either create a subclass of the Thread class found in the java.lang package, or you can inherit the Runnable interface and jump through a hoop or two. Subclassing Thread is by far the easier solution of the two, and until you get the hang of threads you probably want to stick with this method for your initial experiments. To create a subclass of Thread use the following syntax:

```
class YourNewThreadedClass extends Thread {
    public void run() {
        ...stuff you are doing...
    }
}
```

First you are defining *YourNewThreadedClass* as a subclass of Thread. However, this is only half of the battle. In order to get your new thread to do anything you will need to put the active operations of the thread inside a function named *run()* which is being overridden from a Thread method of the same name.

In some cases, however, you aren't going to want to subclass off of Thread to create your new threaded class. In these cases, you must implement the Runnable interface in your code. To do this you will simply declare the Runnable interface as part of your class declaration.

```
class YourNewThreadedClass implements Runnable {
    public void run() {
        ...stuff you are doing...
    }
}
```

If it seems easy, wait till we get to starting threads to see why it is a little more annoying than just subclassing Thread.

Starting Threads

There are two different ways to start a thread depending on how you created it. Starting a thread from a class that is a subclass of Thread is pretty easy; you just ask it to start with the following syntax:

```
YourNewThreadedClass.start();
```

YourNewThreadedClass inherits the start method from Thread and all is well and good.

However, when you are implementing the Runnable interface to create a class that will run in a thread, you are going to have to make a two-step process out of the venture. First you have to create a bona fide instance of Thread and then tell it that it wants to pick up the code from your new class and take it along for the ride:

```
YourNewThreadedClass NewObject = new YourNewThreadedClass();
Thread TheRunner = new Thread(NewObject);
TheRunner.start();
```

What is happening in the above code snippet is that you are first creating an object of YourNewThreadedClass (which we are assuming is implementing the Runnable interface) called *NewObject*.

However, since NewObject really doesn't inherit all of the stuff it needs to be a thread, we need to instantiate a thread and tell it to take NewObject along for the ride. We do this in the second line where we create the Thread object *TheRunner* and pass it NewObject as a constructor variable. TheRunner will now create a thread wrapping around NewObject which you can use to pass NewObject all the normal methods by which you implement thread control.

Once you get familiar with dealing with threads that are subclassed instances of Thread, then spend some time playing around with implementation of the Runnable interface as a thread technique. It looks much more convoluted explaining it than it is in practice.

Common Thread Control

You will need to fully explore the Thread class in the API docs to really get all you can get out of threads. However, there are only a few thread control methods that you really *have* to know in order to get by.

Start and Stop

The *start method* sends your thread to the queue and starts implementing whatever code you put under the run method in your thread object. The *stop method* does just the opposite: It takes your thread out of the queue and then hits it over the head with a hammer, killing it. Once you have stopped a thread, it is gone.

Yield

The *yield method* tells your method to step out of the way so that someone else can use the processor for a while. When you call the yield method, your thread gives up the processor and goes to the back of the queue to wait its next turn.

Sleep

Sleep is akin to yield, except it puts your thread into a blocked state (outside the queue) until a set period of time has passed. When you are using the sleep method, you normally will pass it a long value that equates to the number of milliseconds it should take itself out of circulation:

```
YourNewThreadedClass.sleep(100);
```

Look in the API for alternate constructions of sleep that allow you to specify more precise time intervals. Unlike the other control methods we have just discussed, sleep's declaration says that it throws an InterruptedException. Therefore, you must wrap sleep in an exception handler to use it if your code is going to compile properly.

An Example of Threading in Action

Too much talk and not enough code makes for pretty inferior performance. So let's do a small program that illustrates the use of threads. We will simulate a simple firefight between a group of good guys and a group of bad guys.

```java
/* ShootOut.java. This is a fairly simple example of threading
simulating a shootout between two opposing forces */

class BadGuys extends Thread {

    int totalbadguys = 5;
    void BadShoot() {
    if (Math.random() > .5) {
        ShootOut.totalgoodguys--;
      if (ShootOut.totalgoodguys < 0) {
        ShootOut.totalgoodguys = 0;}
        System.out.println ("Good guy hit." +
                            ShootOut.totalgoodguys +
                            "Good guys left.");

    }
  }

  public void run() {
   while (ShootOut.totalgoodguys > 0 && totalbadguys > 0) {
    for (int i = 0; i < totalbadguys; i++) {
        System.out.println ("Bad Guy" + i + "Shooting.");
      BadShoot();
    }
    try {
        sleep(20);
    }
    catch (InterruptedException e) {
        return;
    }
   }
  }
}

class ShootOut {
    public static int totalgoodguys = 5;

    static void GoodShoot(BadGuys TheBadGuys) {
    if (Math.random() < .5) {
        TheBadGuys.totalbadguys--;
      if (TheBadGuys.totalbadguys < 0) {
      TheBadGuys.totalbadguys = 0;
        }
        System.out.println("Bad Guy Hit." +
                    TheBadGuys.totalbadguys +
                    "Bad guys left.");
    }
  }

    public static void main (String args[]) {
```

```
BadGuys TheBadGuys = new BadGuys();
TheBadGuys.start();
while (TheBadGuys.isAlive() && TheBadGuys.totalbadguys >0)
                                                    {
    for (int i=0; i < totalgoodguys; i++) {
        System.out.println ("Good Guy" + i +
                                "shooting.");
        GoodShoot(TheBadGuys);
    }

    try {
      Thread.sleep(20);
    }
    catch (InterruptedException e) {
      return;
    }
  }
 }
}
```

Now let's pull this code apart and see what we have here. First, we create a class called BadGuys that extends Thread. Here we define two methods: the run method, which is required to be present in all classes that can be scheduled as threads, and a method called BadShoot.

In BadShoot, we are letting the five bad guys who are represented by the totalbadguys integer take a shot at their opposing forces, the good guys, who will be defined later with a variable called totalgoodguys. We call on the static method *Math.random* in the java.lang package in order to create a random number somewhere between 0 and 1, then use that number to determine if we hit a good guy or not. If we hit one, then we deincrement the totalgoodguys variable to represent the fallen fighter. Finally, we tell the world whether we hit anyone and how many of those pesky good guys are left by using the System.out.println method from java.lang.

In the run method we check to make sure that at least one guy on each team is alive to shoot and be shot at, then we announce our intentions to shoot and call the BadShoot method. Once everyone on our team has had a chance to fire, we put the thread to sleep for 10 milliseconds with the sleep(10) call. Note that this sleep is wrapped in an exception handler. If you look under java.lang.Thread.sleep() you will find that it throws an Interrupt-edException as we discussed previously. So we have to wrap an exception handler here in order to catch it or our code won't compile.

Now—for twisted reasons of my own—I want only two threads in this program. So instead of creating another class of GoodGuys, I have wrapped the good guys into the main body of the ShootOut class so we can ride along on the program's main thread of execution instead of having to start a third one. Note this: *There is always one implicit thread of execution in your program, and that is the thread that runs your main() method and actually gets the program going.* So if you start one thread, you have two in your total program.

The GoodShoot method is a repeat of the BadShoot method with the names changed to protect the innocent. We have declared this method static so that we can use it without instantiating a ShootOut object.

In the main method of ShootOut we first instantiate a BadGuys object named TheBadGuys and then use the start() method it inherited from Thread to start it going as a thread. Next we perform a basic repeat of the BadGuys run method, but this time with all of the good guys getting their shots.

Go ahead—compile and run this routine and watch the bad guys and the good guys shoot each other.

Lies, Damned Lies . . .

When you compile and run ShootOut you might see all of the bad guys getting their shots and then the good guys getting their shots and so on. If that is true for you, then everything you have been told up to this point is pretty

---

STATIC IS YOUR FRIEND

The keyword *static* doesn't do the same thing in Java that it does in C++. In C++ a static variable is a persistent variable that doesn't get cleared between calls to a method. In Java however, *static* means the variable or method is shared by all instances of the class.

When you declare some method or variable static, you can access that method or variable without instantiating the class into an object. To get at a static variable you simply use the format <Classname>.variable and you will be allowed to use that variable or method.

However, this comes with a restriction (or else we would make nearly half of everything we write static so that we could just throw back to the bad old procedural days): A static method or variable can't access a nonstatic method or variable. So if you start getting compiler errors belching bile about static and nonstatic access, either you have forgotten to instantiate an object before trying to use a nonstatic variable or method in the class or you have accessed a nonstatic variable or method from a static method.

much accurate on your development platform. However, you might see something else. You might see a bad guy or two take a shot, then a good guy or two take a shot, and so on till one side is dead. In that case, a whole lot of what you have been told up to now is a lie.

The problem is with the multitasking in Java. Unfortunately, the Java language specification is pretty vague about how to implement thread scheduling, a task that is pretty much left up to the underlying system. Here is where things get ugly.

Some environments use preemptive multitasking, whereas other environments use nonpreemptive multitasking. In the *nonpreemptive* environment everything works pretty much the way we have described it: Threads sleep and yield to other threads and they all pretty much wait their turn in the queue. (See Figure 5.4.)

However, not all environments work this way. Some—including the single most popular environment in the world—use preemptive multitasking. In *preemptive multitasking* the environment slices up the processor and gives little slivers of time to all scheduled events in a sequence independent of your queue. (See Figure 5.5.) So each thread you spawn will do what it is supposed to and sleep for as long as you tell it (from a human perspective, each thread will run pretty much at the same time). It becomes impossible to predict the order of execution of different elements in two threads. It might go ABBABAABBBAABAAA, or ABBBAABBAAAB, or any other combination of the steps of an A and B thread.

The purpose of this book is far from presenting a definitive reference on the Java language. Therefore, we have not comprehensively tested the threading behavior of Java on every available platform. But we have deter-

```
Bad Guy 0 Shooting.
Good guy hit. 4 Good guys left.
Bad Guy 1 Shooting.
Good guy hit. 3 Good guys left.
Bad Guy 2 Shooting.
Bad Guy 3 Shooting.
Good guy hit. 2 Good guys left.
Bad Guy 4 Shooting.
Good guy hit. 1 Good guys left.
Good Guy 0 shooting.
Bad Guy Hit. 4 Bad guys left.
Bad Guy 0 Shooting.
Bad Guy 1 Shooting.
Good guy hit. 0 Good guys left.
Bad Guy 2 Shooting.
Bad Guy 3 Shooting.
Good guy hit. 0 Good guys left.
```

Figure 5.4   ShootOut run on a nonpreemptive multitasking system.

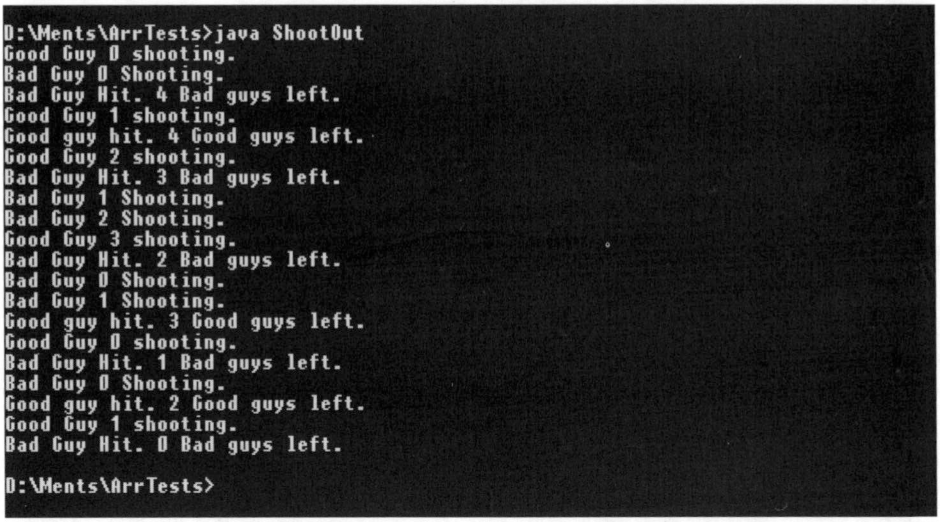

```
D:\Ments\ArrTests>java ShootOut
Good Guy 0 shooting.
Bad Guy 0 Shooting.
Bad Guy Hit. 4 Bad guys left.
Good Guy 1 shooting.
Good guy hit. 4 Good guys left.
Good Guy 2 shooting.
Bad Guy Hit. 3 Bad guys left.
Bad Guy 1 Shooting.
Bad Guy 2 Shooting.
Good Guy 3 shooting.
Bad Guy Hit. 2 Bad guys left.
Bad Guy 0 Shooting.
Bad Guy 1 Shooting.
Good guy hit. 3 Good guys left.
Good Guy 0 shooting.
Bad Guy Hit. 1 Bad guys left.
Bad Guy 0 Shooting.
Good guy hit. 2 Good guys left.
Good Guy 1 shooting.
Bad Guy Hit. 0 Bad guys left.

D:\Ments\ArrTests>
```

Figure 5.5 Representative run of ShootOut on a preemptive multitasking system.

mined the threading behavior of Java on the two development environments we use: Linux on an Intel box and Windows 95 running on an Intel box.

Linux uses a nonpreemptive multitasking scheme. Each thread will work through the queue in order on a Linux box. Win95 uses preemptive multitasking and all of your threads will appear to run concurrently in that environment.

How do you deal with the fact that on some platforms you don't know the exact order of execution for your threads? Well, it is partly voodoo: playing around until you have a good grasp of creating threads that won't get into nasty snarls if they do things in any order possible. However, there are also a couple of threading techniques you can use that will minimize problems. These are *priority setting* and *synchronization.*

Priority Setting

In our examples up to this point we have used threads that have the same priority and thus sidestepped dealing with priority issues. In general, we aren't going to have to worry too much about using priority on systems that use nonpreemptive multitasking. However, on systems with preemptive multitasking we might very well need some way to make sure that threads execute in some kind of coherent order. We can do this with *priority setting.*

Looking in the java.lang.Thread entry in the API docs you will find a method called setPriority. This method allows you to change the priority of a thread so that you will have some control over the number of clock ticks it gets to steal from other threads.

Priority for a thread is set as an integer between 1 and 10, with 1 representing the low end of the scale. A thread with a higher priority than another will get more of the processor time in a clock-tick sequence. By default a thread has the same priority as the thread that spawned it. The default value of Java's running thread (the one that starts up with a main method) is 5.

The higher the priority of your threads, the more clock ticks they will get in the preemptive multitasking environment of Win95. To assure that a thread is going to get to do its stuff before another thread gets to go to work you can set it to the maximum priority, which as we know is 10. But there is also a class constant in Thread of MAX_PRIORITY you can use to make your code more readable.

In order to play with this a bit and get a feel for how it is supposed to work, add the following line to the ShootOut example in the main method of the ShootOut class right after you create the BadGuys object:

```
TheBadGuys.setPriority(10);
```

This makes your new main method look like this:

```
public static void main (String args[]) {
     BadGuys TheBadGuys = new BadGuys();
     TheBadGuys.setPriority(10);
     TheBadGuys.start();
    while (TheBadGuys.isAlive() && TheBadGuys.totalbadguys >0)
     {
         for (int i=0; i < totalgoodguys; i++) {
             System.out.println ("Good Guy " + i +
                                       " shooting.");
             GoodShoot(TheBadGuys);
         }

        try {
         Thread.sleep(20);
        }
        catch (InterruptedException e) {
         return;
        }
     }
   }
```

If you compile and run the new version of this, you will now see that the bad guys all shoot first and whenever they start shooting they finish as a group before any of the good guys get to shoot. If you start lowering the thread priority, the good guys get more and more chances to shoot in between shots of the bad guys until at a 5 priority it is a toss-up as to who is going to shoot at any given time (see Figure 5.6).

Even with priority, it is still hard to control some aspects of thread-behavior scheduling. So let's look at synchronization to get another tool to add to our thread toolchest.

Synchronization

With threads running wild over the processor and your data, it becomes pretty important to have a tool to make sure that some data or instruction blocks can be accessed by only one thread at a time.

The most used example of this deals with a bank balance. If two different locations are doing two different things with a bank balance at the same time, all sorts of errors are going to result. Let's say you are accessing a corporate account at an autoteller at the same time one of your employees (hey,

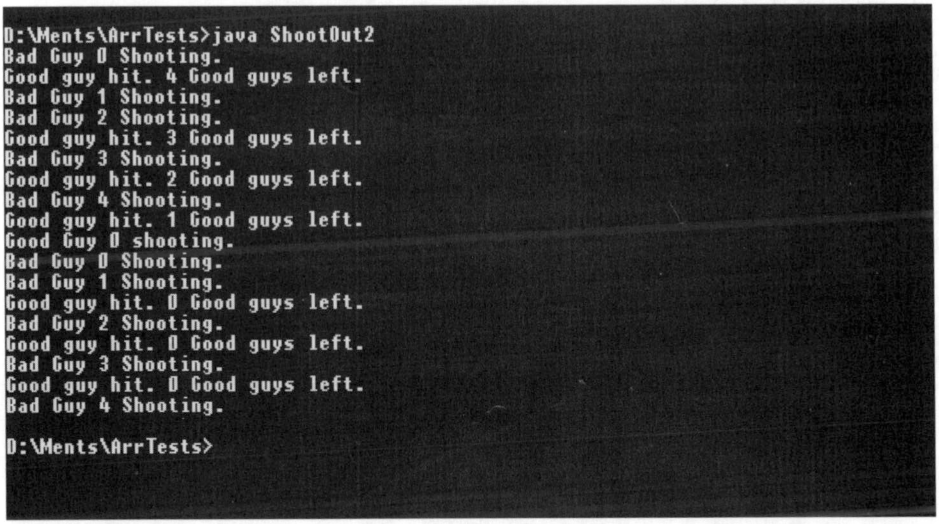

```
D:\Ments\ArrTests>java ShootOut2
Bad Guy 0 Shooting.
Good guy hit. 4 Good guys left.
Bad Guy 1 Shooting.
Bad Guy 2 Shooting.
Good guy hit. 3 Good guys left.
Bad Guy 3 Shooting.
Good guy hit. 2 Good guys left.
Bad Guy 4 Shooting.
Good guy hit. 1 Good guys left.
Good Guy 0 shooting.
Bad Guy 0 Shooting.
Bad Guy 1 Shooting.
Good guy hit. 0 Good guys left.
Bad Guy 2 Shooting.
Good guy hit. 0 Good guys left.
Bad Guy 3 Shooting.
Good guy hit. 0 Good guys left.
Bad Guy 4 Shooting.

D:\Ments\ArrTests>
```

Figure 5.6 ShootOut with priority on threads run on a preemptive multi-tasking system.

we are making it up, so you get to be the boss) is using a debit card that hooks into the same account.

You look in the account and see $1000. At the exact same time, your employee is putting though a debit card purchase for a new wonker that is going to cost a grand. The debit card reader looks in your account and sees $1000. You pull $500 out of the account and walk away whistling with your money. Then the actual transaction goes through on the debit card and pulls $1000 from your account. Now you owe $500 and the bank is upset with you.

Java solves this kind of problem with *synchronization.* You can declare a method or block as synchronized and only one thread at a time can access that method or block. Other threads waiting on that block or method go into a blocked state and only resume running when the synchronized method opens up (the calling thread is done with it).

This is accomplished inside the JVM by assigning a construct called a *monitor* to any synchronized item. A thread may only get access to that item when it gets the monitor associated with the item. When the thread is done with the item, it releases the monitor and the next thread waiting on that item can pick it up. You don't have to worry too much about the details of this process: The JVM handles this whole monitoring thing deep in its innards, but we still need to know the idea of it to make the following discussion a little easier.

To implement a synchronized method you simply add the *synchronized* keyword to the method declaration:

```
synchronized workWithAccount() {
    //stuff to do that only one thread will get to use at a time.
}
```

The technique for synchronizing a block is slightly different. You need to use the synchronized keyword with an argument of an object. The block of code you have marked out is synchronized based on the ability of the calling thread to get the monitor of the object specified in the argument. This object doesn't have to reside in the same class as the code you are synchronizing. (Man, that is a mouthful, but it should become more clear in a moment.)

The syntax for locking a block is:

```
synchronized (theObjectWhosMonitorYouNeed) {
    //The stuff to do that only one thread will access at a
    //time.
}
```

Now this matter of getting a separate object's monitor in order to work with your synchronized block can be a bit confusing (at least it was to me the first time I ran across it). So let's look at a code fragment that might help this make more sense.

Let's say you are printing a file to a printer. Further, that file is being used by many different threads who are adding and deleting data to it pretty much continuously. You have put your access methods to this file in an object called FileAccessObject. Elsewhere you have a block of code that controls printer output. Now most of the time you probably don't need to lock up the FileAccessObject at all. For various reasons you might not care if the data in the file change in a pretty dynamic manner depending on your thread flow.

However, this isn't going to be the case for your printer controls. You are going to want only one thread at a time working with the printer for fairly obvious reasons. So you will make sure that all calls to your printer are in one block that is synchronized. And during the time that your printer is going, you will need to make sure that your file doesn't change under you so you will want the FileAccessObject, which is normally a nonsynchronized object, to be inaccessible to other threads. We can do all this in the following snippet:

```
    . . .
    synchronized (FileAccessObject) {
        //the printing routines go here
    }
    . . .
```

When a thread decides it is going to get ahold of the printing routines, it first will get the monitor for FileAccessObject. This means that FileAccessObject, though it is not normally a synchronized item, is going to be locked to this thread for the duration of this thread's use of the printing routines. Further, no other thread is going to be able to access the printing routines because they are accessible only to a thread that possesses FileAccessObject's monitor.

When the thread is done with the printing routines, FileAccessObject's monitor will be released and it can again be used by multiple threads at once until someone tries to use another print routine. Pretty cool, huh?

Deadlock

To make up for how cool synchronization is, we get deadlock to bring back a little bogus factor into our rosy world. *Deadlock* is when two threads are both waiting on synchronized objects from each other before they are going to release their monitors. They will be waiting for a long time: With a good UPS and a reliable machine we are talking about geologic epochs.

The one positive way to avoid deadlock is to make sure that you never use synchronized methods. This normally isn't going to be feasible in a complex, multithreaded program, but try to minimize your need for synchronization to the absolute minimum that is required to get your job done reliably. Another sure way to avoid deadlock is never to call a synchronized method from another synchronized method. If you don't have two synchronized methods waiting on each other, you can't have deadlock—not an unattainable goal. In most cases if you need to call one synchronized method from another synchronized method, the two of them can have elements that are most critical to lock linked into one method.

Finally, try to make your locking of objects as short a term as you can. If you are going to be locking something for a long period of time, think about doing things some other way that is going to take less time. If you just take reasonable care you can avoid deadlock, but don't go and wholesale synchronize everything you can in your programs, or you are going to be asking for pain.

• • • • • • •
Applets

Now that we have all the basic foundations in place, we can start to deal with applets. So far in all of our discussions we have been relying on stand alone Java programs for our examples. From here on out, the majority of our discussions will be dealing with applet programming.

First of all, we need to define the difference between stand-alone Java programs and applets. A *Java program* is a compiled program that runs by using the Java interpreter launched from a command line. A Java program requires two things. A class definition inside a .java file with the same name as the file, and a main() method somewhere in that file. When the interpreter is called it starts executing the instructions in the main method. You can add a lot more to this, but that is the heart of the Java program. An applet is a slightly different animal. An *applet* is designed to be delivered over the Web and run in a relatively safe environment in a Web browser applet-viewing window. As we will find out in a moment, an applet doesn't look for just a main method, but instead follows a life cycle that calls a number of different methods in order to bring your code to life.

When we are creating an applet, we gain a few advantages. The applet inherits the power of the underlying Web browser and gets an extra kick in that direction by getting some windowing and interrupt advantages. You can program these into a Java stand-alone application, but get them for free with an applet.

However, the double-edged sword of applets is that they are burdened by a number of security restrictions that, although they are good to help prevent the spread of evildoing code on the Net, are somewhat restrictive to us as programmers.

We have three security considerations to deal with in delivering applets.

1. Applets can't do any file access operations on the client machine. You cannot, for example, keep a game-configuration file on the client machine that your applet will look for every time it runs in order to load the preset option configuration your user prefers.

2. The only network connection an applet can make is back to the server. This doesn't create any big problems except in multiplayer gaming situations. There are many reasons you might want your players to be able to connect directly to another player. However, you will have to route all communications between multiple players through your server.

3. Applets can't do anything that is going to result in running code that doesn't get checked by the applet viewer. This means you can't call code native to the platform such as linking DLLs.

We don't have these restrictions in Java stand-alone programs. Later in the book we will be discussing the benefits of building certain types of games as stand-alone games in order to avoid these security restrictions and the way you might want to deliver them to your users. However, for the moment we will build all of the things we are working on in order to work with these restrictions and take advantage of the power of the applet.

Applet Life Cycles

An applet has a number of distinct parts of its life, and each of these cycles has method calls associated with it.

Init

When your applet is first loaded, it will get a call to its *init method*. This doesn't start the applet to running and happens only once during the life of your applet, right after it is loaded into the applet viewer. Use the init phase of the applet's life cycle to implement any initialization that must be done only once at the start of your applet's existence.

In order to perform actions based on the init call, you need to override the init method in Applet, which is defined as follows:

```
void init()
```

Start

The *start method* of your applet is going to be called in order to get it running. This happens once right after it is loaded and the init phase has been accomplished. It will also be called after your applet has been stopped for some reason and it is returned to. This method is basically the same as the main method in a stand-alone program. The method in the applet class is:

```
void start()
```

Stop

The *stop method* of an applet is called when the applet execution should be stopped for an external event, such as the page the applet is on being replaced by another page. The stop method doesn't represent the end of the applet's life cycle, and if the page with the applet is returned to, then the start method will be called again. This might happen many times over the life cycle of the applet. The major use you should have for the stop method is to suspend the running of threads in your applet in order to (1) pause your execution stream and (2) free up some system resources while your applet isn't being viewed. The stop method is defined as:

```
void stop()
```

Destroy

Destroy is telling your applet that the show is over. On the final cleanup phase for your applet, the stop method will be called and then the destroy method. This is where you should destroy all your threads at the end of the program's life. You can rely on the shutdown of the applet viewer to do this for you; since it can prove somewhat unreliable in this respect, you should always clean up after yourself. The method is, predictably enough:

```
void destroy()
```

Some particularly simple applets aren't going to need to worry about overriding every method in the life-cycle chain in order to produce good results. In particular, if you aren't starting any explicit threads or allocating huge chunks of resources, then you probably won't have to worry too much about init or destroy methods. However, with most applets, you will need to make sure that you allocate resources at the start of your applet and clean up after yourself when you are done.

Building a Simple Applet

Let's take a few moments to build a quick applet framework we can use in order to continue our discussions on the topic.

```
/* HelloApplet.java: The basic hello world routine, displayed as an
applet.
*/

import java.awt.Graphics;

public class HelloApplet extends java.applet.Applet {
```

DISTINCTIONS

It is important to understand in your efforts with Java that stand-alone programs and applets are much different beasts and demonstrate different sides of Java programming. Unfortunately, everyone seems to have latched onto applets as the only image of Java programming and programs they have.

Applets weren't particularly intended by the designers of this language to bear a heck of a lot of weight from a complexity point of view. As a result, people tend to think that Java is a pretty clunky language as more and more complex functions are being hammered into applets. This tends to be a bad thing in some ways, as Java applets weren't necessarily intended to bear the weight of more advanced functionality. In the particular field of study we are embarked on, this problem is particularly prevalent. Everyone and their cat has decided to program applet games. Well, applets aren't really all that well suited for many game applications. The overhead produced by the appletviewer welded into many popular browsers really kills the playability of the design.

We will be dealing with these issues at more length later in the book. However, keep in mind as you are learning about applets that they are really neat for some things, but there are tricks that an applet isn't all that well suited for due to increased overhead.

```
public void paint(Graphics g) {
    g.drawString("Hello World!", 80, 50);
}
}
```

This example is about as simple as you can get and have anything at all happen in your applet. However, it does raise a number of interesting questions. First, where is the start method? Second, where does this paint routine come from? Where does this phantom object of the Graphics class, g, get instantiated so that we can pass it to the paint method as an argument? Finally, how do we run this thing?

Well, we are going to catch the answers to these in catch-as-catch-can order. First we will deal with how to actually get this applet to run and work our way out from there.

An applet requires two steps to get to the point that it can run. First, just as with a stand-alone application, you must compile it with the javac compiler to produce a class file. Do this now for the above code. Second, an applet requires an HTML file to call it in order to run. Let's create an HTML stub that will run this (and almost all of our other experiments) right now.

Open a text editor and create the following file:

```
<HTML>
<HEAD><TITLE>Applet Testing Page</TITLE></HEAD>
<BODY>
<APPLET CODE="HelloApplet.class" WIDTH=250 HEIGHT=75>
If you see this message something is seriously wrong.
</APPLET>
</BODY>
</HTML>
```

Save this file with whatever name you like. (I am using the name aptest.html, but make sure that you have the .html extension on the end.)

Now go to the command line and use the appletviewer to bring up the aptest.html file. You start the appletviewer by the following syntax:

```
appletviewer aptest.html
```

You should get a final output that looks something like Figure 5.7.

Well, now we have a whole new set of questions to play with: What are the HTML scripts for dealing with applets and how do they work? Since this is a much quicker topic, let's segue off into this for a moment, and come back to the harder questions of what makes the HelloApplet tick.

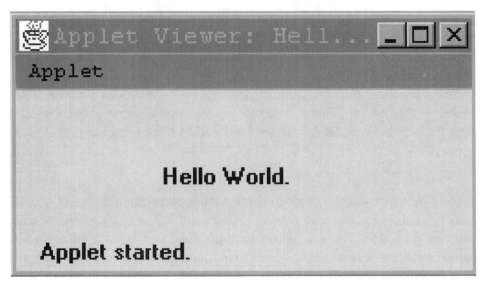

Figure 5.7   HelloApplet output.

HTML and Applets

For purposes of this book I am going to assume that you have a basic grasp of HTML. We don't have time to deal with all of the details of HTML tag scripting here. However, there are a number of tags that relate only to applets and are now implemented on Java-capable browsers that are fundamental to our discussions. The first of these is the most obvious, the <APPLET> tag.

<APPLET>

The *Applet tag* is a non-HTML construct that is recognized only by Java-capable browsers. Browsers that aren't Java equipped (like all four of them left on the planet) will just ignore the contents of the Applet tag (except for the optional text we will be discussing in a moment).

Although the Applet tag isn't technically part of the HTML specification, it still acts like an HTML construct. Therefore, for an opening <APPLET> tag you must have a closing </APPLET> tag in order to have your code execute properly.

Inside the confines of the Applet tag, we will specify a number of different things: the name of the file that represents the applet itself, how to display it, someplace to find the applet, alignment of the applet, as well as a number of other required and optional points.

Required Stuff

There are three required things that must be in an Applet tag: the code, width, and height attributes. The *code attribute* is the name of the file that actually contains your applet. To repeat the salient line from our HTML stub above:

```
<APPLET CODE="HelloApplet.class" WIDTH=250 HEIGHT=75>
```

Note that first we have named the attribute by putting the word CODE after our applet call, then an equals, then the full name of the class file that contains our code. The use of the attribute followed by an equals then a name or value is constant for all of the parameters you will be using with the Applet tag. Also note that we have put the name of the class file in quotes. When you are passing anything that contains any characters but letters and numbers you will need to put quotes around the parameter. In this case, we are using quotes to avoid nasty problems with that dot before class.

The second and third values here are the two other required parameters of the Applet tag, the *width* and *height*. These values, in pixels, determine how big the area running our applet should be. In this case we are telling the appletviewer (or browser or whatever) that a window that is 250 pixels wide and 75 pixels high needs to be created to run our applet.

Additional Parameters

The following parameters are optional.

codebase. *codebase* is a specification for the base URL of the applet. By default, the appletviewer is going to look for the file specified in the code parameter in the same place it found the HTML file that is calling your applet.

When you only have one applet running on a page and have structured your directories in such a way that there aren't too many files associated with any given page, this might be fine. But in most instances you are going to want to have all of your HTML in one place, all of your graphics and sound in another, and all of your applets in yet a third location. This is where codebase comes in.

Codebase can be either a relative or absolute URL that points to your class file. If you had your code in a directory called applets that was right under the location with your HTML file, then the following line would produce a relative URL that would point to your class file:

```
codebase="applets"
```

Note that we didn't really need the quotes here, but I like to stay in the habit of using them for any URL or file reference so that I don't make stupid mistakes when I do need them.

However, if you wanted to, you could also provide a full URL in this location that would point to the directory with your applet.

```
codebase="http://www.imadethisup.com/notreal/donttrytofindit"
```

Name.   The *name attribute* gives this applet a virtual identifier that can be passed to other applets on the same page so that they can trade information with this applet.

Align.   The *align attribute* represents the alignment of the applet's box on the page. The following values are accepted by the align attribute: left, right, top, texttop, middle, absmiddle, baseline, bottom, and absbottom.

Vspace.   The *Vspace value* is used to define a vertical space, in pixels, around the applet. This and the Hspace attribute coming up next only work when the align value is set to left or right.

Hspace.   Does the same that Vspace does, only for horizontal space.

Applet-Specific Parameters

In addition to the above parameters, you can also pass applet-specific arguments inside the applet tag. This is done with the *param name* parameter. This parameter is followed by a label name for the parameter and then the parameter itself. Look at the following example.

```
<APPLET CLASS="DestructoApplet.class" WIDTH = 300 HEIGHT= 100>
<PARAM NAME=Thing=Blood>
<PARAM NAME=Color=Red>
<PARAM NAME=Location="In Bodies">
```

In this example we have passed the DestructoApplet the following labels and values: Thing=Blood, Color=Red, and Location="In Bodies".

When you are creating an applet that is going to require outside parameters in order to customize it, you can do so by this method.

Let's do a quick example of this. Modify your HelloApplet to read as follows:

```
import java.awt.Graphics;

public class HelloApplet extends java.applet.Applet {
    String output;

    public void init(){
        output = getParameter("output");
    }
    public void paint(Graphics g) {
        g.drawString(output, 80, 50);
    }
}
```

And add the following line inside your applet tag:

```
<PARAM NAME=output="Howdy, Folks!">
```

Now when you run this combo through the appletviewer you should get a screen like that in Figure 5.8.

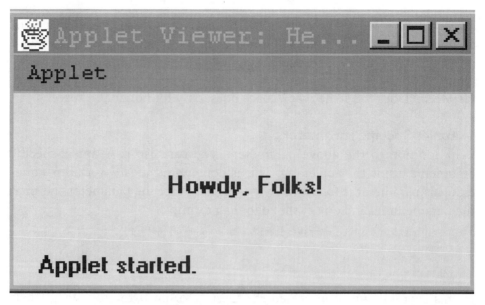

Figure 5.8   Howdy World output.

Anything named in a Param Name tag can be grabbed in the init method of your applet with a getParameter method call, which returns a string. The only thing you need to keep an eye on with this is that the name in your Param Name parameter and the name of the argument string in your getParameter call must match exactly, including capitalization. Any mistakes will provide you with a nasty null-pointer exception. In fact, it is a good idea to either wrap any getParameter calls in a NullPointerException handler or test in some other way for a null return value to keep your code from spontaneously combusting over a simple misspelling.

Default Lines

You will note that in our generic HTML stub for running our experimental applets, there is a suspicious line right in the middle of the applet tag that says, "If you see this message, something is seriously wrong." This is a default line and will appear on browsers that don't have Java capability. You can use any normal combination of HTML tags to create this message and it

---

HEY, WHAT ABOUT MY STAND-ALONES?

Some of you reading this might be wondering how to get command-line arguments into your stand-alone programs. Well, basically the method isn't that far off of C and you have been sort of using it in all of the examples so far in this book.

Remember our main declaration always looks like:

```
public static void main(String arg[]) {}
```

Well, your arguments are that arg[] near the end (you can name that anything you want, by the way, but traditionally it is arg[] or argv[]). You can get at your arguments in order by moving through this array. The 0 index in the array is the first argument after the name of the class; each time the interpreter hits a space it puts the next argument after the space in the next string in the array. In order to pass an argument that has a space in it, put the argument in quotes.

Note the fact that this argument is chock-full of arguments only, although the name of the program isn't anywhere in here. This deviates from C usage and is another case of something in Java looking so much like C it will lure you into a false sense of security and botch up your code.

won't be seen by those who can run your applet. The traditional use of this default message is to notify anyone seeing it that it might be good to get out of the Stone Age and get a browser that supports applets.

Back to Applet Behavior

Now that we know how to call up an applet with the proper HTML tags, get it to display where we want it, and how to pass it arguments, we are back to our burning questions about how it works. One of the most pressing: Where is that annoying paint routine coming from?

If you are a quick person (and of course you are, or you wouldn't be reading this book), you have probably already looked in the class definition of java.applet.Applet and realized that Applet doesn't have a paint method. So where did that puppy come from? For that you are going to have to go back a ways. Applet extends Panel which extends Container which extends Component. So when you are using an Applet, you have the methods in all of these classes to call upon also. Until you start to see in the next couple of chapters the toy chest that opens, it isn't going to seem all that significant, but trust me, there are lots of cool things in the Java Advanced Windowing Toolkit and by working with an Applet you get them all.

However, knowing where paint came from still doesn't explain how it got up on the screen. We didn't do anything to actually bring our applet to life in a start method, so it just rose up on its own in some amazing computer version of spontaneous generation.

Well, actually, the paint method is one of the methods that isn't always being called from your code, but is occasionally called from the appletviewer or browser you are working in. When your applet is first created one of the first things the environment does is call the paint method. This method is also called after another window has hidden your applet or when you switch to another page and come back to it. So you get the paint method for free.

In much the same way, you get a Graphic object for free that goes with it. The Graphic object is part of the environment and you will be manipulating it (and in some cases downright abusing it) in order to get something for your paint method to paint.

The one important point to remember here is that while you get the free Graphic, you do need to put up an include line for java.awt.Graphics at the top of your applet files. In most cases you will just be using java.awt.* since the entire Abstract Windowing Toolkit is a pretty nifty thing to have laying around. These are going to be a constant feature of 99.9 percent of all of the applets that you write, since the only way to talk with the screen is by using this include. If you have a handy macro function on your programming editor, you might want to add this line now.

•
What We Have Learned

We have covered a lot of useful ground in this chapter. Let's quickly recap.

Arrays

Arrays in Java are actually objects in the language. As a result you must instantiate the array, instantiate the objects that are going to go in the array, and then fill up the array slots with the newly created objects. However, for basic types and strings, the Array class will take care of some of the tedious work for you; you can start to use the array immediately, just as you would in C or C++. If you want an array to hold different types of objects, make the array of type Object and it will hold any other object you can create.

Vectors

Vectors are a specialized class of objects designed to hold other objects. The Vector class automatically creates an array of type Object and then will take care of adding or subtracting members for you without any worries about overflowing the array index. In order to manipulate members in a vector you must use the methods in the Vector class.

Wrappers

Java has classes designed to give object functionality to all of the basic types in the language. These classes have the same name as the basic type, but are initial capped to denote they are *wrapper classes.*

Strings

Instead of C's null-terminated arrays, Java *strings* are actually objects, and as a result come with a full load of methods to help manipulate them. Among the useful functions of the String class are length, substring, and equals.

When dealing with string literals, it is important to remember that they cannot span over two lines of code; when you put a return in the middle of a quoted string, Java gets upset with you. Instead use the language defined + overloaded operator to concatenate two quoted strings.

The only real drawback of strings: Once defined, they are constants. To manipulate the contents of a string, you need to use the StringBuffer class that allows modifying data.

Exceptions

Java error handling is exceptionally robust, and all you need to do in order to set up an error-handling routine is to couch any suspect code inside a try/catch loop that will allow you to handle most exceptions gracefully and recover.

When a method can throw an exception that should be caught, Java tells you by appending a throws statement to the end of the method definition in the API documentation. You may choose to either trap for the exception in the calling method, or implement throws in your method to chuck the exception up the call stack. However, at some level in your code, there must be an exception handler that will catch the exception, or else Java won't let you compile.

Threading

Java supports spawning concurrent lines of execution in the form of *threads*. A thread is always in one of five states: newborn, runnable, running, blocked, or dead.

You may create and start threads in one of two ways. First you can sub-class Thread and then instantiate your new threaded object and call its run method. This is the easier process. You may also create a new thread by having your class implement the runnable interface and instantiating an object of the class. Then you must instantiate a new thread and pass it your threaded object as a constructor argument. You can then call the new thread object's run method and it will take your runnable object along for the ride.

Nonpreemptive versus Preemptive Multitasking

On some systems, Java threads of equal priority will wait for one thread to finish its work and cede the processor before the next starts. However, in preemptive multitasking environments threads will run in a less predictable simultaneous manner. The best way to deal with this is to use thread priority to ensure that more important threads get more of the clock ticks of the processor.

Synchronization

You can use the synchronized keyword to make sure that only one thread at a time can get at your methods or data. To *synchronize* a method, you simply place the synchronized keyword at the start of the method definition. However, you can also synchronize blocks. In order to do this you use the synchronized keyword also, but you pass an argument of another object. This block will be locked based on the ability of a thread to get control of the argument object. While this seems a bit cumbersome, it can be extremely handy for locking down normally nonsynchronized objects for some sensitive operations.

Deadlock

When two threads are each locking down synchronized resources that the other thread is waiting on to continue, it is called *deadlock* and it will stop the execution of both threads indefinitely. To avoid deadlock, minimize your use of synchronization to only where you need it, don't call a synchronized method from another synchronized method, and try to make sure that the use of synchronized resources takes as little time as possible before releasing them.

Applets

Applets are small Java programs designed to be delivered over the Net and run in a special environment in a browser. In order to maintain some semblance of security, applets can talk only to the server they were downloaded from and can't do any file access or writing on the host machine.

An applet has the following life cycle: init, start, stop, and destroy. Each of these phases has a method of the same name that is called by the environment at the appropriate part of the applet's life and that you use to control the applet's response to external events.

An applet must be run from a page of HTML-tagged script. There are a number of different parameters that you can control with the <APPLET> tag, including the size of the applet window space and the location of the applet either in relative or absolute terms.

You can also use the <PARAM NAME> tag to pass parameters to the applet which can be caught in the applet's init method with the getParameter method, which, in turn, will return a string based on the matching <PARAM NAME> tag in the HTML file. Stand-alone programs are passed parameters in the command line in a similar manner, but these parameters are placed in a string array that is an argument to the main method of your stand-alone code.

An applet inherits from a number of different Abstract Windowing Toolkit classes that give it a great deal of functionality. One of these inherited characteristics is a paint method which is called when the applet is first called and when it becomes visible again after some external windowing event. In connection with this painting process, the applet is given a Graphics object by the environment that allows it to work the paint method to send output to the screen. However, in order to use these functions you must import java.awt.Graphics into your applets.

From Here

Now that we have enough information to be able to function a bit in Java and follow the flow of the code for both stand-alone and applet programming, it is time to move on to getting some more involved fun happening. In the next chapter we will be examining graphics and sound programming with Java, which has plenty of built-in tools to make both jobs fairly easy.

So turn the page and let's get started with the cool bits.

CHAPTER 6
• • • • • • •
GRAPHICS, SOUND, AND EVENTS

In this chapter we are going to look into the two most important programming elements for a game: *graphics* and *sound*. Along the way we will be picking up a little bit on input control and then finally showing how to bring them all together into a working game. And along the way we might even get to see a couple of examples of how a game design evolves into a finished product on a small-scale project.

With a huge amount of ground to cover, we should get started.

• • • • • • • • • • • • •
Graphics Coding

Java makes basic graphics coding pretty open and shut with the huge number of included methods available for drawing functions. Instead of having to code methods for simple graphic functionality yourself, or rely on an external graphics library, most of the graphics functions you could want or need are built right into the Java API. However, in order to use these functions, you will first have to get used to the ways that Java communicates with the screen.

As you know, when you are dealing with an applet, talking to the screen is handled with a paint method that is included in your applet. The JVM automatically calls this method when your applet starts or when something happens that causes the visibility of your applet to be altered (it is covered by another window and then uncovered, the user switches to another page and switches back, and so on).

Your paint method takes one argument, a Graphics object. This object is generated by the environment and handed to your paint method. To actually use graphics on the screen, you will be making modifications to this Graphics, which will then be displayed.

As you will see in the next few pages, drawing simple shapes on the screen is a piece of cake. In order to do some simple experiments, create the following code stub:

```
/* Stubby.java--A simple little graphics stub we are going to use to do
some of our experiments */

import java.awt.*;

public class Stubby extends java.applet.Applet {

        public void start() {
        repaint();
            }

        public void paint (Graphics g) {

        }

}
```

Also create an HTML file that calls this applet in a 300-by-300 window.

As we go through the code to draw the various shapes on the screen add the code lines for the graphics calls inside the paint method, then compile the program, and run it in the Appletviewer in order to see the results.

X and Y

The coordinate system for Java is based on whole pixels as the primary unit and starts at 0,0 in the upper lefthand corner of the drawing area (the total area of your applet). X values run from 0 to the length of your applet to the right and Y values run from 0 to the height of your applet going down. In a 100-by-100 applet, 50,50 would be a point right in the middle of the screen. Look at Figure 6.1 and you can see the coordinate system laid out in a grid.

Later in the chapter we will be working with the program that produced this chart in order to see a bit more about the use and abuse of the basic graphics system.

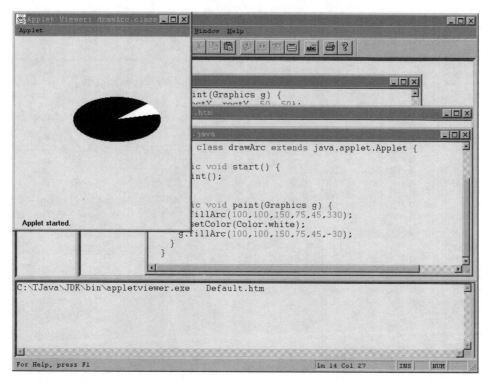

Figure 6.1   Output of Chart2.java showing the graphic coordinate system.

Drawing Basic Shapes

The following methods of Graphics (to follow along in the Java API docs—a pretty good idea—you can find Graphics under java.awt) allow you to draw various basic shapes on the screen.

draw3DRect
The *draw3DRect method* paints a shaded 3D rectangle on the screen.

```
draw3DRect (int x, int y, int width, int height, boolean)
```

The x and y values define the starting point for the upper righthand corner of your rectangle, the width and height values are how long and high your rectangle is going to be, and the boolean value tells whether your rectangle is going to be raised or sunken.

The following lines of code, added to your Stubby class, will produce Figure 6.2.

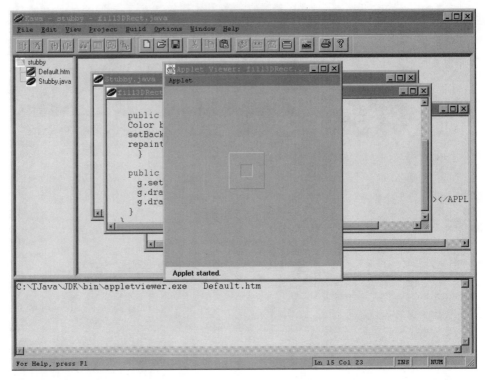

Figure 6.2   A pair of 3D rectangles.

```
g.setColor(Color.gray);
g.draw3DRect(110,110,60,60,true);
g.draw3DRect(130,130,20,20,false);
```

In order to assure that this displays properly (we will be talking more about this when we get to color), make your start method look like the following:

```
public void start() {
    Color bg= new Color(128,128,128);
    setBackground(bg);
    repaint();
    }
```

Now run this and you will see a lowered rectangle inside a raised rectangle.

fill3DRect
The *fill3DRect method* creates a 3D rectangle in the current drawing color.

```
fill3DRect(int x, int y, int width, int height, boolean)
```

The arguments to this method function the same as the arguments to draw3DRect. The following code will produce Figure 6.3:

```
g.setColor(Color.lightGray);
g.fill3DRect(110,110,60,60,true);
g.fill3DRect(130,130,20,20,false);
```

drawOval

The *drawOval method* draws an oval on the screen within the bounds of a specified rectangular area.

```
drawOval(int x, int y, int width, int height)
```

X and Y are the starting point (this is always the upper righthand corner in any rectangle specifications from here on out) for the bounding rectangle, and width and height specify the length and height of the rectangle.

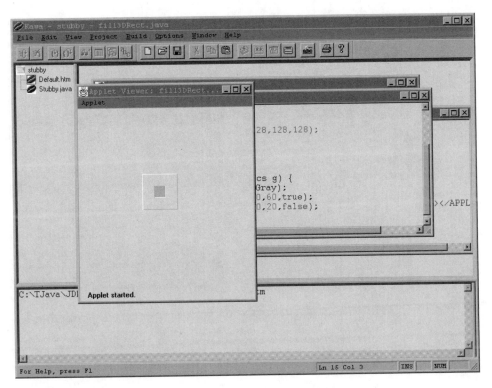

Figure 6.3 A filled-rectangle version of Figure 6.2.

The following code inserted into your Stubby class will produce Figure 6.4.

```
g. drawOval(75,100,150,75);
```

fillOval

Pretty much as you would suspect, *fillOval* is identical to drawOval, except that it fills the oval in the current drawing color. The following lines will produce Figure 6.5.

```
g.setColor(Color.darkGray);
g.fillOval(75,100,150,75);
```

drawArc

The *drawArc method* allows you to draw arcs out of an oval within a defined rectangular bound. If you don't remember your geometry, you might want to play with this one a while to make sure you get the hang of the angles.

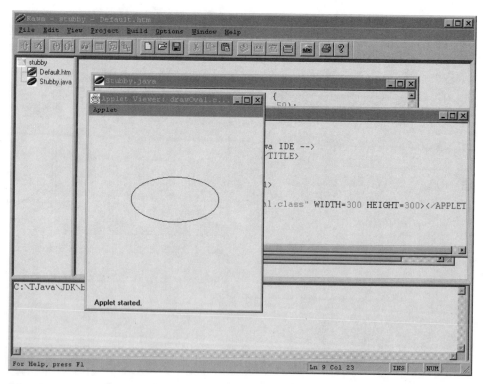

Figure 6.4　An oval.

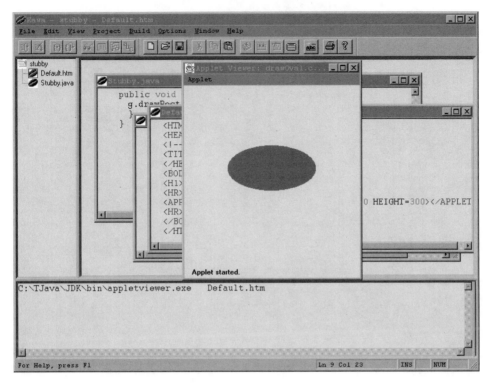

Figure 6.5 A dark gray filled oval.

```
drawArc(int x, int y, int width, int height, int startAngle, int arcAngle)
```

X, Y, width, and height define the rectangular bounds of the ellipsis your arc is going to be drawn from. *startAngle* is the starting angle for your arc from a 0 degree line in the three-o'clock position. *arcAngle* determines not only the angle of your arc, but how it is drawn. Positive arc angles are drawn counterclockwise and negative arc angles are drawn clockwise.

To see this in action, use the following code in Stubby to produce the arc displayed in Figure 6.6.

```
g.drawArc(100, 100, 150, 150, 45, 80);
```

Now, if you are a bit geometry challenged, change the line in Stubby to the following code in order to produce Figure 6.7:

```
g.drawArc(100, 100, 150, 150, 45, -80);
```

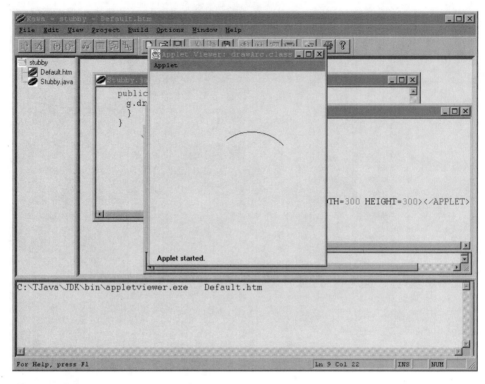

Figure 6.6   Positive arc angle.

Now note that we are drawing the same arc here. However, in Figure 6.6 the arc is being drawn in a counterclockwise rotation from the 45-degree point set in our startAngle. Figure 6.7 represents the same angle being drawn with a clockwise rotation from the same point.

If you are having problems understanding what is happening here it might help you to remember to think of the arc as being a slice of an oval created by the bounding box. To demonstrate this, let's change our example line just a bit in order to see the underlying oval this arc would demonstrate if it were to move just a bit further (Figure 6.8).

```
g.drawArc(100,100,150,150, 45, 330);
```

Now if we change the bounding box producing the underlying oval, we can see a little more of what is happening.

```
g.drawArc(100, 100, 150, 75, 45, 330);
```

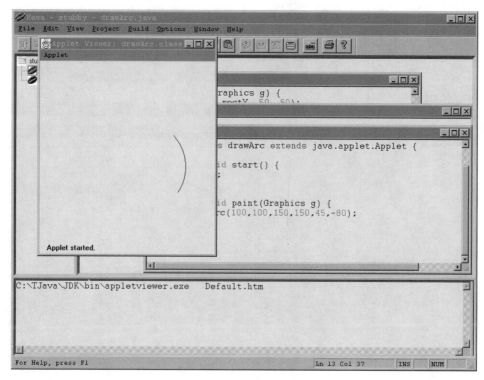

Figure 6.7 Negative arc angle.

Figure 6.9 should now make the details of drawArc clear. If you are still having problems seeing what is going on, then play around a bit with the numbers and you should be able to get the hang of it pretty quickly.

fillArc

Just like the other fill methods we have seen here, the *fillArc method* fills an arc with the current drawing color. It uses the same arguments as the drawArc method in the same way. However, unlike other fills, fillArc doesn't just fill the arc; instead it fills the arc out to the center point of the underlying ellipse it describes. This creates a pie-shaped wedge. The most obvious use for fillArc is to create pie charts of various types (see Figure 6.10). Let's use our example to do just that.

```
g.fillArc(100,100,150,75,45,330);
g.setColor(Color.lightGray);
g.fillArc(100,100,150,75,45,-30);
```

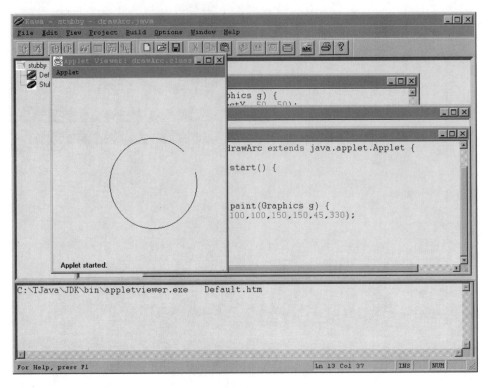

Figure 6.8 Almost complete circle of arc.

drawPolygon

The *drawPolygon method* draws multiple lines on the screen using a pair of arrays to mark the points to be drawn. These lines, if the first and last points are the same, end up as polygons.

```
drawPolygon(int x[], int y[], int nPoints)
```

The x array is an array of all of the x points marking vertices and the y array is an array of all of the y points marking vertices. nPoints is the total number of points delineated in the x and y arrays. When the drawPolygon method is called, it will take the first value in the x array and the first value in the y array and start a line that goes to the second x and y values. Then the second x and y coordinates will be the start of a line going to the third x and y coordinates, and so on.

The drawPolygon method doesn't automatically close your polygon, so if you want an actual polygon as opposed to just a random collection of lines,

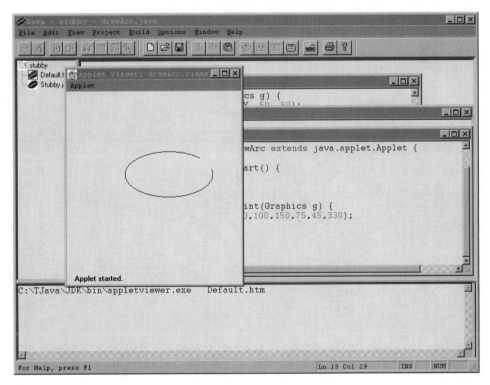

Figure 6.9   Another arc defining most of an oval.

you need to put the coordinates for the first point as the last coordinates in your arrays in order to close things up.

The following example code will produce an octagon like the one in Figure 6.11.

```
int x[] = {75,125,175,225,225,175,125,75,75};
int y[] = {125,75,75,125,175,225,225,175,125};
int pts = 9;
g.drawPolygon(x, y, pts);
```

If you wish, you can create a Polygon object and pass it to drawPolygon as the argument and get the same results. The Polygon object has exactly the same information contained in the arguments to drawPolygon, but is simply easier to manipulate depending on what you are doing in your code. fillPolygon can be used to fill your polygon in the same manner that all of the fill methods work.

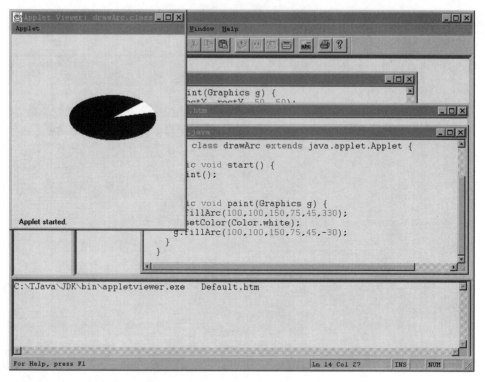

Figure 6.10   Pie chart made out of fillArc.

drawLine

By now, drawing a line is going to seem pretty self-explanatory.

```
drawLine(int startX, int startY, int endX, int endY)
```

where startX and startY are the starting point of your line and endX and endY are the ending points of your line.

```
g.drawLine(0, 0, 300, 300);
```

This will draw a line diagonally from the upper lefthand corner of your Stubby applet to the bottom righthand corner.

One point to be made about lines, and all of these graphics elements we have been working with so far, is that Java has decided that you only need lines of a single pixel. At this time, there is no provision for drawing anything with line-width specifications. Therefore, if you want something thicker, you are going to have to draw another line one pixel away from your original line in order to produce a thicker line.

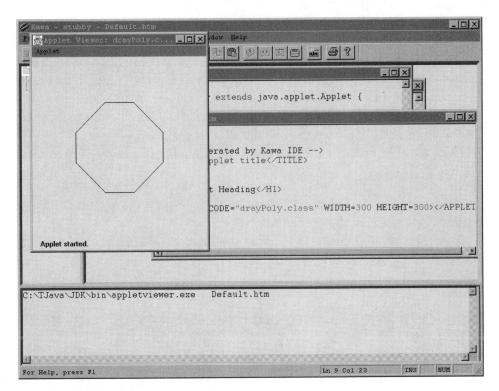

Figure 6.11 Octagon polygon.

drawRect

By now you might have seen my logic of introducing the harder stuff first. At this point, we get to save a lot of ink on drawRect. This draws a rectangle on the screen.

```
drawRect(int X, int Y, width, height)
```

The X, Y, width, and height values work the same as they have for all other rectangle-bounded graphic elements.

```
g.drawRect(50, 50, 200, 200);
```

This code will produce a huge rectangle in your Stubby applet. If you want to fill it, then you can use the fillRect method.

drawRoundRect

The *drawRoundRect method,* which provides us with a way to create rectangles with rounded corners, needs a slight bit of explanation. Instead of the usual four arguments, this method takes six.

```
drawRoundRect(int X, int Y, int width, int height, int
arcWidth, int arcHeight)
```

We are already familiar with the first four of these arguments. The arcWidth determines how far the corners round on the x axis and the arcHeight determines how far they round on the y axis. If you specify an arcWidth of 30 and an arcHeight of 25, the corners are going to round 30 pixels in from the corners on the x axis and 25 in from the corners along the y axis.

The following pair of code examples should make this fairly easy to see.

```
g.drawRoundRect(50, 50, 200, 200, 25, 25);
```

This code produces the rounded rectangle in Figure 6.12. The rounding occurs 25 pixels from the corner points.

To make this a bit clearer, the following line of code produces the decidedly more rounded rectangle in Figure 6.13.

```
g.drawRoundRect(50, 50, 200, 200, 150, 150);
```

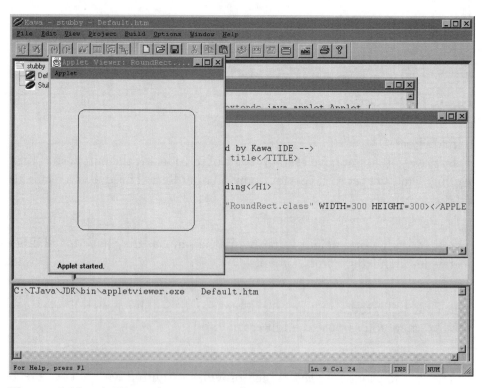

Figure 6.12 A 25-pixel corner rounding on a rectangle.

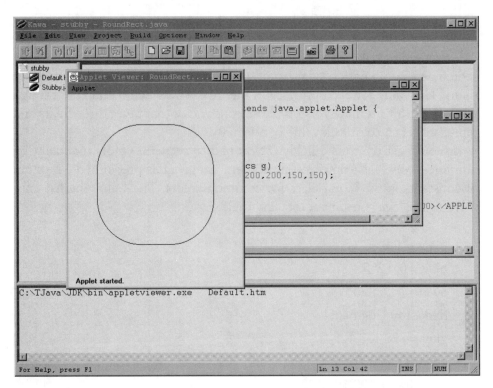

Figure 6.13   A 150-pixel corner rounding on a rectangle.

Colors

Now we get to find out about those setColor calls we have been making from time to time. Java, in its typical object fetishism, has an object called *Color* that is used to deal with colors. When you are inside the paint method, you get a free color object along with your free Graphics object (wow, pretty soon we will be able to start a game show with all of this free stuff!). You can use this Color to do all sorts of color setting, as you have seen.

The primary method you are going to use to do this is the *setColor method* of the Graphics class. When you make a setColor call, it is going to set the current drawing or filling color in your applet to the color you have called.

The details of the method are:

```
setColor(Color c)
```

where the c argument is a color object set to the color that you want to start displaying. However, this begs the question of how to get a color object to display our chosen color. To do this, you first need to understand how Java thinks about color.

Java handles color in a 24-bit RGB format. That is, all colors are represented as a combination of the red, green, and blue primaries that produce them. The value for each primary in the mix is between 0 and 255 (though you can use an alternate version of the constructor that takes three floats and represents each color as a value between 0 and 1).

It would get onerous quickly if you had to set your colors manually by numerical code each time you used them. So Java has predefined a number of constants in the Color class for common colors. The following list enumerates the Java constant colors and their values:

> black = 0,0,0
> blue = 0,0,255
> cyan = 0,255,255
> darkGray = 64,64,64
> gray = 128,128,128
> green = 0,255,0
> lightGray = 192,192,192
> magenta = 255,0,255
> orange = 255,200,0
> pink = 255,175,175
> red = 255,0,0
> white =255,255,255
> yellow = 255,255,0

To actually make a color, create a color object with the proper values:

```
Color c= new color(0,127,0);
```

This line will produce a nice dark green that is handy for felt background (which you will see used at the end of this chapter).

Now with your new color object in hand, you want to do something with it. You have already seen our use of the setColor method. However, there are some other things you can do with colors. First, you can set the background color of your applet. This is done using the *setBackground method* of the Applet class.

This method is used as follows:

```
setBackground(Color c);
```

where the argument is a color object set to the background color you want to use. Note that if you want this to work in an applet that is going to be viewed in a browser (and obviously you want your applet to be viewed in a browser or there isn't much point in creating one) you are going to need to set your background color initially in your init or start method and then set it again to the same value at the start of your paint method. This might seem like overkill, but different browsers work a hair differently when it comes to the setting of the background, and you are well served to make your code run on all of them: This multiple setting will make your life a lot easier in that direction.

Along with setBackground, your applet also has a method (well, inherits a method, actually) for *setForeground* that changes the color of all drawn elements. It is the same as the setBackground method in usage:

```
setForeground(Color c);
```

That is pretty much it for color for the moment. However, one thing to remember is that the JVM conforms to its environment, so your panoply of cool colors might not be capable of displaying on your user's system. In this case Java will filter down to the closest match. As a rule of thumb, I pretty much assume that most machines that are going to be viewing applets are running in 256 color mode as a minimum, but there are sure to be a host of people running mono or 16 color out there who aren't going to see your color settings the way you intend for them to.

A Bit about Text

As we have seen, Java has quite a few methods devoted to the display of basic graphics shapes. Even though a good legend is worth a thousand graphics primitives (hey, I like text, okay?) there are also methods for dealing with strings and font manipulations.

The main way you are going to display text on the screen is with the Graphics object's *drawString method* which has the following syntax:

```
drawString( String yourString, int x, int y);
```

where yourString is the string you wish to display and x and y are coordinates on the screen where you wish to display the string.

Alternatively, you can use the *drawChars method* with syntax as follows:

```
drawChars (char yourCharacters[], int offset, int length,
int x, int y);
```

where yourCharacters is an array of characters that you wish to draw to the screen, offset is the place in the array to start, length is the number of characters from the offset to draw, and x and y are the starting position on the screen.

In most cases, you are going to want to use the drawString method. However, the drawChars method occasionally comes in handy. One case in point: When you are printing words that run vertically rather than horizontally you might want to use drawChars.

These are the only two methods you really need to output characters to the screen. Without using anything else you can get words to print to the screen in the default font of your applet's environment. However, in most cases you are going to want a lot more control than just the ability to print raw characters where you want them—for example, you are going to want control of the point size of your text and to be able to use effects such as bold or italics—not to mention how handy changing fonts can be. For this, you are going to need to manipulate a Font object.

The Font Object

Java deals with different fonts as instances of the Font class. The running environment you are using has a default setting for this object that is available to your applet just like the default Color and Graphics objects. If you want to make any changes to these default text display properties, you are going to need to instantiate your own font object with the proper characteristics.

```
Font f = new Font(String TheFontName, int style, int size);
```

TheFontName is the name of one of the fonts available to your applet and *size* is the point size you wish to have displayed. Style, however, takes a short bit of explanation.

Style controls the application of bold and italics to your text. This is an integer that is the sum of the style elements you want. Plain text is 0. Bold is 1. Italics is 2. Bold and Italics are going to sum to 3. While you can specify this value as just a number, in most cases you are going to want to use the three class variables provided for this purpose, PLAIN, BOLD, and ITALIC. This makes life much easier on anyone reading your code.

```
Font f = new Font("TimesRoman", Font.PLAIN, 12);
```

This line creates a new Font object containing the specifications for plain, 12 point TimesRoman text.

However, in order to actually use this font, you will have to switch the font of your Graphics object to the new font. This is accomplished by the *set-Font method,* which takes a single argument of a Font object. The example line below would set your font to the font object we defined above:

```
g.setFont(f);
```

In general, an applet isn't going to have a heck of a lot of fonts available to it. We are going to show you in a few moments how to determine what fonts are available on a given system, but it is an annoying and burdensome process. Java is fairly good, in that if you call for a font that isn't available, it will default to an available system font. However, in general you can rely on having Courier almost anywhere your applet is going to be running. Helvetica and TimesRoman are also pretty safe. Past that, you are likely to be running into a system default font on many user's machines.

FontMetrics

Although being able to set your font and attributes is a good thing, being able to know the display properties of those fonts is a much better thing. You can do this with the FontMetrics class. A *FontMetrics* object provides methods that give you information critical to figuring out how to properly display your strings, such as the height and width of a given string given the settings in a Font object.

In order to use FontMetrics you must instantiate a FontMetrics object and pass it a font object you wish to find out information about. For example, the following snippet would provide a FontMetrics object for the Font object we have been using in our examples so far:

```
FontMetrics fm = new FontMetrics(f);
```

FontMetrics provides a number of methods for finding out the gory details of your font, but there are only two that really concern the vast majority of the world.

The *stringWidth method* returns a number that represents the number of pixels wide the string will be when displayed. It must be passed the string you wish to check as an argument.

```
fm.stringWidth(SomeString);
```

The above line would give us the number of pixels that SomeString would be when displayed with the settings in the Font object that fm was derived from.

charWidth works exactly the same as stringWidth, just with a character for an argument. The other method that concerns us (I am not counting char-Width as one of our two important methods, considering it more of a poor cousin of stringWidth) is getHeight. *getHeight* takes no argument and returns the total height of our something printed in the font that our FontMetric object is derived from.

```
fm.getHeight();
```

This line would give us the height in pixels of something printed in the font represented by our f object we derived the fm object from.

Using these two methods you can figure out how to display something on the screen centered properly and without anything you write running over any other text.

Getting a List of Available Fonts

If you decide you need it, you can query the environment for what fonts are available to your applet. However, you can't do this as directly as you might like.

Before you can query for fonts you must first get a Toolkit object. *Toolkits* bind various abstract methods used to deal with the underlying system to the objects that are used for building your interface. We have been working with one of these building objects in the form of the Applet object. There is a Toolkit customized for applets yelling at the system for things, such as FontMetrics and other such information.

However, the implementation of the Toolkit changes depending on some factors in how you construct your program. Hence, you can't just instantiate a Toolkit and use it. Instead, you have to request a Toolkit that is going to work with your program setup and then put this into a Toolkit reference built to hold it.

This sounds pretty complex, but in real life it is fairly easy to actually use. In order to get a Toolkit, use the following line of code:

```
Toolkit Tools = getToolkit();
```

You now have a Toolkit in the Tools object that has all the bits that work for your program.

You can use this Toolkit to help you to get the list of system fonts by using the *getFontList method* which returns an array of strings with the names of the available fonts. The following line provides an example of doing this:

```
String listOFonts[] = Tools.getFontList();
```

The String array *listOFonts* will now contain a number of strings that provide the name of the available system fonts.

• • • • • • • • • • • •
Example Time

We have gone quite a few pages without any real example of code that uses what we are learning. So let's deal with a couple of examples that will help us work with what we have learned. The first is *FontShow*, a simple applet that will find out what system fonts are available to us and then display them on the screen so we can get an idea of what we have to work with.

```
/* FontShow.java--This program demonstrates the use of fonts and some
associated methods by getting and displaying the local system fonts
available for Java to use. */

import java.awt.*;

public class FontShow extends java.applet.Applet {

    public void start() {
    repaint();
    }

    public void paint(Graphics g) {
    //First we need a Toolkit to get a list of system
    //fonts.
    Toolkit Tools = getToolkit();

    //Now we need to get a list of Fonts from the toolkit.
    String listOFonts[] = Tools.getFontList();

    //Get the total number of fonts we are dealing with.
    int numFonts = listOFonts.length;
```

```
//Get a placeholder for total height of all fonts.
int totalHeight = 85;

//Now do something with all this. . .
for (int i = 0; i < numFonts; i++) {

    //Make a font object for the font we are on.
    Font f = new Font(listOFonts[i], Font.PLAIN, 14);

    //Get the metrics of the font.
    FontMetrics fm = getFontMetrics(f);

    //Get the height and length of the font from the
//fm object.
    int fHeight= fm.getHeight();
    int fLength= fm.stringWidth(listOFonts[i]);

    //Use these to produce our x and y values for
//display.
    int x = (size().width - fLength)/2;
    int y = fHeight + totalHeight;

    //Update our placeholder so we know how far down
//the screen we are.
    totalHeight = y;

    //Print font name centered with enough height not
//to overlap.
    g.setFont(f);
    g.drawString(listOFonts[i],x, y);

    }
  }
}
```

This little bit of code is pretty straightforward. First, we get a Toolkit we place in Tools and then we use this to get a list of fonts that we put in listO-Fonts. We determine how many fonts we are dealing with by using the length method of Array on listOFonts, then we start a loop that will run through all of the fonts. In the loop we change to the fonts one at a time, get their height and length from a FontMetrics object we create, and put in fm. Then we center the fonts on the x axis, keep a running total of how far we are down on the y axis using totalHeight and display the font on the screen (see Figure 6.14).

Note that the initial setting of totalHeight is pretty much an arbitrary spacing number that will center the display on my system. If you wanted to make this a better piece of code that would make sure that the display was centered on the y axis no matter what the size of the applet window or the number and size of the fonts in the users system, you could create another

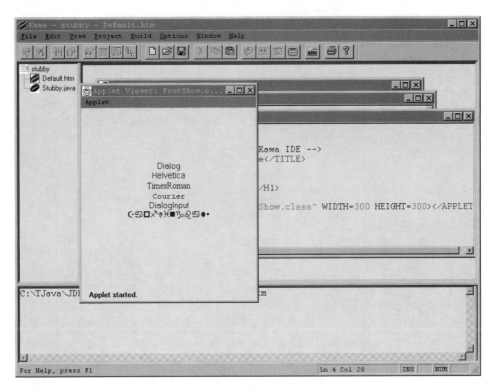

Figure 6.14 Output from FontShow.

loop that would rapidly run though all the fonts without displaying them and add up their total height. Then it is a stupid math trick to figure out where to start your display using the total height of all of the fonts and the size( ).height function of the applet itself. Then again, for sheer brutality, you could just display the fonts where you wanted them and then forcibly resize the applet window around them to make them centered.

Even though FontShow demonstrates a few things about font metrics and setting fonts, it isn't likely we are going to be using fonts in this way in our own applications. Instead, we are much more likely to be mixing fonts and graphics calls to create meaningful displays. To this end, look back at Figure 6.1 at the start of the chapter. Instead of just creating a chart to produce this graphic, we coded a fairly simple applet to produce the image we needed. There are two versions of this applet, one without using any fancy font tricks and one using good font practices to make things look better.

Here is the initial run at producing our X and Y chart, Chart.java.

```java
/* Chart.java--This code produces a chart that shows the
X and Y coordinates on a screen. */

import java.awt.*;

public class Chart extends java.applet.Applet {

    public void start() {
    setBackground(Color.white);
    repaint();
    }

    public void paint(Graphics g) {
        setBackground(Color.white);
        // Display our axis identifiers centered on their
    //axis.
        g.drawString("X", (this.size().width/2),20);
        g.drawString("Y", 5, (this.size().height/2));

        // Create the X and Y numbering legends.
        for (int x = 50; x < (this.size().width); x = x +
    50) {
            g.drawString("" + x, x, 40);
        }
        for (int y = 50; y < (this.size().height); y = y +
    50) {
            g.drawString("" + y, 20, y);
        }

        //Create our X and Y 10 pixel lines in light gray
        //starting at 50 pixels and going to the end of
        //their axis in display.
        g.setColor(Color.lightGray);
        for (int x = 50; x < (this.size().width -10); x =
    x + 10) {
            g.drawLine (x, 50, x, this.size().height -10);
        }
        for (int y = 50; y < (this.size().height -10); y =
    y + 10) {
            g.drawLine (50, y, this.size().width-10, y);
        }

        //Create our X and Y 50 pixel major division lines
        //in black starting at 50 pixels and going to the
        //end of display.
        g.setColor(Color.black);
        for (int x = 50; x < (this.size().width -10); x =
    x + 50) {
            g.drawLine (x, 50, x, this.size().height-10);
        }
```

```
        for (int y = 50; y < (this.size().height -10); y =
    y + 50) {
            g.drawLine (50, y, this.size().width-10, y);
        }
    }
}
```

From a code standpoint, this program is fully as obvious as FontShow. (See Figure 6.15.) We set our background to white, then draw legends labeling the two axes we are working on, and then lay down legend markers every 50 pixels on each axis.

Next, we change our color to gray and draw lines from the 50-pixel mark to the end of the applet display space in both the x and y axis. These lines are 10 pixels apart and form our minor division lines. We start at the 50-pixel point for a couple of reasons, but the main one is to make sure that we have room for the labels we have already laid down.

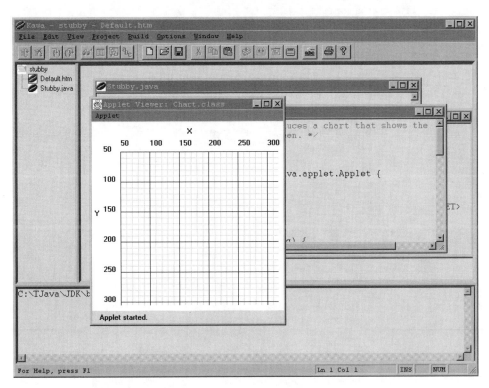

Figure 6.15 First run of Chart.java.

Finally, we change colors to black and draw our major division lines in the X and Y axis. These are drawn last to overdraw all of the gray lines so that we won't get any breaks in our major division lines as they are intersected by minor division lines. We draw these starting, again, at the fifty pixel mark and run them out to the length and height of the applet.

Looking at Figure 6.14, however, we can see there are some minor problems with this simple drawing code, problems that have to do with our labeling. While our labels start at the 50-pixel mark, they then run out from this, making things a bit confusing. If the labels were centered over the divisions they represent, things would be much improved. By adding font metrics, we can easily take care of this problem.

```java
/* ChartB.java--This code produces a chart that shows the X and Y
coordinates on a screen and makes some use of font metrics. */
import java.awt.*;

public class ChartB extends java.applet.Applet {

    public void start() {
        setBackground(Color.white);
        repaint();
    }

    public void paint(Graphics g) {
        setBackground(Color.white);

        //Get a FontMetrics for the default font.
        FontMetrics fm = getFontMetrics(getFont());

        // Display our axis identifiers centered on their
//axis.
        g.drawString("X", (this.size().width/2),20);
        g.drawString("Y", 5, (this.size().height/2));

        // Create the X and Y numbering legends.
        for (int x = 50; x < (this.size().width); x = x +
50) {
            //Turn x into a string we can work with.
            String XString = String.valueOf(x);

            //Determine offset from fm.
            int xOffset = (fm.stringWidth(XString)/2);

            //Draw the legends.
            g.drawString(XString, x-xOffset, 40);
        }
        for (int y = 50; y < (this.size().height); y = y +
50) {
            //Get the offset for height of Y legends.
            int yOffset = (fm.getHeight()/2);
```

```
        g.drawString("" + y, 20, y+yOffset);
    }

//Create our X and Y 10 pixel lines in light gray
//starting at 50 pixels and going to the end of
//their axis in display.
        g.setColor(Color.lightGray);
        for (int x = 50; x < (this.size().width -10); x =
x + 10) {
            g.drawLine (x, 50, x, this.size().height -10);
        }
        for (int y = 50; y < (this.size().height -10); y =
y + 10) {
            g.drawLine (50, y, this.size().width-10, y);
        }

        //Create our X and Y 50 pixel major division lines
//in black starting at 50 pixels and going to the
//end of display.
        g.setColor(Color.black);
        for (int x = 50; x < (this.size().width -10); x =
x + 50) {
            g.drawLine (x, 50, x, this.size().height-10);
        }
        for (int y = 50; y < (this.size().height -10); y =
y + 50) {
            g.drawLine (50, y, this.size().width-10, y);
        }
    }
}
```

Now in this example we have added a FontMetrics created from getting the default font for the environment. From this we calculate offsets that equal half of the width or height, respectively, of the X and Y major division legends. Then we apply these offsets when we display the legends so that the characters now bisect the pixel line they label. (Look back to the beginning of the chapter at Figure 6.1 and you will see the output from this revised code.)

As you can see, the application of font metrics allows you to place your text on the screen with the precision necessary for some of the more exacting game applications (and just general neatness).

• • • • • • •
Images

Although drawing graphics primitives is a fine thing, more robust applications are going to require using pregenerated images. Java supports two popular graphic file formats, GIF and JPEG. You can easily retrieve and use files in these formats with Java's built-in image management facilities. Using images in Java is accomplished through the Image class.

In order to produce a member of the image class, you must use getImage in order to put the image you want into the object. The *getImage method* takes a URL as an argument or a URL and a string name. The following code snippets will both retrieve an Image:

```
Image imageOne = getImage(getCodeBase(), "Butch1.jpg");
Image imageOne = getImage(new
    URL("http://www.ianet.com/~withers/Butch1.jpg");
```

The first example uses getCodeBase to retrieve the base directory URL where the applet is running and pulls Butch1.jpg from it. The second example produces a new URL that gives explicit directions to getting the file you want. Unless otherwise noted you will find that all of the examples of absolute URLs in this book, like this one, don't really lead to anywhere, so don't try to use them.

Once you have an Image you can use the drawImage method of the Graphics class to draw them. The drawImage method takes four arguments:

```
drawImage(Image YourImage, int x, int y, ImageObserver
    YourObserver);
```

The first argument is the image that you want to display, the x and y integers say where you want the origin for your image, and the ImageObserver is the ImageObserver instance that is watching over this particular image loading. That last bit is going to take a slight amount of explaining.

When you decide you are going to use an image, you have already created an instance of the Image class and told it where to get the raw data to use for its painting. However, just because you have told your Image to load something doesn't mean it actually gets done with the job before you decide you are going to perform some operations on that data (oh, let's get wild and say you are going to do something crazy and try to display it). This is particularly prevalent when Java is used in its foremost environment, the Web, where your image source files might be halfway around the planet from the machine where your applet is running.

To work with this problem, you need to pass along with your image an instance of a class that implements the ImageObserver interface. The function of the ImageObserver interface is to make sure that a method called imageUpdate is available to your Image class instance. This method keeps repainting your Image when more pieces of it come in over the wire for use. Therefore you might call a repaint that is going to use an Image that isn't finished loading, the repaint will paint as much of it as is available and the imageUpdate method will make sure that as more information becomes available it gets painted.

Now, before you start getting nervous at the need to know all of this stuff, realize that while you need to have some kind of understanding what is going on behind the scenes, you aren't going to need to really worry about dealing with all of this yourself for one simple reason: way back the inheritance chain at Component the ImageObserver interface got implemented. This means that your Applet object implements the ImageObserver, so all you need to do with applet (or any other Component you might someday end up using for drawing) when using Image is to pass it the keyword *this* as the ImageObserver argument and everything will be fine.

There was a good reason for going through all of this explanation, however: It helps us somewhat when we talk about the media tracker. The *MediaTracker* object is a handy little bit of code that helps you keep track of where your Image objects are in the loading process and can keep your code from messing with your Images until they are fully loaded.

The constructor for MediaTracker takes a single argument of a component object for which MediaTracker is going to be keeping track of image flow. Since Applet is a component, just pass it a *this* keyword.

In order to add an image to MediaTracker to be tracked, use the following method:

```
addImage( Image yourImage, int idNumber);
```

The Image object *yourImage* is an instance of the Image class that you want MediaTracker to keep track of. The *integer idNumber* is what image group yourImage belongs to. Image groups are how MediaTracker keeps up with your images. You can have multiple images assigned to one group id, or you can put each of your images in a different group. However, MediaTracker will load your images by the order of their group ids. Lower numbered groups will be loaded before higher numbered groups.

So what use is all of this? Well, by using MediaTracker's methods you can ensure that you don't start working with groups of images until you have them fully loaded. Let's take a quick look at a few of MediaTracker's methods to see how we do this.

```
checkAll();
```

This method checks to see if all of the images that MediaTracker has logged are fully downloaded or have gotten zapped by errors.

```
checkID(int idNumber);
```

This works the same as checkAll, only just for the Images objects in the selected idNumber group.

```
waitForAll()
```

Now this one is great—*waitForAll* will block execution of the thread it is called from until all of the Image objects that are logged get done downloading. Note that this throws an InterruptedException that you must trap for.

```
waitForID(int idNumber)
```

This works the same as waitForAll, but only for the Image or Images in the selected group number you feed it. Using this you can block a thread until all of the images you are going to be using for the first few moments of your applet, such as a sign-in screen or splash graphics get downloaded, and then have the rest of the Images downloading in the background while you start using the first group.

An Image Example

Everything we have been talking about up until now can seem pretty esoteric. However, a quick example should suffice to make things a lot clearer if you pay attention. The example we are going to present here is called Dying-Butch. In this example we are going to use seven images of a simple stick man (Butch) to create a looping animation. Originally this was going to be called DancingButch, but the totally inept art capabilities of your humble narrator forced the name change. While the actual quality of the animation is admittedly inferior, the program does serve to illustrate our discussions up to this point.

```
/* DyingButch.java--A horrible hack to demonstrate some points about
image loading. */

import java.awt.*;

public class DyingButch extends java.applet.Applet

                                          implements Runnable{
```

```java
Thread runner;
Image butchImg[] = new Image[7];
int counter;
MediaTracker tracker;
Image dispImg;

public void init() {
      tracker = new MediaTracker(this);

      //Get all of our files into image slots and
//register their loading with the media tracker
//object.

      for (int i = 0; i < 7; i++) {
            butchImg[i] = getImage(getCodeBase(), "Butch"
                  + (i+1) +".jpg");
            tracker.addImage(butchImg[i], i);
      }
      //Start our thread.
      runner = new Thread(this);
      runner.start();
}

public void run() {
      //Make the thread sleep and wait for images to get
 //into their respective slots.
      try {tracker.waitForAll();}
      catch (InterruptedException e) {}

      //Loop to make Butch cycle 10 times.
      for (int times = 1; times < 10; times++){
            //Loop to run through Butch animation series.
            for (int i = 0; i < 7; i++) {
                  counter = counter + 1;
                  dispImg = butchImg[i];
                  //Put a delay between frames;
                  try {Thread.sleep(150);}
                  catch (InterruptedException e) {}
                  //Paint it.
                  repaint();
            }
      }
}

public void paint(Graphics g) {
      //If any image loading errors came up, tell us.
      if (tracker.isErrorAny()){
            g.drawString("Error", 200,200);
      }

      //Tell us what frame we are on.
      g.drawString(""+ counter, 10,10);
      //Display our picture, but if it is null don't
//bother.
```

```
if (dispImg != null) {
    g.drawImage(dispImg, 50,50,this);
}
    }
}
```

This class isn't much more complicated than anything else we have dealt with to this point, but from the use of threads and the MediaTracker to control our displaying you might manage to fall off the one true path, so we will explicate it.

After setting up our variable declarations, we instantiate a MediaTracker object called tracker. Then we load all seven Butch images (which need to be in the same directory that the HTML stub is being served from) into the slots of an Image array called butchImg.

Right after that, in the same loop, we add the butchImg images to tracker, giving each one a separate group id. This is pretty much arbitrary. We could have assigned them all to the same group just as easily, since we have no real need to load parts of the image base at different times in this simple an applet.

While still in the init method we also start a Thread called runner and assign our applet to it. Now we can easily pause everything from time to time in order to make our display run the way we want it to. In the *run method,* the first thing we do is use tracker.waitForAll to stop everything until everything we are loading in butchImg is ready for use. Note that we have wrapped this in an exception handler to catch the possible InterruptedException.

Next we initiate a couple of loops that are designed to run us through the entire series of seven Butch pictures ten times. We are keeping a counter that will tell us what frame we are on at any given time when we display it later in the paint method and we are moving our current butchImg into another Image object called dispImg. The reason for this is fairly obvious: When we go to our paint method we are going to be getting outside the scope of our counter, i, and the easiest way to deal with that is just move the Image we want to display right now into a new reference before we call paint.

After we are done with these simple chores, we put everything to sleep for a pretty arbitrarily determined 150 ms so that we get some delay between frames. Without this, we go through our frames too quickly to see any of them painted.

This might be a good time to talk very briefly about what would happen if we didn't include this delay. If you make calls to a paint method quicker than it can paint, it starts keeping a *call stack.* Instead of running through that stack one at a time as it gets done with each paint, it jumps to the last call in the stack. This means that if you are on a fast machine and don't slow things down when you are doing animations, you only get the last frame or so of data actually painted to the screen.

Finally, in the paint method, we first use an error-checking method of tracker, *isErrorAny,* to check and see if our MediaTracker had problems loading any of our images. If it did, we want to know about it, so we throw up an error message.

Then we spit out our count number to the screen so that we know where we are at in our execution. Note the little trick we have used here to use drawString to spit out an integer. By concatenating an integer onto the end of an empty string, Graphics will let you slide by on the drawString method and display the integer without your having to convert it to a string value. A cheap trick, but you use what works.

Finally, we display our *displmg,* which actually draws the painted image to the screen. You might be wondering a bit about why we have wrapped this in null check for displmg. Well, do you remember our earlier work with HelloApplet.java a chapter back? Well, if you look at the listing for that code, you will note that it doesn't have a start or run method. One of the first things that is done with an Applet in the JVM is that it gets a gratuitous call to the paint method. Nothing is wrong with that if you are ready for it. However, in this case what is going to happen when paint is called before we hit our run method is that paint is going to try to draw displmg and will find out that there isn't anything there, throwing all sorts of nasty errors. By skipping display if we have a null value in the Image we are trying to display, it skips drawing on that first call and makes all right with the world.

Now we could have made a much easier example sans threading and a MediaTracker in order to demonstrate throwing up images. However, that would have been pretty misleading. In real, useful, Java work you aren't going to be doing much straight book-example type of display action. Instead, your applets and applications are going to require the use of threads and using MediaTrackers to make sure that what you want to display is actually around for use. By diving in right now, we get used to the fact that we are going to have to deal with Threads and such when we are working with Images (and graphics in general).

Another point here is that when you are doing graphics-intensive work, you are also going to need to use threads and good OOP technique for another simple reason: Although Java's automatic garbage collection is a fine and wonderful thing, if you try to build monolithic programs that don't use threads and don't pass off to method calls at reasonable rates, you will end up confusing the garbage collector in the Appletviewer or Browser environment and can suffer from memory leaks. Later in the book, we will talk about this a little more and show you some examples.

Double Buffering

Although our DyingButch example works reasonably well and at a pretty good clip (at least on our test machines here; your results may vary—no warrant of fitness is implied; tax, title, and license fees may vary from state to state; keep hands and feet away from moving blades), that is because it is stupidly simple. There aren't many images here; we are just throwing them up one at a time and keeping them in pretty much the same place on the screen.

As you start to get into more advanced animations, and particularly situations where you are throwing up a number of different animation sequences on the screen at once (can anyone say sprites? I knew you could), things are going to get much uglier for your little animations and the speed at which they execute.

However, there are a few things you can do about this, and one of the most important is double buffering. *Double buffering* is a fairly simple technique. The whole idea is that you set up an off screen image buffer where you throw up your next screen view and then import it to the machine when you are going to show it instead of painting each element on the screen individually. This allows the box to take care of figuring out all of its rendering stuff in the background and show you the finished product only. Remember when we talked about how ImageObserver's imageUpdate method would repaint stuff to the screen as more data comes in? That ends up making for annoying flicker and other such problems—problems that double buffering pretty much eliminates. Although double buffering isn't a be-all and end-all for speedy graphics, it is extremely handy.

Implementing double buffering is just about as easy as talking about it. All you need to do is add an offscreen graphics object and an offscreen image object to your code, then you do all of your graphics work there and paint it in a lump sum.

These two lines set up your references to your offscreen surface. Then you instantiate them so that they are going to be usable:

```
Image oImage = createImage(this.size().width,
     this.size().height);
Graphics oGraphics = oImage.getGraphics();
```

Now what we have done here is create an Image the size of our applet that is offscreen and then a graphics context that links to that graphics. We can now use this context just the same way we would a call to the screen:

```
public void paint(Graphics g) {
    oGraphics.drawString("Using double buffering.", 150,
              120);
    g.drawImage(oImage, 0, 0, this);
```

Note that we used the drawImage method from our screen graphics context, g, and then drew our offscreen image to it, placing the origin point at 0,0. We have set this image to be the size of the applet; therefore, it will paint over the entire screen when it is put up as an image.

Clipping

There are situations where double buffering isn't going to be your best friend. If most of your animation pain is coming from redrawing the screen with straight graphics primitives (drawRect and suchlike) then you might not get that much of a speed boost out of double buffering. And double buffering is an unrepentant memory hog. Probably the best deal for your processor ticks is using clipping, a bit more complicated to implement, but generally a good way to speed things up. First of all, we need to understand something that you have probably picked up by now, but if not, you need to understand to keep going. A Graphics object isn't anything unto itself but a pipe with some cool methods hooked to it. When you are drawing to a Graphics object, you aren't drawing to a Graphics object at all, but to an image surface underneath it. This is why double buffering works the way it does. When you create a new Image and then hook a Graphics object to it, you can then draw on the new image surface created. The default image surface you are drawing to in paint with the free Graphics object you get there is the screen.

Up until now, you really haven't had much call to figure out or work with this. However, when you use clipping it is kind of important that you get this because you are going to need to open up two different Graphics objects to the same drawing surface. This isn't that big a trick, because the Graphics class gives you a simple method called *create* to do it.

To create a new Graphics object that is a copy of a given Graphics object, use the following line:

```
Graphics clippedGuy = g.create();
```

This will make a new Graphics object, clippedGuy, that is a copy of the original graphics context, g.

Now why did we need to learn to open up two identical windows to the same drawing surface? Because we are about to clip one. *Clipping* is declaring only one area to the screen to get painted. When you are clipping you give it a rectangle on the screen, and from then on all graphics operations are limited to that rectangle of the screen. Obviously, this makes things much quicker in drawing since only the tiny little bit of the screen you are working with actually needs to get updated.

The drawback here, and why you have to create another Graphics object to make this really work right, is that when you start clipping, you can't stop. Clipping is a one-way street: When you have clipped a graphics context, it stays clipped from then on. So instead of using your main graphics object for clipping—which means you lose control of the rest of your screen from then on without jumping through some annoying hoops—you create another graphics context that matches your original one, and then clip that one down and use it.

The *clipRect* is the method to use for clipping and it works as follows:

```
clipRect(int x, int y, width, height);
```

where x, y, width, and height define the area you want to clip.

Once you are done with a clipped graphics context you probably want to get rid of it. You can do that by calling the *dispose method* of that context, with no arguments. That will throw away the graphics context.

A Brief Bit about Update . . .

And finally on the graphics front, we come to update. When your applet calls repaint it doesn't just jump to paint. Instead it calls an inherited method called update first. *Update* clears the screen for you by filling the whole graphics context with the background color set for your applet. It does this to clear the screen. When you are drawing a number of different objects, a little apart from each other let's say, this update method keeps everything you have already painted from staying on the screen during your later drawing operations.

Now this is a good and laudable goal; however, it can help lead to slow graphics performance and flickering. To help prevent this, you can override the update method in your own applets by writing your own update method. One way you can override update is to clip the area being redrawn. If you are just changing one element on the screen and the rest of it is staying the same, then it is an easy matter to use the clipping methods outlined above and only clear the sections of the screen you are going to be using.

• • • • • •
Sound

Sound is pretty open and shut with Java. First, at the moment you can use only Sun au files. If you don't happen to be on a Sun box, there are various pieces of software you can use to convert your native sound formats to the Sun au. For Wintel boxes, the excellent CoolEdit95 sound editing package available all over the Net is highly recommended.

The quickest way to get sound into your program is to use the *play method* of your Applet. The play method takes one or two arguments just as for the getImage method. You can feed it either an absolute URL or a relative URL and a file name string.

Either of the following methods would work to get and play the sound SoundOne.au.

```
play(getCodeBase(), "SoundOne.au");
play(new URL("http://www.ianet.net/~withers/SoundOne.au"));
```

Although play is fine, it needs to be explicitly called each time for our sound in question; it won't stop before the end of the clip without using some brute-force method like killing the thread it is running in; and it only loads when you call it, causing an annoying wait. To solve these problems (though not enough of them to make most sound programmers happy) we have the AudioClip object.

An *AudioClip object* is acquired by calling the getAudioClip method of an Applet object and, again, you can use either a relative or absolute URL calling method. AudioClip has three methods; loop, play, and stop.

`loop()`	This method will play your clip in a continuous loop.
`play()`	This method plays the clip and stops when done.
`stop()`	This method will stop a currently playing clip.

The following code snippet will demonstrate getting and using a couple of sounds.

```
AudioClip cardFlip = getAudioClip(getCodeBase(),
                "cardflip.au");
AudioClip cardShuffle = getAudioClip(getCodeBase(),
                "cardshuffle.au");
//the next line plays the cardFlip sound.
cardFlip.play();
//the next line loops the shuffle sound till you stop it.
cardShuffle.loop();
//and now we stop it.
cardShuffle.stop();
```

And, sad as it may seem, that is about it for sound in Java. There are rumblings that in future implementations of the JDK we are going to see more advanced sound features, but don't hold your breath till you see them.

• • • • • •
Events

Java notifies your program of things happening in the system environment though *events.* Most events we don't really care all that much about, as Java will handle them for us (e.g., a window being resized); but there are a couple of events that we really need to have an understanding of, and those are key strokes and mouse events. These are going to form our control features.

Dealing with common events is a piece of cake. There are default event handlers built into the AWT component classes (your applet is a subset of these, remember) that get called when an event occurs. All you need to do is override these methods in your applet.

For many applets, the most important events are going to be those that deal with mouse action. There are only a few methods here we need to deal with. Each of them is going to take three parameters; an event object, the one that Java generated to tell us what was going on, and two integers that are our x and y values of the event source. All of these methods also return a boolean value. This is to tell various other components that we have dealt with this event. If you deal with an event, return a true value and if you don't deal with it return a false. When you are making complicated programs this ends up making your life a lot easier.

Here are the methods and what they do:

mouseDown: called when the mouse button is clicked.

mouseDrag: called when the pointer moves and button is down.

mouseUp: called when button goes back up.

mouseMove: called when pointer is moved.

mouseEnter: called when pointer enters applet's display area.

mouseExit: called when the pointer leaves the applet's display area.

Here would be an example mouse handler for a button click:

```
public boolean mouseDrag(Event et, int x, int y) {
     paintX = x;
     paintY = y;
     repaint();
     return true;
}
public void paint (Graphics g) {
     g.drawString("Mouse is at " + paintX + " ,"+paintY+".",
          50,50);
}
```

Now with the normal trimmings around it (stick it in Stubby) this will produce an output that shows the mouse coordinates when the mouse is dragged. When you aren't in drag mode, it won't be painting. Pretty simple stuff.

To hook keys you do pretty much the same thing, just with another set of events. The important one to keep your eye on here is the *keyDown method.* This method gets an event object and an integer representing the ASCII value of the key that got pressed.

Further, the Event class has some predefined variables to help us out with some of the extended keys. Here is a list:

Event.HOME: home

Event.END: end

Event.PGUP: page up

Event.PGDN: page down

Event.UP: up arrow

Event.DOWN: down arrow

Event.LEFT: left arrow

Event.RIGHT: right arrow

So if we wanted to create an event handler that took in a letter and moved it to a variable for display, or would check for end, we could use the following code snippet:

```
public boolean keyDown(Event et, int key) {
displayChar = (char)key;
if (key == Event.END) {
        . . .code to handle the end event. . .}
return true;
}
```

This would turn our incoming key value into a character and send it off to the displayChar for something to be done with it later, while we are also checking for the END key and doing something separate with that.

Finally, Java also recognizes three modifier keys, which can be pressed in conjunction with other keys in order to add more functionality to your keyboard: These keys are the shift, control, and meta keys. Three methods of the Event class will test for these keys being pressed: shiftDown( ), meta-Down( ), and controlDown( ). Each of these will return a true if that key is pressed while a keyDown event has been generated from the pressing of one of the regular keys.

Let's do a very quick example that demonstrates the use of keys to control our applet.

```
//MoveRect.java: a simple example of handling key events.
import java.awt.*;

public class MoveRect extends java.applet.Applet {
      int rectX=50;
      int rectY=50;

      public boolean keyDown(Event evt, int key) {
            int multi=1;

            if (evt.controlDown()) {
                multi = 3;
                }
            if (evt.shiftDown()) {
                multi = 10;
```

```
        }
    if (key == Event.UP) {
        rectY=rectY-(5*multi);
        }
    if (key == Event.DOWN) {
        rectY=rectY+(5*multi);
        }
    if (key == Event.LEFT) {
        rectX=rectX-(5*multi);
        }
    if (key == Event.RIGHT) {
        rectX=rectX+(5*multi);
        }
    if (rectX > this.size().width) {
        rectX = this.size().width;
        }
    if (rectY > this.size().height) {
        rectY = this.size().height;
        }
    if (rectY < 1) {
        rectY = 1;
        }
    if (rectX < 1) {
        rectX = 1;
        }
        repaint();
        return true;
    }
public void paint(Graphics g) {
    g.drawRect(rectX, rectY, 50 ,50);
    }
```

Now this example looks relatively long but is actually quite simple. All we are doing here is defining two variables, *rectX* and *rectY* which are going to be used for the origin points for a 50,50 rectangle. Then we catch keyDown events and check to see if they are any of the arrow keys. If they are, then we increment or deincrement the rectX and rectY values to the proper degree to move our rectangle around the screen.

By using the boolean check methods for controlDown and shiftDown, we add a multiplier to the basic movement values that make our rectangle move more rapidly when these keys are pressed in combination with our movement keys. Note that we aren't catching anything else. If spurious keys are pressed it just goes by the wayside.

There are quite a few different methods and variables you can play with in the Event class and it would behoove you to look them over carefully. If you need a control method, it is probably there.

• • • • • • • • • • • • • • • • • •
What We Have Learned

We have covered a huge amount of ground in this chapter. Let's do a quick recap of what we have learned.

Graphics

When dealing with graphics we are working through an instance of the Graphics class found in the awt package. We get a free Graphics object when we work with our applets and this Graphics object writes to an image-drawing surface that puts things on the screen.

When we wish to draw lines or shapes, we use the various methods of the graphics class that handle all the basic drawing jobs for us.

Color

When we want to create a color, we instantiate a Color object, which we then set to specific color. Colors are defined as combinations of red, green, and blue primaries in Java and we can use any mixture of these values we wish (within a 0–255 range) in order to create our colors. We may also use the preset color constants in the Color class to do our setting work for us.

By passing color objects to various other objects, we can set the colors either for individual drawing elements or for the entire applet.

Fonts

Fonts are also objects, this time of the Font class. When we wish to change a font in a graphics context (specific Graphics object) we pass an appropriate font. We can use present constants in the Font class in order to get our fonts to have effects such as italics or bold.

FontMetrics

In order to really work with Fonts however, we are often going to need to know many things about their display characteristics in order to line them up on the screen properly. This is accomplished by creating a FontMetrics object from a specific Font object. The methods of FontMetrics allow us to determine a stupid number of details of how a font is going to display so that we can make sure our font is lined up with other elements in our display.

Images

We can load images into Java easily by creating an Image object and loading in a file from a specific URL. Our images can then be displayed on the screen with a simple call of a Graphics method in our paint routine. However, to handle loading of Images we probably want to instantiate a Media-Tracker object, which can help us make sure that our images are loaded from our source before we start messing with them.

Double Buffering

In order to more rapidly draw our various graphic objects, we might want to double buffer them. In most cases, this process will make our graphics work more quickly. In order to do this, we instantiate a new Image object that has the same size as our applet's display region. Then we link a new Graphic object to this Image and use it for our drawing surface. When we want to display this image, we simply use the default Graphic object in the paint method to show our new image.

Clipping

In order to speed up our graphics operations, we can also use clipping, which allows us to limit our working surface to only a predetermined rectangle out of a whole graphics object. The only thing we need to remember about clipping is that in most cases we are going to want to instantiate a new Graphics object to our drawing image in order to use it, because once a Graphics context is clipped it can't go back to a larger size.

Update

The update method, by default, blanks the whole screen in preparation for the next draw of a paint method. We can override this behavior, depending on our application, in order to help speed up our drawing process.

Sound

Sound support in Java is a pretty limited beast. It uses only Sun's sound format, au, for audio work.

You can start a sound directly from an applet with the play method. However, for slightly more robust sound capabilities, you can load your sound files into AudioClip objects which will allow you to play them, loop them, or stop them. The AudioClip objects also have the advantage of loading your sounds asynchronously; therefore, if you load your AudioClips well before you are going to use them, then you don't need to worry about a delay before playing while they are loaded.

Events

Java uses events in order to communicate system events to your program on an ongoing basis. In order to use these events, all you have to do is override the default event handlers in your applet and Java will call your overridden event handlers when something happens.

Java has a pretty robust set of event handlers to hook keyboard and mouse input and by using these handlers you shouldn't have any problems establishing control of your games.

Moving On

We gave pretty short shrift to double buffering and some of the other more advanced graphics techniques in this chapter as far as presenting examples. The reason is that the next chapter is going to be pretty much one example after the other of how to implement full-blooded games in Java.

If you have been wondering when we were going to get to showing you the actual games, well, wait no longer. In the next chapter we are going to go blow by blow though the implementation of not just one but a number of full games in order to show you exactly how to start working with all the things you have learned up to this point.

CHAPTER 7
• • • • • • •
IMPLEMENTING DESIGNS

We have just completed a huge chunk of basic foundation work, and if you learn the way I learn, you have been playing around with all of the things we actually set down in the book to date and have learned a few incidental things besides. Between all of the Java foundation and game-design theory, we have been pretty long on concept and short on applications up to this point. Well, here is where we make up for it with a vengeance: This chapter is totally devoted to applying what we have learned and implementing some games.

To this end we will be designing and implementing a small-scale game to show in detail the thinking process used to create and program a game in Java.

We have quite a bit on our plate for this chapter, so let's dive in.

The Evolution of Poison Pair Hand Solitaire

When I first started writing this book, I knew that I was going to want to implement at least two games for demonstration purposes, some type of card game and either a war or computer role-playing game (CRPG). I also knew that the card game would be the first game implemented. So before the actual writing process started there was already some noodle work going on for a card game.

Naturally, the first question is: Why limit ourselves to card-based games, CRPGs, or war games for our considerations at all? Why not just run wild and do a first-person shooter or something really ambitious? Well, if you were paying attention to all that droning about game-design theory back in Chapter 2, the reason should pretty much jump out at you: the toolset.

The topic of this book is game design in Java. And while we will be looking at some instances where it might be better to implement a Java game as a stand-alone application, the vast majority of the people picking up this book are going to be thinking of Java only in terms of Web development features. If this book doesn't deliver information mostly oriented to applets, there are going to be some readers who will feel ripped off by a cheap technicality.

So we are trying to limit our toolset not only to Java, which in current incarnations has some inherent speed limitations, but to Web-delivered Java, which has some huge speed and security restrictions. We will deal with the security restrictions at a much later point, but the speed thing is going to be on top of us right from the get-go. Running Java in a Web browser is only slightly faster than drawing your screens one at a time by hand and FedExing them to your recipient.

Therefore, we need to look at genres where speed isn't going to cripple us too badly, and that means turn-based games. That isn't to say that people don't try to implement simple action games in Java. As a matter of fact, the Gamelet Toolkit we will be dealing with in a later chapter is heavily balanced in that direction, but Web-delivered Java is just not all that well suited at this time for games requiring speed. Turn-based games aren't all that much damaged by speed restrictions. The fact that the game stops after every turn to wait on more user input gives you plenty of time to fool around with.

Now just because you are doing a turn-based game doesn't mean that it has to be cheesy. Nethack is basically a turn-based game, as is Panzer General and its descendants. You can do a lot of perfectly cool stuff in a turn-based game, and with careful planning and good execution turn-based games can be just as compelling to a large segment of the gaming market as a shooter.

So we have decided to limit our field to turn-based implementations for our first example game and we want it to be a pretty simple effort so that we can demonstrate the fundamentals of implementing a game in Java without getting overly complicated. However, even a fairly simple demo is worth doing right, so we want a game that is going to actually provide some play-ability and demonstrate good game-design principles.

This screams for cards. A few different considerations narrow things down from all turn-based games to cards. A couple are game-design issues and a couple are book issues. First, we are looking for a fairly modest game type that one programmer can reasonably expect to do a decent job at. Card games are limited enough in scope that one person can program a halfway interesting card game with a bit of thought. Then there is the matter of all of the card games out there that make Java look bad because not enough thought has gone into the execution. Let's face it, half of the world has done a card game, the majority of which are clearly inferior products. If we can make a compelling card game, we can prove that any genre can be done decently if you use good game-design technique. Finally, card games are a natural for exploiting some of the reusable code features of an OOP approach.

Now that we have cards, we want to go a bit deeper. What kind of card game? Card games encompass everything from War on one end of the scale to Contract Bridge on the other. Well, even within the realm of card games we want to keep it simple. A really good poker or bridge game is going to require lots of multiplayer trash we don't want to get into with a simple example, or it is going to require pretty sophisticated AI. That leaves us looking at Black Jack or Solitaire. Black Jack has been done to death. Who honestly can generate enthusiasm for another Black Jack game, no matter how well executed? So that leaves us looking at Solitaire.

Now the same argument about being done to death can be made about Solitaire, but solitaire is an entire class of games and not just one particular configuration of rules that happens to be popular right now. Any game meant to be played with a deck of cards solo is a solitaire game. With enough spin and good design, there is still room for yet another Solitaire. And, once again, if we can make a compelling version of solitaire, after all the bad or cookie-cutter versions that have come before us, we know that we are practicing some good game-design principles.

So even at the earliest stages of the design, we have gone through quite a bit of thinking to get down to the general class of game we want to make.

Just to get to this point we have taken into consideration our toolset, how the users are going to be using the game (Web-delivered), and our overall purpose in creating the game (doing a decent, simple game that is good for a demonstration of basic Java and game-design principles).

However, we still have a huge amount of ground to cover. Saying we are going to make a solitaire game is like saying we are going to build a house out of all of the possible buildings in the world someone could build. There are still the little matters of what kind of house and what it is going to look like. This is the bit that requires some judicious decisions as well as some inspiration.

Well, more common solitaire configurations are right out there. Klondike and the like have been done about a billion times and while many of them are inferior, some of them are really good. Why do a cheap clone of something that has already been done right when you can do something new? What kind of things can you do with a deck of cards that are interesting but you can put a new spin on?

One of the great ways to get ideas is through synthesis. Instead of just trying to rip some great idea out of the ether, take two things that don't normally intersect and see how you could put them together to make an interesting new something. What about concentration-type games and poker machines?

Concentration games lay down the cards in a five-by-five or ten-by-five pattern and then you flip a couple of cards at random to see if they match. Flip them back over and then flip two more. Repeat until you have matched out all cards. The trick is in memory. Poker machines on the other hand are solitaire games in the guise of slot machines, but they are supersimple solitaire games, basically relying in some way on the making of a poker hand to get paid.

Now if you are going to crunch these two things together you have two ways to go about it. The first is to somehow add a memory factor to a poker hand–based game. That seems like a pretty complicated way to go (though at some point or another it would be an interesting game to tinker with). But what if you took the grid layout from a concentration-type game and rolled in trying to make poker hands?

Now this has some promise. If you are dealing with poker hands, a five-by-five grid naturally presents itself. And if you have a five-by-five grid, you have a potential for 12 total hands, all the hands by the columns, all the hands by the rows, and the two hands from the diagonals.

So how do you make a challenge of it? Just throwing hands up wouldn't work. You could do a draw poker–like thing, where you got a grid filled with cards and could discard so many. But that doesn't seem to have all that good a hook. The way that seems like the best way to make a game with some teeth is to give players a deck of cards and let them lay down one card at a time in the grid. Then they are scored based on how many good poker hands they can make out of the potential 12 hands. A lot of luck here, but still a real feeling of skill and working a pattern to try to win. Now with a game even slightly more complicated than this, we would want to do a whole lot more design work before we even considered doing any coding, but with something this quick to make (and simple to change), we might as well make an alpha before we go any further and then see what obvious design improvements the alpha presents us with.

Please note that this isn't particularly good design practice for any game with any complexity at all. The reason we are doing it with this game lies totally with the simplicity of the design and the short period of time required to code it. In a more complicated game, you want to think every detail out at least somewhat before you go to alpha. The reason is that with more complicated structures, it can be a real pain to make major engine overhauls on the fly. In the beta stage of a game you are always going to have to do a good bit of tuning work to your design, but it is discouraging to have to change the basic foundations of your engine because you didn't put in enough brain work at the onset. And then the fatal *good enough* starts creeping into your thinking, as in "Well, recoding the entire object structure in the game would take weeks. This is probably good enough. Who is going to notice such a small problem anyway?"

Simple rule: Good enough never is. A game will never be perfect, but it always must work the way it should. It doesn't matter how brilliant or original your design, the game doesn't cut it if it doesn't work right and fully implement its scope. In the time I have been working in the industry, there has been only one game (and I am not going to go into which one it was) that was so brilliantly conceived to make me overlook flaws in the engine and still think of it as a great game. For that one game there are dozens of others that would have been really great games if it weren't for minor loopholes or flaws that blemished them. The designers obviously settled for good enough and seriously damaged all their hard work on the rest of the game by being lazy or careless in minor matters.

During your learning process about game design you are going to make mistakes. Even the best of the pros do so once in a while, but come by your mistakes honestly, not by going into good enough mode. Do the best you can with the tools and the skills at your disposal at any given time. If you see a mistake, fix it. And learn to look honestly for mistakes. If the effort to get the game right starts to get you down, then lower your scope instead of turning out a more ambitious but flawed effort.

Initial Coding Considerations

The first thing we are going to want to do in making a card game is figure out how we are going to structure our objects. Things in a small card game can be fairly simple or fairly complex depending on how we approach the structure. We can make little objects for everything and go psychotic with our OOP approach, or we can try to throw back to procedural and roll everything we can into a single huge class and pray it works.

Well, for something of this scope, we are probably better off taking the middle ground. Break the biggest elements into separate objects of reasonably good size.

What immediately presents itself is a cards class that takes care of all the things that are going to be common to using a deck of cards. Using a cards class and developing it first makes a lot of sense from many different points of view. But the main consideration here is *reusability of code.* If we make a really good cards object, then we can use it in a whole series of card games. If this particular game doesn't work out the way we have planned, we will still have a good code basis already written to work on another card game.

Here is the cards class we came up with:

```
//////////////////////////////////////////////////////////////
// Cards.java playing card class with sound enhancement
// Copyright (C) 1996 John Withers and Robert J. Osborne
//////////////////////////////////////////////////////////////


// Reference the packages required in any of the objects listed in this
file
import java.awt.*;
import java.util.Vector;  ✕ 我不用
import java.applet.Applet;
import java.applet.AudioClip;
```

```
/** ACard is a primitive class holding the basic information for each
of the card objects. The Cards object place these is a vector. */
class ACard {

    // xwid and ywid are the size of any cardface or
    // cardback in the deck
    public static int xwid=50;   ✓
    public static int ywid=70;   ✓


    /**
    How the Card IDs are arranged:
    (Group 0) The first 13 (0-12) are Clubs,
    A,2,3,4,5,6,7,8,9,10,J,Q,K.
    (Group 1) The second 13(13-25) are Spades, A..K.
    (Group 2) The third 13 (26-38) are Diamonds, A..K.
    (Group 3) The fourth 13 (39-51) are Hearts, A..K.
    Card 37 would be the 11th card of the third group of 13. (37 /
13=2)
    It is the (11th card, Queen) of Diamonds. */

    int id;

    // These are the x and y positions of each of the card
//objects
    int xcards=0;
    int ycards=0;

    // Describe how to show the card:
    // 0= invisible (but clickable!)
    // 1= show cardback
    // 2= show card face-up
    int showcard=0;

    // This is the card's face image
    Image cardface;

    // ACard constructor -- assigns an ID to a card
    ACard(int i) {
        id = i;
    }

    // Return the identification of a card
    int getID() {
        return id;
    }
}

public class Cards {
```

inner class? for what

```
/**
    This class handles a virtual deck of cards. Cards are numbered
0..51.
*/
    // Number of cards in a standard deck
    static final int MAXCARDS = 52;
    // This holds the ACard objects
    Vector deck = new Vector();
    // Order in which cards are painted.
    Vector cardstack = new Vector();
    // Count into the deck to find the next available card
    int deckcount = 0;
    // Only need one cardback since it is the same
    Image cardback;


    // Sounds played during the manipulation of Cards.
    AudioClip cardflip;
    AudioClip shufflesnd;


    boolean soundOn= true; //We default to playing sound


    /** Constructor for a Cards object */
    Cards(Applet ob) {

        MediaTracker tracker = new MediaTracker(ob);

        ob.showStatus("Loading card images. Please wait.");

        Image img;
        // Load the ACard objects into the deck vector.
        for(int i=0; i<MAXCARDS; i++) {
            ACard C = new ACard(i);
            deck.addElement(C);
        }

        // Load the cardback graphic
        img = ob.getImage(ob.getCodeBase(),"images/0.gif");

        // Add image tracking
        tracker.addImage(img,0);
        try {
            tracker.waitForID(0);
        } catch  (InterruptedException e) {}

        // Load the card faces
        for(int i=0; i<MAXCARDS; i++) {
            ACard temp;
            temp=getCard(i);
```

For background?

This is why?

```
            temp.cardface=ob.getImage(ob.getCodeBase(),
                "images/"+(i+1)+".gif");

            try {
                tracker.addImage(temp.cardface, i+1);
                tracker.waitForID(i+1);
            } catch (InterruptedException e) {}

            setCard(temp);
        }

        // Load the audio clips
        cardflip = ob.getAudioClip(ob.getCodeBase(),
          "images/cardflip.au");
        shufflesnd = ob.getAudioClip(ob.getCodeBase(),
            "images/shuffle.au");
    }

    public void cardSound(boolean snd) {
        soundOn = snd;
    }


    public void cardSoundToggle() {
        soundOn = !soundOn;
    }


    /** Change the Image used to portray a face-down card */
    public void changeCardback(Image img) {
        cardback = img;
    }


    /** Return the graphic image placed as a cardback.      Could
be usedto draw a pile representing a deck of           cards, for example.
*/
    public Image getCardback() {
        return cardback;
    }


    /** Retreive an ACard element of the V vector by its         ID*/
    public ACard getCard(int ID) {

        for (int i=0; i<deck.size(); i++) {
            ACard temp = (ACard) deck.elementAt(i);
            if (temp.getID() == ID)
                return temp;
        }
        return null;
    }
```

```
/** place ACard object over the equivalent one in the deck vector.
*/
    public void setCard(ACard updated) {
        // Find out which card we have.
        int id = updated.getID();

        // Find the card in the deck and update it.
        for(int i=0; i<deck.size(); i++) {
            ACard temp = (ACard) deck.elementAt(i);
            if (temp.getID() == id) {
                deck.setElementAt(updated,i);
            }
        }
    }

    /** Given an (x,y) coordinate, find which card is top-???most at
that position. Returns -1 if no card is at that position. */
    public int locateCard(int x, int y) {
        Integer c;

        if (cardstack.size()==0)
            return -1;
        // Begin at most recent entry and move deeper into
    // the pile
        for(int i=cardstack.size(); i>0; i--) {
            c= (Integer) cardstack.elementAt(i-1);
            ACard t = getCard(c.intValue());
            // Does this ACard object exist at (x,y) on the
        // screen?
            if (((x - t.xcards) < t.xwid) &&
                (x - t.xcards > -1) &&
                ((y - t.ycards) < t.ywid) &&
                (y - t.ycards > -1)) {
                // ... if so, return its ID.
                return t.getID();
            }
        }

        return -1; // If no card was found, return -1.
    }

    /** This internal method removes a card from the
    cardstack and shrinks the array to fill in the hole left behind.
*/
    private void killfromstack(int i) {
        if(i>=cardstack.size()) return; // Bulletproofing
        cardstack.removeElementAt(i);
    }
    /** Removes a card from the table
    */
```

```
    public void takeCard(int ci) {
        // Is the card on the table?
        boolean foundcard = false;

        for(int i=0; i<cardstack.size(); i++) {
            Integer cs = (Integer) cardstack.elementAt(i);
            if (cs.intValue()==ci)  {
                foundcard = true;
                // Remove the card from the paint cardstack
                killfromstack(i);
            }
        }
        // If the card was found on the table, clear the
// object.
        if (foundcard) {
            ACard t = getCard(ci);
            t.xcards=0;
            t.ycards=0;
            t.showcard=0;
            setCard(t);
        }
    }


/** Place card c at (x,y).
    If f=0, the card is invisible.
    If f=1, the card is face-down.
    If f=2, the card is face-up.   */
```

hand annotation: card id   *hand annotation: show status*

```
public void placeCard(int c, int x, int y, int f) {
        if (c<0 || c >MAXCARDS) return; // Bulletproofing

        // Is the card already in the cardstack?
        for(int i=0; i<cardstack.size(); i++) {
            Integer co = (Integer) cardstack.elementAt(i);
            // If it is, remove it.
            if (c==co.intValue())  {
                killfromstack(i);
            }
        }
        // Update the ACard's parameters
        ACard t = getCard(c);
        t.xcards=x;
        t.ycards=y;
        // Place the card in the cardstack
        cardstack.addElement(new Integer(c));

        if (f>-1 && f<3)  {    // Make sure f is in range
            t.showcard=f;
        }
        else t.showcard=1; // If not, default to face-down.
```

```
        setCard(t);
        // Play the sound of a card being flipped.
        if (soundOn) cardflip.play();
    }


    /** Draw the next card from the deck. If we're out, return
-1 */
    public int nextCard() {
        if (deckcount==MAXCARDS)
          return -1; // Are we out of cards?
        ACard t = (ACard) deck.elementAt(deckcount);
        int c = t.getID();
        deckcount++;
        return c;
    }


    /** Paint all cards where they belong on the screen.*/
    public void paintCards(Graphics g, Applet ob) {
        for(int i=0; i<cardstack.size(); i++) {

            Integer tempi = (Integer)
                        cardstack.elementAt(i);

            ACard c = getCard(tempi.intValue());

            if (c.showcard ==1) // Paint face-down
              g.drawImage(cardback, c.xcards, c.ycards, ob);
            if (c.showcard ==2) // Paint face-up
              g.drawImage(c.cardface, c.xcards, c.ycards,
                  ob);
        }
    }


    /** Shuffle the deck. WARNING -- This collects all
cards and assumes it has no cards already drawn from it! */
    public void shuffle() {
        double R;
        ACard H;

        if (soundOn) shufflesnd.play();
        // No cards on the table
        cardstack.removeAllElements();
        deckcount=0; // No cards taken from the deck yet

        for(int i=0; i<24; i++) { // Shuffle 24 times
            // Replace each card with some other from a
    // random place
            for(int j=0; j<MAXCARDS; j++) {
                R=(Math.random())*MAXCARDS;
                H=(ACard) deck.elementAt((int)R);
```

```
                    deck.setElementAt(deck.elementAt(j),(int)R);
                    deck.setElementAt(H,j);
            }
        }
    }
}
```

This looks complex (and is quite a bit more complex than the simple, do nothing, examples we have been seeing up to this point), but it actually isn't all that hard to see what is going on if you take it one piece at a time.

First, what we are doing here is representing a card deck and the operations you might need to perform on one in order to make a game. This isn't meant to work on its own, but instead be a generic part of an applet that implements a card game.

In order to do this, we are going to need a few things. The first is a *card*. We define a card in the Acard class, which is nothing but a few place holders that will allow us to deal with a card. First we have the width and height of our card which we are going to need to know in order to paint it on the screen. These are our *xwid* and *ywid* values. We are also going to need to be able to know what specific card out of the 52 standard cards our Acard object represents—this is the *id variable*. Then we must know the screen position for the origin of our cards, represented by the *xcards* and *ycards* values. Also we are going to need to know the status of the card, if it is face up, face down, or invisible (we aren't going to be using invisible in our demonstration, but thought it might be handy for some games). This is represented in the *showcard variable*. Finally, we are going to need to know what graphics file to use to show our card face. This is the *Image cardface*.

That is all there is to a specific card. The actual fleshing out of cards happens in our Cards class. First we define the size of a deck in the MAXCARDS constant. Then we create a vector that is going to allow us to work with our deck and another vector called cardstack.

The key to making this code easy to comprehend is in the relationship between the deck and cardstack vectors, so we should spend a moment dwelling on it. The *deck* represents all the cards. It doesn't matter where these cards are at, still in the stack being dealt from, in hands, on the table, discarded—they are still a part of the deck. The cardstack vector exists only in order to show the order in which the cards are painted. In this way, if you lay a card over top of a card that is already on the table, then the later card will paint. But if you move another card over top of a later card, the program needs to know that even though one card was laid on the table later, its painting is superseded by the card on top of it.

One more time, the *cardstack* is just which Acard objects from the deck are going to be painted on the table the next time the paint routine is invoked and what order they are being painted in. If this is firmly understood, the rest of the class falls to easy examination.

The constructor for the Cards object takes one argument, the applet that is calling the Cards object. This is so that the applet and Cards can easily pass data and painting back and forth. The first thing the Cards object does is load all the Acards into the deck in order. Think of this as opening the pack of cards and fanning them out. At this point the deck is in order.

Next we load the cardback graphic and wait to make sure we get it using a MediaTracker called tracker. Then we do the same for all the card faces and the audio clips. Note we are using methods defined in the Applet class to do our loads by calling on the methods of the ob object where we have stored a reference to our calling applet.

Next we set our sound options on and create a method after that allowing us to toggle the sound should we wish to. What you are seeing here, by the way, is actually the second generation of the card object. Originally, as I have alluded to much earlier in the book, we had no sound, but for reasons that will become quite obvious later on, we added it in.

After taking care of the sound there is a method that will allow you to change the cardback: a pretty simple one-line addition that can allow more options to the game. This, along with some other method calls here, we didn't actually use in our final game, but this Cards class isn't just for this one game—it is a good foundation that will allow the creation of a number of different card games.

The next major method is *getCard*. This method allows us to return a specific Acard object in order to examine it. Let's say we wished to find out if the King of Clubs was in the deck or had been removed. We could use get-Card(13) to return the King of Clubs if it was in the deck.

The setCard method might be a bit more obtuse. *setCard* allows us to find a particular Acard id in the deck and replace it with another Acard of the same id. While at first glance this might appear to be somewhat self-defeating, it actually is pretty handy, since this allows you to change an Acard with one set of x and y coordinates for another Acard with different ones, allowing you to change the position where the card is painted. *locate-*

Card is pretty self-evident. It moves through the cardstack from the end looking for Acards with a specific set of x and y coordinates. Since the Acards to be painted are put on the cardstack in a last-in, first-painted order, the first card found matching the coordinates when running through the stack backwards is going to be the last card laid at that position.

killfromstack and *takeCard* both remove cards from the cardstack, but killfromstack takes a position in the cardstack as an argument and takeCard searches through the cardstack for a specific card id to do it. This is the equivalent of saying "Burn the first card in the stack" or saying, "Find the Jack of Clubs and pull it out."

placeCard puts a specific card from the deck in the cardstack and sets its coordinates for painting to a passed x and y value. This is how you get a card to get painted.

nextCard, pretty self-evidently, pulls the next card off the top of the deck and returns the card id. When you want to pull the next card and place it on the table, you would use a combination of nextCard and placeCard.

paintCard is pretty open and shut, simply going through the cardstack and then drawing the appropriate cards in their proper position on the screen.

shuffle uses a straightforward random-number generation routine to mix up all the cards. Now Cards.java might not be the most elegant piece of code ever written, but it does get the job done in forming a basis from which we can create a number of card games.

Next we are going to need to create our alpha of the game that uses this class. For right now, we will call this game Hand Solitaire for lack of anything else to call it.

```
//////////////////////////////////////////////////////////
////   Hand Poker java applet
//////////////////////////////////////////////////////////

// Reference the packages required in any of the objects listed in this
file
import java.awt.*;
import java.applet.Applet;

public class Poker extends java.applet.Applet {

    Cards CA;
    Image ibuffer; // This holds the double-buffering.
    int[] gameboard = new int[25]; //The table of cards
    int[] wins = new int[10]; //Count of each type of win.
```

just an array?

```
    // Make the size of the cards easy to access
    final int xwid = ACard.xwid;
    final int ywid = ACard.ywid;

    // Offset from the top left hand corner of the applet to //
start the card layout
    final int xoff = 25;
    final int yoff = 25;

    // Spacing between cards on the screen for x any y //
directions
    final int xsp = 10;
    final int ysp = 10;

    int drawncard = -1; // Card last drawn from the deck

    // Prepare to display the scores in times roman bold.
    Font trb = new Font("TimesRoman",Font.BOLD,18);
    Font gof = new Font("TimesRoman",Font.BOLD,65);

public void init() {
      CA = new Cards(this);
      setBackground(Color.black);
}

// Things to do each time before we play.
public void start() {
      for(int i=0; i<25; i++) {
          gameboard[i]=-1;            // 每个 block has nothing
      }

      for(int i=0; i<10; i++) {
          wins[i]=0;
      }
      CA.shuffle();
      drawncard=CA.nextCard(); // Put out the first card
      showhole();
}

public void showhole() {
    CA.placeCard(drawncard,350,375,2);
}           P231

private int xeq( int i) {
  return ((i%5)*(xwid+xsp)) + xoff;
}

private int yeq( int i) {
  return ((i/5) * (ywid+ysp)) + yoff;
}
```

```
public void paint(Graphics g) {
    // Draw the boxes where the cards can be placed
    g.setColor(Color.white);

    for(int i=0; i<25; i++) {
        if(gameboard[i]==-1) {  // If a card isn't placed,
            // Draw a white rectangle
            g.drawRect(xeq(i),yeq(i),xwid,ywid);
        }
    }


    // Prepare to draw the scores in times roman bold.
    g.setFont(trb);
    g.setColor(Color.yellow);
    // Scoring
    g.drawString("Royal Flush "+wins[9],350,100);
    g.drawString("Straight Flush "+wins[8],350,125);
    g.drawString("Four of a Kind "+wins[7],350,150);
    g.drawString("Full House "+wins[6],350,175);
    g.drawString("Flush "+wins[5],350,200);
    g.drawString("Straight "+wins[4],350,225);
    g.drawString("Three of a Kind "+wins[3],350,250);
    g.drawString("Two Pairs "+wins[2],350,275);
    g.drawString("One Pair "+wins[1],350,300);

    // Draw the cards on the screen
    CA.paintCards(g,this);
}

// Find out which position on the table the user is
//clicking on. If it returns -1, they were not in a box on //the
table.
public int locatebox(int x, int y) {
    int b=-1;  //he ID of the box we're clicking on.

    for(int i=0; i<25; i++) {
        if ((((x - xeq(i)) < xwid) && (x - xeq(i)>-1) &&
        ((y - yeq(i)) < ywid) && (y - yeq(i)>-1)) {
        b=i;
        }
    }
    return b;
}


// How good is this hand? 9=Royal Flush.. 0=nothing, -1 //=
unfinished.
public int ratehand(int[] c) {

    // Is the row/column/diagonal finished?
    for(int i=0; i<5; i++) {
```

```
        if (c[i]<0) return -1;
}


// Are all cards of the same suit?
boolean samesuit = true;
int s=c[4]/13; // Integer divide by 13 checks suit 0..3
    // for last card
for (int i=0; i<4; i++) {
    // Are the first cards the same as the last card?
    if ((c[i]/13) != s) samesuit = false;
}


// Next, check to see what the distribution is.
int dis[] = new int[14]; // We will move Ace high so
                    // add an extra slot.
for(int i=0;i<5;i++) {
    dis[c[i]%13]++; // Modulo removes suit from card
            // identity
}


// Moving Ace high.
dis[13]=dis[0];


// Now count frequencies of cards.
int H1=0; // Highest card frequency
int H2=0; // Second highest card frequency
for(int i=1;i<14;i++) {
    if (dis[i] >= H2) {
        if (dis[i]>H1) {
            H2=H1;
            H1=dis[i];
        }
        else {
            H2=dis[i];
        }
    }
}


// Find out how many cards we have in sequential order
int seq=0; // This will hold our sequence count.
int sc=0; // This will hold a temporary count.
for(int i=0; i<14; i++) {
    if (dis[i]>0) {
        sc++;
    }
    else {
        if (sc>seq) {
            seq=sc;
        }
        sc=0;
```

```
      }
   }
   if (sc>seq) seq=sc;

   // For scoring, first check for a Royal Flush...
   if ((samesuit) && (seq==5) && (dis[13]==1) &&
(dis[9]==1)) {
      return 9;
   }


   // Check for a Straight Flush
   if ((samesuit) && (seq==5)) {
      return 8;
   }


   // Check for a Four of a Kind
   if (H1==4) {
      return 7;
   }


   // Check for a Full House
   if ((H1==3) && (H2==2)) {
      return 6;
   }


   // Check for a Flush
   if (samesuit) {
      return 5;
   }


   // Check for a Straight
   if (seq==5) {
      return 4;
   }


   // Check for a Three of a Kind
   if (H1==3) {
      return 3;
   }


   // Check for Two Pair
   if ((H1==2) && (H2==2)) {
      return 2;
   }


   // Check for One Pair
   if (H1==2) {
      return 1;
   }
```

```
   return 0;
}

public void checkforwin() {
  int a[] = new int[5]; // This is the parameter given to
                // ratehand();
  int r[] = new int[12];

  // There are 12 ways to win on the board

  // Check the 5 rows
  for(int i=0;i<25;i++) {
      a[i%5]=gameboard[i];
      if ((i%5)==4) {
          r[i/5]=ratehand(a);
      }
  }

  // Check the 5 columns
  for(int i=0;i<5;i++) {
    for(int j=0;j<5;j++) {
      a[j]=gameboard[i+(j*5)];
      if (j==4) {
          r[5+i]=ratehand(a);
      }
    }
  }

  // Check the 2 diagonals
  for(int i=0;i<5;i++) {
    a[i]=gameboard[i*6];
  }
  r[10]=ratehand(a);

  for(int i=0;i<5;i++) {
    a[i]=gameboard[(i*4)+4];
  }
  r[11]=ratehand(a);

  for(int i=0; i<10; i++) {
      wins[i]=0;
  }

  for(int i=0;i<12;i++) {
   if (r[i]>0)
   wins[r[i]]++;
  }
}
```

```
public boolean mouseDown(Event evt, int x, int y) {
    int box = locatebox(x,y);
    if (box>-1) {    // If we have clicked on a box...
    // If we don't have a card here, drop one.
        if (gameboard[box]<0) {
            CA.takeCard(drawncard);
            CA.placeCard(drawncard,xeq(box),yeq(box),2);
            gameboard[box]=drawncard;

            drawncard=CA.nextCard();
            showhole();
            repaint();
            checkforwin();
        }
    }

    return true;
}
```

Because of the foundation work we did in the Cards class, the actual game implementation is pretty simple. First we get a Cards object in CA and then initialize a number of class variables we are using, all of which are pretty self-explanatory from the comments. As a matter of fact, most of this code is pretty obvious. We create an array of 25 ints to serve as our gameboard. These ints will hold our card ids. Since we already have a card painting method in our Cards class, we don't need to worry about actually painting these cards, but just what card is in a given slot in order to score properly.

To understand Hand Poker reasonably well, you should probably look at the mouseDown event-handler at the very end of the code first. This is where most of the real work is being done. There is some dealing with boxes that might be a little obtuse at this point, but the boxes are just our playable areas on the screen. Now look at what we do: We simply use our Cards class to get a card, move a card, and then draw our cards on the screen. Then we check for a win.

Although the details of the painting and mechanics of the game are pretty obvious on simple inspection starting from the mouseDown event-handler, the one place it is possible to get lost is in the *checkforwin() method,* where we actually figure out who won what. Looking at checkforwin you will see that it goes through the five-by-five grid of the board and checks performs a check on each column and row of cards and then on the two diagonals. That is pretty easy to see, but how it checks is with the ratehand method. rate-hand can seem a bit more complicated.

ratehand takes the array of five ints representing the cards that checkfor-win passed it and first checks to see if the hand is the same suit. Next it puts the cards in an array by their values so it can easily check to see if they are in a row. Then it breaks down the two highest frequencies of cards occurring in the hand. Finally, it checks the number of cards in sequential order.

Now even though this might seem a bit onerous to produce all this data, it makes checking for the existence of various hands a cakewalk. Start look-ing through the hand checks and you will see that as long as we have gener-ated this basic information, it is a simple matter to find out if we have a winning hand.

Now at about this point it would be a good idea for you to fire up Hand Solitaire at home (see Figure 7.1). Start the game now and play with it for a

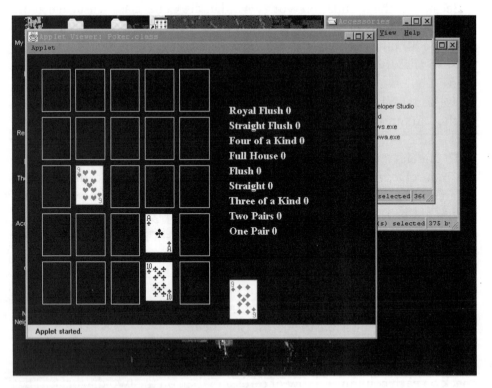

Figure 7.1   Hand Solitaire.

second, because without having an idea of the playing of the game, the next few pages aren't going to do much good.

Alpha Redesign

Since we have decided to forge ahead without the benefit of a firmly thought out design, we need to look at our alpha code of Hand Solitaire and see what we can do with it.

Well, the first thing we can see is that the play paradigm is going to work. This whole challenge of laying the cards down in a pattern to get a good score seems to be pretty clever. But this alpha obviously is going to need a lot of work before it is even in the ballpark of being a game we can work with.

First, there is a serious need for veracity. In the version you are playing there is sound. But in the original first attempt there wasn't, so that was the first thing we added. However, even with the sound, this game is way below par. But veracity is quick to gain in such a simple world. First, we need a green background. Next, we can add a deck as opposed to having a card just hanging out there in space. Between sound, a deck, and a green background this game is going to gain a world of good.

But there is more than just veracity to deal with in redesigning a game. We are going to need a good scoring system. Putting a little number after how many hands you get just doesn't cut it. No, we need real scoring. Real scoring with dollars is a pretty good idea. So we rate each hand with a dollar multiplier based on how difficult it is to get the hand—that would do the trick.

Although the scoring thing is pretty cool, we also need to make the game a bit more of a challenge. As it sits the game is only mildly challenging. Since there is no easy formula to make a game like this harder as it progresses, we are going to need to have it pretty hard from the get-go. So let's throw a loop in there: We will make single pairs score a negative amount of money. So you need to make killer hands, but single pairs will sink you. Ah, now that is a much more challenging game.

Further, we are going to need to make the game compelling over more than one play. As it is, we don't even have anything that tells someone when the game is over. You just have to figure it out from the slots being filled. So let's add first of all a "game over" sign. And then let the money you won stay around. So now you are playing to build up a pot. But each game costs you $50 dollars to buy into. Now it is pretty hard to get $50 bucks out of a board with the way we are going to weight the value of the hands and with the poison pairs, so this is going to be a very challenging game.

Now, I am not going to bore you with the actual code of the beta we came up with at this point, but it was challenging. The problem is that it was too challenging. So we made a number of revisions to the code based on the beta. First, we added an option for second card that you could decide to use if you didn't like the one you had face up. We like to call this the "wimpy option" because it makes the game easy to beat. Second, we changed the amount of money that you had to pay for each new game in order to give more difficulty options. We added a sound toggle and a secondary scoring system based on points for those who don't like the money-scoring system. Finally, we implemented double buffering at this stage to make the game paint clean on slow machines. So let's put our revised code here so you can see the changes we made.

```
///////////////////////////////////////////////////////////////
////   Poison Pair Poker java applet
////
////   The final version of the Poker class.
///////////////////////////////////////////////////////////////

// Reference the packages required in any of the objects
// listed in this file
import java.awt.*;
import java.applet.Applet;

public class Poker extends java.applet.Applet {

    Cards CA;
    Graphics gbuffer; // Used to draw to the ibuffer.
    Image ibuffer; // Image for double-buffer.
    Color felt; // Felt will be darker than Color.green.

    int[] gameboard = new int[25]; // Table of cards

    int[] wins = new int[10]; // Count of each type of win.
    int tmpwin = 0; // Temporary winnings
    int winnings = 100; // Start off with $100.00

    // Make the size of the cards easy to access
    final int xwid = ACard.xwid;
    final int ywid = ACard.ywid;
```

```
        // Offset from the top left hand corner of the applet to //
start the card layout
    final int xoff = 25;
    final int yoff = 25;
    // Spacing between cards on the screen for x any y
    final int xsp = 10;
    final int ysp = 10;

    int drawncard = -1; // Card last drawn from the deck
    int choicecard = -1; // Another face-down card if you
                // don't like the drawn card

    // Prepare to display the scores in times roman bold.
    Font trb = new Font("TimesRoman",Font.BOLD,18);
    Font gof = new Font("TimesRoman",Font.BOLD,65);

    Button restartbutton;
    Button optionbutton;

    Frame  DFrame;
    PDialog optd;

  public void init() {
        CA = new Cards(this);

        // Configure our button and dialog of choices for        //
the game

        DFrame = climbToFrame();
        optd = new PDialog(DFrame,this);
        optd.resize(250,210);

        restartbutton = new Button("New Game");
        optionbutton = new Button("Options");
        setLayout(new FlowLayout(FlowLayout.RIGHT));
        add(restartbutton);
        add(optionbutton);

        // Define a dark green color background
        felt = new Color(0,127,0);
        setBackground(felt);

    // Create a new image to place our screen graphics on
    ibuffer = this.createImage(600,450);
    gbuffer = ibuffer.getGraphics();
  }

// Things we must do each time before we play the game.
public void start() {
```

play ground.

```
        // Clear the game board
        for(int i=0; i<25; i++) {
            gameboard[i]=-1;
        }

        // Clear off how many hands we have won
        for(int i=0; i<10; i++) {
            wins[i]=0;
        }

        // Each game costs $50.00

        winnings += tmpwin;
        tmpwin=0;
        winnings -= optd.gamedifficulty();

        CA.shuffle();
        drawncard=CA.nextCard();   // Put out the first two
                                   // to choose from
        choicecard=CA.nextCard();
        showhole();
}

void showhole() {
  if (dropcount()<25) {
    CA.placeCard(drawncard,350,360,2);
    if (optd.getdealtype()) {
      CA.placeCard(choicecard,450,360,1);
    }
    else {
      choicecard=-1;
    }
  }
}

int dropcount() {
  int c = 0;
  for(int i=0; i<25; i++) {
      if (gameboard[i]>-1) c++;
  }
  return c;
}

int xeq( int i) {
  return ((i%5)*(xwid+xsp)) + xoff;
}

int yeq( int i) {
  return ((i/5) * (ywid+ysp)) + yoff;
}
```

```
void laytable(Graphics g) {

    // Place a few cards to represent a "deck"
    for(int i=0;i<3;i++) {
        g.drawImage(CA.getCardback(),475+(i*4),335-
            (i*4),this);
    }


    // Draw the boxes where the cards can be placed
    g.setColor(Color.white);

    for(int i=0; i<25; i++) {
        if(gameboard[i]==-1) { // If a card isn't placed,
            // Draw a white rectangle
            g.drawRoundRect(xeq(i),yeq(i),xwid,ywid,15,15);
        }
    }
}


void drawscore(Graphics g) {
    // Prepare to draw the scores in our font times roman
//bold.
    g.setFont(trb);
    g.setColor(Color.black);
  if (optd.getscoretype()) {
    // Counted scoring
    g.drawString("Royal Flush "+wins[9],350,100);
    g.drawString("Straight Flush "+wins[8],350,125);
    g.drawString("Four of a Kind "+wins[7],350,150);
    g.drawString("Full House "+wins[6],350,175);
    g.drawString("Flush "+wins[5],350,200);
    g.drawString("Straight "+wins[4],350,225);
    g.drawString("Three of a Kind "+wins[3],350,250);
    g.drawString("Two Pairs "+wins[2],350,275);
    g.drawString("One Pair "+wins[1],350,300);
  }
  else {
    // Point scoring
    g.drawString("Royal Flush "+wins[9]+" x 250 = "
      +(wins[9]*250)+".00",350,75);
    g.drawString("Straight Flush "+wins[8]+" x 50 = "
      +(wins[8]*50)+".00",350,100);
    g.drawString("Four of a Kind "+wins[7]+" x 25 = "
      +(wins[7]*25)+".00",350,125);
    g.drawString("Full House "+wins[6]+" x 10 = "
        +(wins[6]*10)+".00",350,150);
    g.drawString("Flush "+wins[5]+" x 5 = "
        +(wins[5]*5)+".00",350,175);
    g.drawString("Straight "+wins[4]+" x 4 = "
        +(wins[4]*4)+".00",350,200);
    g.drawString("Three of a Kind "+wins[3]+" x 3 = "
```

```
                +(wins[3]*3)+".00",350,225);
          g.drawString("Two Pairs "+wins[2]+" x 2 = "
              +(wins[2]*2)+".00",350,250);
          g.setColor(Color.yellow);
          g.drawString("Poison Pairs "+wins[1]+" x -10 = "
              +(wins[1]*-10)+".00",350,275);
          g.setColor(Color.black);
          tmpwin = (wins[9]*250)+(wins[8]*50)+(wins[7]*25)+
                  (wins[6]*10)+(wins[5]*5)+(wins[4]*4)+
                  (wins[3]*3)+(wins[2]*2)+(wins[1]*-10);

          if (tmpwin<0) tmpwin = 0;

          g.setColor(Color.white);
          g.drawString("Total winnings: $"
                  +(tmpwin+winnings)+".00",350,315);
      }
  }


// By replacing update(), we remove screen erasing and //flicker. We
are now responsible for clearing the screen.
    public void update(Graphics g)  {
        paint(g);
    }


    public void paint(Graphics g)  {
        gbuffer.setColor(felt);

    gbuffer.fillRect(0,0,this.size().width, this.
            size().height;
        laytable(gbuffer); // Draw the white card shadows,
                    // "deck", etc.
        drawscore(gbuffer); // Put the scoring on the screen.
        CA.paintCards(gbuffer,this); // Place active cards

        // "Game Over" message when finished placing cards.
        if(dropcount()==25) {
        gbuffer.setFont(gof);
        gbuffer.setColor(Color.black);
        gbuffer.drawString("Game Over",10,230);
        }

        // After ibuffer is finished draw it.
        g.drawImage(ibuffer,0,0, this);
    }

// This is called whenever an event occurs- we want to //manage
buttons and choices.
    public boolean action(Event evt, Object arg)  {
      if(evt.target instanceof Button) {
```

```
      // If a button has been pushed...
          handlebutton((String) arg);  // Pass the name of the
                                    // button pressed
    }
    return true;
  }


  void handleconfig()  {
    if (optd.getdealtype()==false) { // Can we select a
                //card from the top of the deck?
            if (choicecard>-1) CA.takeCard(choicecard);
            choicecard=-1;
    }
    else  {
            if (choicecard<0)  {
                choicecard=CA.nextCard();
                showhole();
            }
    }


    CA.cardSound(optd.getsoundstate());
    repaint();
  }


// What to do when each button is pressed. String s //holds the text
name of the button
  void handlebutton(String s)  {
    if (s=="New Game")  {
       start(); // Re-start the game.
    }


    if (s=="Options")  {
        optd.show();
    }


    repaint();
  }


// Find out which position on the table the user is
//clicking on.
// If it returns -1, they were not in a box on the table.
  int locatebox(int x, int y)  {
    int b=-1;  // This holds the ID of the box we're
      // clicking on.


    for(int i=0; i<25; i++)  {
      if (((x - xeq(i)) < xwid) && (x - xeq(i)>-1) &&
      ((y - yeq(i)) < ywid) && (y - yeq(i)>-1))  {
      b=i;
      }
```

```
        }
      return b;
  }


  // How good is this hand? 9=Royal Flush.. 0=nothing, -1 // =
unfinished.
    int ratehand(int[] c)  {

      //  Is the row/column/diagonal finished?
      for(int i=0; i<5; i++)  {
          if (c[i]<0) return -1;
      }


      // Are all cards of the same suit?
      boolean samesuit = true;
      int s=c[4]/13; // Integer divide by 13 checks suit 0..3
          // for last card
      for (int i=0; i<4; i++)  {
        // Are the first cards the same as the last card?
        if ((c[i]/13) != s) samesuit = false;
      }


      // Next, check to see what the distribution is.
      int dis[] = new int[14];  // We will move Ace high so
                       // add an extra slot.
      for(int i=0;i<5;i++)  {
          dis[c[i]%13]++; // Modulo removes suit from card
              // identity
      }


      // Moving Ace high.
      dis[13]=dis[0];


      // Now count frequencies of cards.
      int H1=0; // Highest card frequency
      int H2=0; // Second highest card frequency
      for(int i=1;i<14;i++)  {
          if (dis[i] >= H2)  {
              if (dis[i]>H1)  {
                H2=H1;
                H1=dis[i];
              }
              else  {
                  H2=dis[i];
              }
          }
      }


      // Find out how many cards we have in sequential order
      int seq=0;  // This will hold our sequence count.
```

```
int sc=0;  // This will hold a temporary count.
for(int i=0; i<14; i++) {
    if (dis[i]>0) {
        sc++;
    }
    else {
        if (sc>seq) {
          seq=sc;
        }
        sc=0;
    }
}
if (sc>seq) seq=sc;

// For scoring, first check for a Royal Flush...
if ((samesuit) && (seq==5) && (dis[13]==1) &&
(dis[9]==1)) {
    return 9;
}

// Check for a Straight Flush
if ((samesuit) && (seq==5)) {
    return 8;
}

// Check for a Four of a Kind
if (H1==4) {
    return 7;
}

// Check for a Full House
if ((H1==3) && (H2==2)) {
    return 6;
}

// Check for a Flush
if (samesuit) {
    return 5;
}

// Check for a Straight
if (seq==5) {
    return 4;
}

// Check for a Three of a Kind
if (H1==3) {
    return 3;
}
```

```
    // Check for Two Pair
    if ((H1==2) && (H2==2)) {
        return 2;
    }

    // Check for One Pair
    if (H1==2) {
        return 1;
    }
    return 0;
}

void checkforwin() {
    int a[] = new int[5]; // Parameter given to ratehand();
    int r[] = new int[12];

    // There are 12 ways to win on the board

    // Check the 5 rows
    for(int i=0;i<25;i++) {
        a[i%5]=gameboard[i];
        if ((i%5)==4) {
            r[i/5]=ratehand(a);
        }
    }

    // Check the 5 columns
    for(int i=0;i<5;i++) {
      for(int j=0;j<5;j++) {
        a[j]=gameboard[i+(j*5)];
        if (j==4) {
            r[5+i]=ratehand(a);
        }
      }
    }

    // Check the 2 diagonals
    for(int i=0;i<5;i++) {
      a[i]=gameboard[i*6];
    }
    r[10]=ratehand(a);

    for(int i=0;i<5;i++) {
      a[i]=gameboard[(i*4)+4];
    }
    r[11]=ratehand(a);

    for(int i=0; i<10; i++) {
        wins[i]=0;
    }
```

```
      for(int i=0;i<12;i++) {
       if (r[i]>0)
       wins[r[i]]++;
      }
    }

    public boolean mouseDown(Event evt, int x, int y) {
      int box = locatebox(x,y);
      if (box>-1) {    // If we have clicked on a box...
      // If we don't have a card here, drop one.
          if (gameboard[box]<0) {
            CA.takeCard(drawncard);
            if(choicecard>-1) CA.takeCard(choicecard);
            CA.placeCard(drawncard,xeq(box),yeq(box),2);
            gameboard[box]=drawncard;
            drawncard=CA.nextCard();
            choicecard=CA.nextCard();
            showhole();
            repaint();
            checkforwin();
          }
      }

      // Else, if it is one of the hole cards, turn it over       //and
select it to place. This will change drawncard
      else {
          if ((choicecard>-1) &&
          (CA.locateCard(x,y)==choicecard)) {
          // Turn the card over
          ACard t;
          t = CA.getCard(choicecard);
          t.showcard = 2;
          CA.setCard(t);

          CA.takeCard(drawncard);
          drawncard=choicecard;
          choicecard=-1;
          repaint();
          }
      }
      return true;
    }

// Climb components of the awt until we reach the
// current frame of the applet -- start with a THIS.
  Frame climbToFrame() {
          // Association of components to start climbing with       //
-- the applet
      Component climbMe = this;
```

```
        do  {
                // step up the hiarchy...
                climbMe = climbMe.getParent();
                // Until we find the Frame
        } while (! (climbMe instanceof Frame));
        return (Frame) climbMe;
    }
}
/////////////////////////////////////
////  Poker Configuration Dialog
////  PDialog
/////////////////////////////////////

public class PDialog extends Dialog  {

    Panel DPanel;

    // Declare the button and drop-down choices for the game
    String scorestring = "Use simple scoring";
    String dealstring = "Can draw card from top of deck";
    String soundstring = "Use Sound";
    Checkbox scorebox;
    Checkbox dealbox;
    Checkbox soundbox;
    Choice difficulty;
    Poker app;

    public PDialog(Frame parent, Poker app)  {
        super(parent, "Game Options",true);
        this.app = app;

        difficulty = new Choice();
        difficulty.addItem("Hard");
        difficulty.addItem("Medium");
        difficulty.addItem("Easy");
        difficulty.select("Hard");

        setLayout(new GridLayout(5,1));
        add(scorebox = new
        Checkbox(scorestring,null,false));
        add(dealbox = new Checkbox(dealstring,null,false));
        add(soundbox = new Checkbox(soundstring,null,true));
        add(difficulty);

        DPanel = new Panel();
        DPanel.add(new Button("OK"));
        add(DPanel);
    }
```

```
    public boolean getscoretype() {
        return scorebox.getState();
    }

    public boolean getdealtype() {
        return dealbox.getState();
    }

    public boolean getsoundstate() {
        return soundbox.getState();
    }

    public int gamedifficulty() {
        String howhard = difficulty.getSelectedItem();
        if (howhard=="Hard") return 50;
        if (howhard=="Medium") return 25;
        if (howhard=="Easy") return 5;
        return 0;
    }

    // Handle the big "X" in the window bar, ALT-F4 and        //
Close.
    public boolean handleEvent(Event e) {
        if (e.id==Event.WINDOW_DESTROY) {
            dispose();
            return true;
        }
        else return super.handleEvent(e);
    }

    // Handle the "OK" button.
    public boolean action(Event evt, Object obj) {
        if ("OK".equals(obj)) {
            dispose();
        }

        // Make sure the screen is updated after our
    // changes.
        app.handleconfig();
        app.repaint();
        return true;
    }
}
```

Now basically this code is pretty much just a jumped-up version of what we were working with before. If you step through it, carefully looking at the comments, it is easy to follow if you see what we are doing in the final prod-

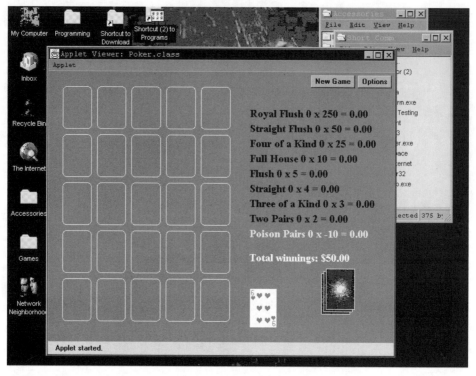

Figure 7.2   Improved Poison Pair Poker applet running.

uct. However, right at the beginning you are going to take a couple of mental hits. What is all this stuff about Buttons and Frames? Did you miss a chapter somewhere along the way?

Well, not exactly. What you are seeing is the application of the *Advanced Windowing Toolkit* (AWT) that comes with Java, and it would behoove us to have a short discussion about it.

The AWT and You

So far we have avoided any discussion of the AWT and what it really does. You have touched on different components of it from time to time in passing, as evidenced by the fact that you have imported it to use things like Images.

Unfortunately we don't have the space to fully explore the AWT and what you can do with it. However, to make up for it there is a complete AWT tutorial on the Web support site that will take you all the way through the care and feeding of your AWT. But we are still going to need to touch on some of the higher points of the AWT here so that you are familiar with the basic concepts in the toolkit.

Basically the AWT exists mainly to allow you to create GUI stuff that you might need: menus, list boxes, and such. In order to do this, AWT tools are split into two major classes: components and containers.

Containers are user-interface gadgets that hold other user-interface components. Containers can hold other containers if you want, or they can hold smaller components such as list boxes and buttons. Your applet is a container because it descends from the Container class way back when.

Components, as you have probably figured out by now, are user-interface objects that can be held by Containers. There are a whole slew of components available to you such as text fields, check boxes, choice menus, and buttons. Basically, there are components that do all the things you expect to find in a windowing interface.

So far this is pretty simple. You can stop right now and take a quick look in the API docs and look through the java.awt class again; beside a lot of the more familiar classes you have been using so far in this book, you will find some stuff that makes a lot more sense with your new knowledge—scroll bars and file dialogs, for example.

Now you can pretty much figure out how to use all this on your own just from the API docs except for one minor detail, layout. The way layout is handled is pretty botched up. Not that it doesn't make sense and isn't for a good reason, but it is still botched up.

For reasons of interoperability, Java doesn't let you just put a component where you want it in a container as would be the case in a sane world. You can't tell a button, for instance, that you want it at 222 x and 234 y. Instead, you must flow it into a layout.

The *layout* is how your components are going to be aligned on the screen when they are displayed. You have a number of different layouts you can use on your container; you implement a layout by calling a *layout manager object.* The layout manager objects available to you are FlowLayout, Border-Layout, CardLayout, GridLayout, and GridBagLayout.

In order to call a layout manager, you use the following syntax:

```
this.setLayout(new GridLayout());
```

You can look up each of these layout objects under the API docs and there are pretty good explanations of what they do and code examples of how to use them.

However, we do want to touch on one of the layout objects right now, and that is the FlowLayout. The *FlowLayout* is the default layout for your containers. In the FlowLayout, components you add to your container are added one at a time and centered. If you put enough components into a layout to fill a line, then components will start flowing down to the next line.

If you want to change this, you use a new FlowLayout object, with arguments and a constructor so that things will move to new positions. You can find the options available to you in the layout manager object write-up in the docs.

In order to deal with things that happen to your components, such as pressing them or checking them or otherwise doing something that you will want to deal with in your code, you are given the action method.

The *action method* is an event handler, just like the mouseDown we are quite familiar with at this point. An action method gets passed two things, the first of which is an Event object, called the target, that represents the type of object that threw the event. This will be Button, Checkbox, or some other type of UI component that expects to get something done when it is messed with. The other thing you get is an object that depends on the type of UI component throwing the event in the first place. The exact argument object that is thrown by a UI is defined in the API write-up for the UI component in question.

This might seem a little confusing, but is really no more difficult than dealing with mouse events. For example, let's look at how we handle a button in our example above.

```
public boolean action(Event evt, Object obj) {
    if ("OK".equals(obj)) {
        dispose();
    }
```

Now, we aren't really worried about performing any action off of anything in our dialog box but the OK button. This is because every time we move through the execution of our Poker game we are checking the state of all of the applicable checkboxes in the option box manually from the body of the Poker class. Hence, all we need to worry about is the OK button to get rid of the dialog box. Here we trap the event, but don't bother to check it because we only care if it is a button. Button actions return a string in their argument object that equals the label on the button. So we know that if our obj argument equals "OK" we got the button in question. Since the function of the OK button is to get rid of the dialog box itself, we just take care of it on the spot.

Back to Poker

Now with a tiny view of how the AWT works, we should look at the Poker applet to see how we used the AWT to make our Option box work properly. The rest of the stuff in Poker is pretty cut and dried at this point, but this bit about getting that box up there is tricky.

First you can see that in Poker we have defined a Frame object called Dframe and a Pdialog object called optd. Now Frame objects are a container class that is handy for holding various types of UI objects. What concerns us is that you have to have one to hold a Dialog object, and as we will find out in a moment, that is what Pdialog class is an example of.

In order to get a Frame to hold Pdialog, we have a couple of options. The first is that we can create a Frame and place it on the screen. This is a perfectly valid option, and later in the book we will present an example of doing just that. But what we are doing here is cheating to get our Frame. Anything running an applet has a Frame around the applet. If you go far enough up the feeding chain in an applet (this isn't true of an application, so don't try it) you will find out that it is running in a Frame. So what we have done is use a method called climbToFrame that just uses the getParent method Applet inherits to run up the feeding chain until it hits a Frame object. Since we didn't create one, we know it must be the environment's frame. When it gets to that Frame it returns it. We then present that to the new Pdialog object we are creating in order for it to get displayed properly.

Now let's jump down to Pdialog and see what we are doing there. It is tacked on to the end of the Poker listing. First we create a number of references we are going to need. We create a number of UI component references, a Frame, and we create a few strings that are going to make our code more concise a bit later. Then we create our constructor, which is where all the work in a dialog comes in.

The first call in our constructor builds the dialog box we end up seeing on the screen and calling our Options box. In order to create the box, we go to the class with the keyword *super,* give it the Frame we got passed when Poker called us, name the box, and set a boolean value of true. This boolean tells us whether our dialog is visible or invisible.

Next we create a Choice box for our difficulty. Choice objects take a number of items with labels and display them in a pulldown choice menu. A good thing to note here is the addItem method we are using to add our labels headings to the Choice object. When you are dealing with UI components, this is how you add them. Containers have an addItem method they have inherited and to add anything to them you use this method. You will see us using it constantly when we are working with the AWT.

In the case of the difficulty Choice we are adding Hard, Medium, and Easy settings and defaulting to Hard by selecting it.

Next we are setting our layout by calling the GridLayout manager with a constructor. Then we add a few Checkbox objects, giving them our predefined strings as arguments. These Checkbox objects give us our options for sound on/off, type of deal, and type of scoring. If you are getting lost here, play the game and go to the option box. It should look like Figure 7.3.

The last thing we add is our OK button. We are going to use this button to close the Option dialog when we are done with it. Instead of just adding our button, we add it to a Panel and add this to our Dialog: This is to get things lined up the way we want.

Now we have three methods. These methods simply return the value of various things in our Options box. This is where Poker is going to get its information about the state of the various options to find out how to conduct its game.

After this we create an event handler that catches the system event WIN-DOW_DESTROY. This is the event that comes from the system when you close a window. We use this to clean up after ourselves. If the event we are catching isn't a WINDOW_DESTROY then we pass it on up the chain and don't deal with it right now.

The handler for the OK button we have already discussed. It is there just to do basically the same thing as catching a WINDOW_DESTROY, except in response to our pressing the OK button. We also make sure that when the OK button is pressed our Poker applet does some housecleaning and knows to update all our options.

You will note that one thing you aren't seeing here is a paint method of any sort. When we use UI components, a good side effect is that we don't

Figure 7.3 Option box.

have to worry about painting them. Java makes sure that our UI components get painted for us.

We will be using the AWT in further examples as we go along and taking particular care to explain what we are doing with it.

What We Have Learned

In this chapter we haven't covered much new ground. Instead, we have cemented what we have already seen by applying it in practice with an example that is close to the kind of real-world games you will be creating. However, the one thing we did pick up that was brand new this chapter was a taste of the AWT.

AWT

The AWT is broken up into two basic categories, user-interface containers and user-interface components. Containers hold other UI stuff, including other containers, and components are what get things done.

Add

When we wish to add something to a container we use the add method of our container. Since Applet is descended from container we can add UI components to it.

Layouts

To control how our various UI elements are displayed, we use a layout manager object. The default layout manager is FlowLayout, which puts our components on the screen in a centered line. In order to use a layout manager we use the setLayout method of the container to call up the specific layout manager object that will control the display of our components.

Actions

Dealing with things that happen to our UI components is much like dealing with mouseDown events; we override a container method called action that catches events generated by various UI components.

When a UI component generates an event, it does two things: It throws an event specific to itself, which is called the target. By checking to make sure the event we are catching is the right target, we can tell which of our UI components generated the event. There is also an argument object thrown that is different for each type of UI component. By using this object, we can tell what happened to that component and then act on it.

In order to understand the specific targets and arguments, we need to look in the API docs, where the entry for each component will tell us what happens when our component is activated.

Painting

Although the way the AWT works seems a little complex, we do get one free ride out of it. We don't need to worry about painting our UI components and containers. Java takes care of all display issues with UI items, freeing us from at least one hassle.

• • • • • • • •
From Here

In the next chapter we are going to be learning a bit more and working with another large example. While doing single player games is great, part of the point of Java is networked communication. Now we move on to how to deal with networking and then we implement another game based on the cards class, this one a multiplayer poker game. We also spend some time learning the fairly severe restrictions on Java communication from applets.

CHAPTER 8
• • • • • • •
MULTIPLAYER GAMING

Web delivery of applets is one of the more important functions of Java. Let's face it—if it weren't for the applet, Java probably wouldn't be making all that much of a splash.

But while an applet game has appeal, that appeal can dull rapidly. Let's look a bit at the limitations. First, everything has to be delivered over the wire, and for most users in this world that wire is connected to a 14.4 modem. That makes downloading a game with large graphics, sound, or code chunks pretty nasty. We have the fact that an applet doesn't allow you to do any file work on the client box. That's unfortunate because you lose specific configuration information relevant to the user. This is also bad because you also have to reach your image and sound information each time you first load up the game. For a humble effort that isn't all that big a deal, but you get into a really complex game and this can be a pretty nasty hit.

So where does Java get back the juice? Why should you continue learning to program in it?

Well, a couple of reasons have presented themselves over the course of the book. One is that Java is an easy language to program in with a high degree of portability. And no matter if there are security bugaboos that limit our effort when dealing with applets, there isn't anything else that is deliverable over the

Web with the ease of Java right now. Those with a more technical background aren't going to have too much of a problem dealing with downloading programs, decompressing and installing them, and then running them over top of a TCP/IP link to get at an on-line content game, but the majority of the world is going to consider this a pain. With Java in applet form it just *happens*.

But the greatest promise for on-line games isn't the static, single-player game. These sorts of games, in the size requirements to make for a decently quick load and play, aren't going to build the kind of sexy highly involving games that are going to keep users coming back for more over the long haul.

The real pot of gold is the multiplayer game. In games with multiple players the dynamic interaction of other human beings, filtered through the rules and world of the game, provide the kick; that kick keeps up for a much longer period of time than with a single-player game.

Java provides a lot of code in the standard package set that allows you to hook up to the Web and other players. At first glance it would appear to make multiplayer gaming pretty much a lead-pipe cinch. Well, in a perfect world, that would actually be the case. But in reality, implementation outperforms the vision in a couple of important cases, and creating multiplayer games in Java isn't quite as easy as it should be right now.

In this chapter we look at the good points and the pitfalls of Java multiplayer implementations, as well as see where things are going to be with the patches that will be implemented in Java 1.1, due out in a few months.

Applets versus Apps

As we know, Java presents us with two different modes of dealing with the delivery of our programs: applets and applications. Applets run in the Web browser and don't require anything else on the client box. Applications, on the other hand, require users to have the JDK set up on their machine.

We need to look at the different issues posed by these two different forms of Java structure when it comes to hooking up players to other players.

Applets

Applets would always appear to be the preferred method of delivering on-line content programmed in Java. Since by nature two players who are hooking up to play a game against each other are going to be wired at the time, the applet would seem to be the only logical choice for multiplayer game delivery.

But there are some very serious drawbacks to using applets to deliver your multiplayer games. These come from the extreme paranoia over the possibility of dangerous applets running rampant over the Net. The applet security restrictions destroy an applet-delivered multiplayer game.

First, we have the issue we touched on earlier about delivery times. Everything has to come down the wire each time the game is fired up. You get a game that has 100K+ of content and you are getting what some people would consider unacceptable delay in the startup time. Then that 100K+ has to be processed by the Web browser and actually fired up to run, which takes a while in itself. More time lag.

Then we have to deal with player information. For all but the simplest, one-shot games, such as most board games, you are going to have player information to deal with. For instance, in a continuing war-game campaign you will have information about status of forces for each player that is going to need some persistence. That is, it will have to exist between games.

To illustrate this, think about Panzer General. Let's say you and a friend were playing an on-line, networked version of the game. There are two persistence issues here. The first is what if you can't get done with a scenario in one sitting? Do you lose an hour of playtime just because you got called away from the computer in the middle of a game? Well, that would be stupid. Obviously there needs to be an ability to save a game in the middle and resume it later.

Second, if you are running a campaign, and in many games one of the major hooks is seeing your forces and abilities advance from scenario to scenario in a progression, you are going to need to keep unit and score data from scenario to scenario.

So we need to be able to deal with persistent information. The problem with applets is that we can't deal with that information in the users' machines. Instead, we need to keep all the files that would store this kind of data on the server machine. That isn't the end of the world, but it is a real pain and a consideration we need to keep in mind during our design. We are going to have to have some method of finding the right file and getting it to the user as well as think about where these files are going to live on the server and how big they are going to be. Since we can't assume that we own the server—the majority of the people who are reading this book probably have to deal with an ISP as opposed to owning their own hookups to the Net—this file storage can actually start costing money if there are too many files of too big a size and override our account limits.

But the file and persistent information problem pales in comparison to the other big problem with applet multiplayer gaming: communication restrictions.

Communication Restrictions

The real trouble when it comes to creating multiplayer games with applets is *restricted communications.*

Applets aren't allowed to communicate with any place but the server they came from. This isn't only for file storage, but for any type of communication. If you want to start sending information streams, such as your game data, to another player, you can do this only by routing it through the server that sent you the applet.

No good things come of this rule, from the point of view of the game designer. If you want to hook two people playing an applet game together, the logical way to do it would be for one to send the other a message with their communication address and the two games to hook up together without the server getting involved. But you can't do that.

So what has to happen is that both games must start talking to the server and stake out ports (virtual communication addresses) on the server machine to pass information to each other. Now this wouldn't be all that bad in some ways except for the fact that the server isn't listening to you.

WWW software is designed to listen to various communication channels looking for very specific types of information. When your game starts trying to talk to a port, the server doesn't know to look for that data there and will just ignore it. This means that it isn't going to pass it on to the other game applet presumably doing the same thing.

Think about sending normal snailmail through the United States Postal Service (USPS). Let's say you want to play a chess game with a friend by mail. You put your move in a letter, address it to your friend, and drop it in your mail box with a stamp on it. Then your friend waits by his mailbox for the letter to come so that he can get your move, make it on his board, and write and mail you a response.

Everything works just fine as long as the USPS is working well. But let's say that all the disgruntled postal workers in the world quit on the same day and service is delayed until the post office hires a whole new staff and trains them. You could be waiting for weeks for someone to come and take that mail out of your box and deliver it to your friend.

This is the situation we are dealing with on the server side. Both applets can be listening and sending information to ports on the server, but until someone decides to deliver them, nothing is going to happen.

So in order to make a game happen between applets, you are going to have a routine up that passes data between the proper ports and delivers the data between your applets. This is a real hassle from a novice's point of view.

If you have control of your own server, you probably know enough to make this happen without a problem. You can write a CGI routine in C or Perl that will do the job easily. You could also set up your own JDK on the server and write your game server software in Java.

But the problems here are multifold. First, we can't assume that we have our own server. The vast majority of us have to deal with an ISP who runs the server we call into. And we have very little control over how that server is set up. A great number of us can't rely on having a copy of the JDK on our ISPs to support us writing a Java app to take over port-passing duties. And since the JDK has to be installed root on a server in order to operate, we don't have the access to set it up ourselves. We are going to have to rely on the ISP operators to do this and give us access to it—too iffy. Many readers of this book aren't going to have the pull with their ISPs to get anything done there.

Most of us are going to have access, whether we know it, to C, Perl, and CGI from our ISP accounts. These tools are pretty much standard on any well-outfitted server setup and all but the most psychotic sysops realize their power users are going to need access to these tools to get things done.

But we run into a couple of problems with talking about using these tools in the course of these pages. One is from my standpoint as the author and one is from the standpoint of the ISP. We will deal with the ISP problem first.

In order to make our port-passing routine happen we are going to have to create what is called a forking process. UNIX users will know what this is right off. However, readers unfamiliar with UNIX probably haven't heard of a fork. A *forking process* is one that assumes a separate thread of operation in order to execute.

Sysops tend to freak out when they see you playing with forking processes. I know of more than one ISP where writing forking code is grounds for immediate revocation of your account, and I know a few others where it would be such grounds if the sysops actually knew what they were doing.

The reason, as the experienced UNIX hacker can tell you, is the possibility of creating a "fork bomb" no matter how inadvertently. A *fork bomb* is a piece of recursive code that continues to call its forking functions infinitely. Within seconds of a fork bomb going off, the server will grind to a halt and crash as the entire processor of the machine ends up taken up with spawned processes from your bomb. And, a fork bomb can creep into code by fairly simple mistakes.

The result of a fork bomb originating from your account will almost certainly be the cancellation of your account as well as the long-term ire of your sysop.

The other problem in going deeply into the server-side solution here is from the standpoint of the scope of the book. Just like a game, we have our little world here and that world is Java programming for games. In order to work with the server-side mechanics in a way that the majority of our users could actually put to use would require talking a good deal about how servers are set up to communicate and, more onerously, talking about C or Perl CGI scripting, because that is all we can reasonably expect to find in the average ISP environment.

These subjects are way beyond our scope. There are books with more pages than this one devoted to only these topics. Just covering the surface of them would require a hundred or more pages, and we don't have the space to spare.

As a result, we are going to skip this solution in print. We will be discussing it at length on the Web support site, as well as pointing out resources for learning more about each of these topics that are available for free on-line. You will also find our Perl and C solutions to this problem located there, where we can talk about the ins and outs of using them at some length.

But while we are placing that particular point on the on-line site, that doesn't mean that we still don't have a huge hit of data to learn and work with in this chapter. We still have applications to talk about.

Applications

While applets present a large group of restrictions to our designs for security reasons, applications don't throw up these particular barriers. The runner of the application, just as with any other piece of code you choose to run on your local machine, is responsible for making sure the code they are running isn't a nasty Trojan in disguise. Applications are permitted full-file access to the local box.

Applications also don't have the communications millstone hanging around their necks. Applications are free to talk to anyone on the Net they want to, when they want to. No server tricks are required to hook two apps to each other.

This would seem to be the obvious ticket. We have the Holy Grail of Java-distributed gaming right in our hands. But if we turn it over and look on the bottom we will see the words "Made in China" etched on the bottom of the cup.

There are two problems with applications for multiplayer games, one minor and one major. We will deal with the minor problem first.

The minor problem is sound support; there isn't any. The sound support functions of the applet actually come from the environment the applet is running in, the Appletviewer or your Java-capable browser. This is what interfaces with your actual operating system to give you the rudimentary sound capabilities that Java provides. When you are running a stand-alone application, it doesn't have any interface to your underlying system in order to use your sound hardware.

We could get around this by writing machine-specific code and patching it into our Java games, but that is pretty self-defeating. If we are going to write machine-specific patches, then why are we working in Java in the first place?

However, even though well used sound can add to the veracity of your game, in most designs it isn't irreplaceable. It is the rare game indeed that can't get by without sound. So this problem isn't all that crippling, just annoying.

The other problem dishes out much larger doses of damage. The way that Java hooks up to other locations on the Net is broken, and while it isn't totally unusable, it sure isn't very functional in its current state.

In order to understand what is wrong, and what it means, we are going to have to know a little bit about how we communicate over the Net.

Net Communications

When we want to hook up from our machine to another machine on the Net, the first thing we do is open a socket on our end that goes from our machine, through the Net (normally through the intermediary services of our ISP), and ends up connected to our destination. The actual details of what a socket is and all of the details of how it works really don't matter to us right now; that is taken care of at a fairly high level by Java. We just need to know that a socket is the opening of a data pipe between our machine and our target.

However, in order to get that socket open, we need to tell it where it is going to connect to. It knows that one end is going to be our program by default, but we need to have the other end hooked to the machine we want to talk to. In order to do this, our socket is going to need an address.

The Internet Protocol (IP) defines a dot notation addressing system, the full and exact details of which don't really concern us here. An IP address is just a group of numbers separated by dots that act as an address for machines connected to the Net. A representative example would look like 204.14.203.5 (I have no idea if this is a real machine or whose it may be, so don't use it).

Well, for those of us who have been around long enough to remember when raw IP addresses were all that existed we know how tedious it got to be to remember the numbers for everywhere you connected to. If you think phone numbers are bad, try to keep track of a few dozen IP addresses in your head.

So the masterminds of Net engineering came up with a much easier system, called domain names. *Domain names* are alphabetic sequences mapped to IP addresses and since these alphabetic sequences are normally words, they are much easier to remember. www.microsoft.com or www.yahoo.com are infinitely easier to remember than a string of numbers with dots in them.

But even though domain names are cool they don't really denote the place you are going—the addressing system of the Net is still IP addresses. It is almost like dealing with text on a computer. As far as the machine is concerned, things are still ones and zeros; we have just all agreed that a pattern of ones and zeros in the right place will be mapped as a specific character.

Therefore, there must be a big master list of all of the domain names and the actual IP addresses they represent so you can punch in the domain name and your machine can go out and get the IP address that it can actually use. This function is provided by dedicated machines on the Net called *Domain Name Servers* (DNSs). You give a DNS a domain name and it will hand you back the IP so that you can actually connect to the machine in question.

And here is where the problem creeps in: The way Java talks to Domain Name Servers is broken. Java refuses to accept a raw IP address as a connection parameter. Big problem.

Details of Pain

In order to communicate over the Net with Java you must open a socket. Like everything else you tend to need, Java has a handy Socket object built in that is fairly easy to use. The most common constructor involves handing it an InetAddress object (we will talk about that next) and looks like this:

```
Socket TheSocket = new Socket(ourAddress, ourPort);
```

where *ourAddress* is an *InetAddress object* with the Internet address we want to connect to and *ourPort* is an integer that represents the port we want to connect to.

This is pretty simple. Once we have created our Socket then we can jack communications up and down, using the various stream objects that Java provides. You should already be fairly familiar with using streams in general from your previous programming background (and the use of sockets for that matter), and looking quickly at the API docs in the java.io package at the stream objects and methods available should be fairly self-explanatory. From your Socket (located in the java.net package) you can use the getInputStream and getOutputStream methods to return streams you can work with to get data across the wire.

So where is the hassle? The hassle is in that InetAddress object we had to create to open our socket.

Creating an InetAddress object is pretty simple. First, InetAddress has no constructor; we must use a static method of the class in order to actually give our InetAddress object a real address. So we create an object first, and then fill it using the getByName method. The process looks like this:

```
InetAddress ourAddress;
ourAddress = InetAddress.getByName("www.ianet.com");
```

The string argument in the getByName method is a string naming the server. However, it can also be a raw IP address in dot notation.

The above example will work like a charm. You have no problem when you give the system the alphabetic name of a location on the Net. It goes to the DNS and pulls up the raw IP address and puts it in your InetAddress object so you can use it in creating your sockets.

The problem comes when you try to feed a raw IP address into the InetAddress. Java still does the same thing it does with the alpha address, it goes to the DNS and looks up the address you gave it. The problem here for those well versed in Net-tech issues is that Java performs a reverse name lookup on the argument of the getByName method no matter if you give it a name or if you give it a raw IP address. For the rest of us this requires a bit more explanation.

A DNS has two cross-referenced lists in it. The first list we will call the *name list.* This is the list of sites by their given names (akin to a baptismal record at a church). The second, which we will call the *number list,* is a list of the raw Net addresses of each site. An entry in each list is linked to one entry in the other list. So the name list might have an entry such as www.this-isjustanexample.com and that might link to the Net address 000.00.000.1 on the number list. A reverse name lookup is the process of giving a DNS a string that is on the name list and having it return the number on the number list.

The problem comes in when you already have the number. When you already have the raw IP address you don't need to go to the DNS to get it looked up. If you know the address, you can just start using it. Java, however, sports a bug that has it go to the DNS and submit the number you give it to the DNS looking for a translation.

So the DNS happily goes through its name list looking for "000.00.000.1" which it isn't going to find since that number isn't a part of the name list at all, but part of the number list. The DNS reports back to your Java program that 000.00.000.1 doesn't have an entry and your InetAddress object crashes.

The moral of this story is that you can't use raw IP addresses to connect two Java applications together over the Net. Java will take only names.

So What's the Big Deal? Just Give It the Names

Well, if only that were a simple trick. However, it isn't. If you are operating from two separate machines, both of which have static IP addresses that have DNS entries, this wouldn't be a problem. But this isn't the normal situation on the Net.

Instead, the majority of the world is going to be using one out of a bank of addresses kept by the ISP for use by their modems and on any given dial in your Net address and lookup name are going to change depending on which modem you are hooked to.

You can get Java to easily report the IP address of the connection it is on by using the toString method of an InetAddress you have created using the getLocalHost method of the same object. What this will do is tell you the IP address that was handed to your box by the ISP when you dialed in. But you can't get it to produce the actual name.

So while you can get the address you are at, and a friend who wants to hook up to play games can tell her address, the connection can't be made with the addresses you can get, just with the names of the addresses.

Getting a name can be either impossible or a real pain depending on circumstances. Doing a finger of the server your friend is on might fess up a name depending on the way the ISP is set up. Or it might not. Life is fairly harsh.

However, the only bright spot in all this is that Sun knows about the problem and has repaired it in version 1.1 which should be out early next year. The JDK 1.1 also has a host of other cool goodies including object serialization, but the important thing is that not too long after you read this, the problem should be repaired.

To this end, we are going to go ahead and include a simple demo that shows the use and abuse of Sockets and how to communicate across the Net in Java. This demo is useful for a number of reasons. The first is that the same basic principles you use to communicate with applications you will be using with the applet communications routines on the Web support site. The techniques are the same; there is just more to handling the server stuff with the applet versions.

Second, this code demonstrates all of the principles just fine, and if you can get the names for the people connected you can use it through the Net. If you can't, you can fire it up twice on the same machine and it will communicate between the two apps without a problem. And when you come into possession of Java 1.1 and recompile the code it will work with addresses as well.

The Demo

This demo is pretty simple, basically the bare minimum to demonstrate the use of socket communications and streams in Java. All we do here is create a simple chat window that is connected between two machines to show how to move data between two different applications. On the Web support site you will find a couple of games that use socket communications to pass their data, but they are the size of houses and with commentary run something over 100 pages, so for space considerations, we are putting a simpler example here in print. However, you follow the same steps for sending text and game-related data. The only difference is that in a game you will be creating your strings to represent the status of your game objects and parsing them at the receiver to replicate game conditions. The particulars of your parsing and string coding are going to change completely from game to game anyway, only the method of socket communications is going to remain the same.

```java
/*
      SimpleChat.java--This is a stupid simple example of socket and
network communication with Java. You can find a number of variations on
this theme scattered across the Net.
      To start a client and a server on the same machine for
demonstration messing around, start the first copy with the /server
command line argument and the second copy with no arguments.
      However, if you wish to connect across the Net, the client can
start with a single argument for the host name.
      With either a client or server setup you can also add the command
line argument /port xxxx where xxxx is the port number you wish to use
for the session.
*/

import java.applet.Applet;
import java.io.*;
import java.net.*;

public class SimpleChat extends Applet  {

        boolean setServer;
        int port = 6005;
        Socket sock;
        String host;

        public static void main (String args[])  {
            new SimpleChat(args);
        }

        public SimpleChat (String args[])  {
            switches(args);

            //Start a client or a server session.
```

```
            if (setServer) setServer();
            else setClient();


    }


    // Here we parse the args string to get the command // line
switches.

    public void switches(String args[]) {
        for (int i =0; i < args.length; i++) {
            if (args[i].equals("/port") ||
            args[i].equals("port")) {
                port = Integer.valueOf
                (args[i+1]).intValue ();
                i++;
                }
                else if (args[i].equals("/server") ||
                    args[i].equals("server")) {
                    setServer = true;
                    i++;
                }
                else if (i != args.length -1) {
                    System.out.println(
                            "Invalid Arguments");
                }
                else {
                    host = args[i];
                    i++;
                }
            }
        }


    // We be a server.

    public void setServer() {
            try {

            //As a server we just need to get the local
        //address, which is provided by the
    //getLocalHost method.
                InetAddress serverAddr =
                InetAddress.getLocalHost();

                //Say where we are crouching in wait.

                System.out.println ("Waiting at " +
                    serverAddr.toString() +
                        " port " + port + ".");

                //Set a ServerSocket waiting on a call.
```

```
                        ServerSocket serverSock = new
                              ServerSocket(port, 50);

                        //Accept any that come our way. . .

                        sock = serverSock.accept();
                        System.out.println("Connected.");

                        //Start the communication threads.
                        new WriterThread (this).start();
                        new ReaderThread (this).start();
                }
            catch (IOException e) {
                    System.out.println
                            ("Failed connection.");
                }
        }


    //We be a client.
    public void setClient () {
        try {

    //As a client, we need to get the argument with the //host. If
this is null, it will default to local.

                        InetAddress serverAddr =
                            InetAddress.getByName(host);

                        //Use the address to open our socket.

                        sock = new Socket (serverAddr.getHostName(),
                                port, true);

                        System.out.println ("Connected to Server.");

                        //Start the communication threads.
                        new WriterThread (this).start();
                        new ReaderThread (this).start();
            }
                catch(UnknownHostException e) {
                System.out.println ("Unknown Host");
            }
        catch(IOException e) {
                System.out.println
                ("Could not make connection to server.");
            }
        }
}
```

```
//The ReaderThread takes data from the socket and throws it //up on the
console.
class ReaderThread extends Thread {
    SimpleChat chat;

    public ReaderThread(SimpleChat chat) {
        this.chat = chat;
    }

    public void run() {
        try {

            //Wrap our System.in stream in a more functional
            //DataInputStream for manipulation.

                DataInputStream in = new
                        DataInputStream(System.in);

                //Generate an output stream to the socket
        //connection.

                DataOutputStream out =
                    new DataOutputStream
                    (chat.sock.getOutputStream());

                //Write data from the console input to the
        //socket stream and sleep the thread to keep
    //from locking up too much of the system.

                while (true) {
                    out.writeUTF(in.readLine());
                    try {
                        Thread.sleep(100);
                    } catch (InterruptedException e) {}

                }
        }
        catch (IOException e) {
            System.out.println("Connection Terminated.");
            System.exit(0);
        }
    }
}

//WriterThread takes the input from the socket connection //and writes
it on the console.

class WriterThread extends Thread {
    SimpleChat chat;
```

```
    public WriterThread (SimpleChat chat) {
        this.chat=chat;
    }

public void run() {
    try {

            // Get an incoming stream from the socket.

            DataInputStream externalIn =
        new DataInputStream(chat.sock.getInputStream());

            //Read the incoming data and throw it up the
//console with some spacing to differentiate
//text.
            while (true) {

                System.out.println(" " +
                        externalIn.readUTF());
                try {
                    Thread.sleep(100);
                } catch(InterruptedException e) {}
            }
        }
    catch(IOException e) {
            System.out.println("Connection Terminated");
            System.exit(0);

        }
    }
}
```

Now after some of the long code we have traced though in this book (and the real doozy is yet to come in Chapter 9 where we get into a game development toolkit) this is pretty much a cinch. By now almost everything here should be pretty much self-explanatory along with the comments.

However, if you haven't taken the time to go to the API docs and look through the input and output streams in java.io, you should do so now, paying particular attention to the DataStream objects, since these are probably going to be your most frequent calls. *SimpleChat* gives a nice clear example of how to use these calls in practice which is pretty obvious once you see it (see Figure 8.1). However, knowing all the methods you have at your disposal for manipulating input and output streams can't be underestimated.

Figure 8.1 SimpleChat in action.

The basic process we are seeing here is pretty simple to understand when you go though the docs, but lets look at the high end of what you do to talk to another application to cement it in your head.

First, the basic unit of communications is the Socket. A *Socket* takes an InetAddress object and opens a communication channel between your machine and another machine somewhere out in the big, bad world (however you can open sockets between different apps on the same machine if you have a need to).

Although the Socket is the prime abstraction of the communication interface, the stream object is the abstraction of actual data transfer. There are two basic varieties of stream, the input and the output stream. But Java doesn't stop there. Instead you are given a dozen different varieties of streams to suit your particular task.

In order to get a stream, you use the getInputStream and getOutputStream methods of your instantiated Socket. If you need something other than plain-vanilla streams (and it is a pretty sure bet that you do) then you use these streams as constructor arguments to the other types of stream you need to wrap them in.

Finally, you use the stream methods to put information into your stream or pull it out.

This is all pretty well illustrated in the SimpleChat code. However, there is one thing that might be slightly confusing in this code, even after you have looked through the API docs: these strange calls to read and write UDF found in the Writer and Reader threads. What is a UDF and why are we calling it?

Well, the odds of your ever needing to use a UDF in anything but this particular example are actually fairly slim, but since we haven't gone into it yet, we should take a quick look at what UDF is and talk at the same time about how Java handles characters.

Early on, we briefly discussed the fact that Java uses the Unicode character set as its native character format. Now the Unicode character set is a pretty cool thing: a multinational character set supporting the basic characters of a host of languages. At this point there are something like 32,000 defined Unicode characters.

However, you don't fit 32,000 characters into the 8 bits we are used to dealing with for characters. This sounds like it could really spawn a nightmare, but in most cases it isn't a problem. The bottom end of the Unicode character set is the standard ASCII/Latin-1 encoding with which we are all familiar. And in almost every case Java will take care of the drudge work of dealing with converting any 8-bit character code that happens to be fed to it.

On the Windows 95 platform, however, this code manages to get into a situation that causes it to gack. Although Win95 supports Unicode (well, it doesn't support all the characters, but it deals with the 16-bit character codes without too much of a problem), when we are running in the DOS box console under Win95 and spitting things over a socket as strings somewhere, those extra bytes (which are all zeros since we are only giving it ASCII in the first place) are coming back to haunt us as blank characters in our output.

However, the people who came up with Unicode understood that some people in this world were going to get into situations where they absolutely, positively had to deal with just 8 bits. As a result they came up with Unicode Transformation Formats, and Java supports UTF in the DataInput and

DataOutput stream classes. If you start having problems with too many bits for your own good (and you know who you are) then start using the UTF read and write methods and you should see your problems vaporize.

What We Have Learned

We have covered a good bit of ground in this chapter, but unfortunately most of it was uniformly depressing. While it is not impossible by any means to implement multiplayer games in Java, things are much more complex than they need to be due to security restraints and broken code. For space reasons, we have offloaded the vast majority of our multiplayer gaming code and discussions to the Web support site where we can handle them in more depth.

However, we did outline some of the considerations we need to deal with in trying to hammer Java into a multiplayer environment, and we broke the majority of these discussions down into Applet and Application considerations.

Applets

When dealing with Applets and multiplayer gaming the problems we run into are of a security nature. Java won't allow you to do any file manipulation at all on the local machine, which is a big enough restriction, but worse than that, you don't have any ability to talk to anyone but the server. This means that you are going to have to create a host on the server that routes communications between Applets where you want it to go. And in many cases the only tools you are going to be able to rely on finding when you go to code on your server are Perl, CGI, and C.

Also by nature you are going to have to be creating forking processes, which should make you much beloved among sysops everywhere if you make a mistake.

Applications

Applications don't have the security restrictions of applets, but they lose easy sound support to make up for some of the difference. The rest of the slack on the inferiority scale is taken up by the fact that name lookup is broken in the current Java implementation, making it impossible for you to use raw IP addresses, the only data it is easy to get your hands on, as to get your games talking to each other.

However, the bright spot on the horizon is that this bug is fixed in the soon-to-be-released JDK 1.1.

Implementing Communications

All was not lost today, however. We did get to deal with the basics of creating sockets and hooking them up with datastreams to load and unload data from your programs.

The process is fairly painless: First you create an InetAddress object with the address you want to use for your communications; then you use the InetAddress to open a socket to your target; then you use the methods of socket to spawn input and output streams that will carry data to and from your application. Finally you use the methods in the streams (seeing a pattern here?) to actually transport your data—a seemingly long process, but not a complicated one—and Java has a large variety of various streams for almost any job.

• • • • • • •
Next Up

Next we are going to deal with the most exciting part of the book, in my humble opinion. In Chapter 9 we will tearing apart the Gamelet Toolkit, a set of utility structures that illustrate a number of great Java game-programming tricks as well as help to make your game-coding worlds quicker. So while it is a meaty and imposing chapter, it is probably the most rewarding also. So let's move on and see the power of Java objects really leveraged to their fullest in a game environment.

CHAPTER 9

• • • • • • •

ADVANCED TOPICS: THE GAMELET TOOLKIT

So far we have learned a lot about dealing with Java and making games. We have learned the most important parts of how to code in Java, some of the nastiness involved in trying to make networked games in Java, and have seen a couple of realistic examples of how to make working Java games. Now we are going to tackle a slightly bigger fish, a reusable games toolkit.

The Gamelet Toolkit

Think back to Chapter 7 and the Solitaire game we coded there. Poison Pair Solitaire isn't a particularly elaborate game, nor is the coding the perfect solution to the problem of making the game. However, it isn't a bad game at all for the type. There is playability, plenty of options, a hook in the form of the running money total, and in general the code does what it is supposed to.

But more important, Poison Pair makes a pretty good demonstration. It is complicated enough that it is an example that actually shows you some of what you are going to have to deal with in the real world, and it contains a big chunk of reusable code in the form of the Cards class.

This matter of reusable code is an important thing to remember when you are creating your code for your own games. In many cases you are going to be able to break down your objects in such a way that you will be able to reuse them a number of times in different games with little or no modification. Many programmers with a procedural background shoot themselves in the foot by not breaking down their object structure into reusable chunks where they can.

You should always be thinking about this. Every time you can take 10 percent more time to save yourself from having to recode something in the next game of the type you create, you should. As you continue your development in Java game programming you will end up with a rich set of personal tools that make each game you write easier and quicker to code than the last one due to legacy code that will be almost 100 percent reusable in your later efforts.

Right now we are going to look at a great example of this, the Gamelet Toolkit (GT), programmed by Mark Tacchi of Next. Where the AWT is Java's package to deal with creating windowing, Mark's Gamelet Toolkit is his package to deal with creating action games.

In order to learn how to work with the Toolkit we are going to look at each object Mark has created and then break them down to see how they operate together. After we have some kind of an understanding of what is going on, we will then look at an example that has been programmed in the Toolkit and see how to use these components to make games.

By now you are probably remembering my strong bias against action games in Java at the current state of development and thinking I have recanted. Well, I haven't, but that doesn't mean that Mark's great use of object orientation isn't instructive for a couple of reasons. First, as more advanced technology gets implemented in browsers the performance of Java applets improves, making these games a more practical option. Second, you might not want to use Mark's tools directly in the type of game you are creating, but seeing how he built the Gamelet Toolkit will show you how to make your own reusable code work together for the types of games you do want to build. Further, Mark has done some pretty neat things here and there, and even if you are just going to go as procedural as you can, and don't give a hoot about reusability at all, there are still some tricks in here you are going to want to steal for your own games.

MICROSOFT VERSUS NETSCAPE: THE BATTLE CONTINUES

If you are going to program in Java you better switch to Microsoft Explorer for browsing and should encourage the rest of the world to do so, now.

I am making this recommendation for sound technical reasons that have nothing to do with market position or monopolistic theory. The simple fact is that Netscape does not perform well when it comes to running Java applets on Wintel platforms.

At the time of this writing, Explorer and Navigator are both at Version 3.0. Running my personal benchmarks on both browsers has shown that Explorer runs Java applets about a third faster than Navigator and on some basic math stuff is over ten times quicker. Don't believe me? You should have enough Java knowledge at this point to write your own tests. Load and display a few images, draw a few basic shapes and do a few thousand math ops. Unless something is severely strange in your setup, you are going to find out that Explorer is markedly faster than Navigator.

I like Netscape quite a bit and am all for market diversity, but until they get a decent JIT applet viewer they don't deal with Java effectively. With Explorer you can get at least a functional speed for some action games that turn into unplayable beasts on Navigator. The example code with the Gamelet Toolkit we will see later in the chapter is a case in point. With Navigator on a P120 Wintel box the Boinkaroids example is pretty much useless. With Explorer it's a pretty fun game.

I am sure that Navigator will sooner or later toss the inept Borland applet viewer code they are running for Java viewing, but until that point Explorer is by far the best option for use with Java.

Overview

The Gamelet Toolkit appears at first glance to be a pretty complicated beast, and it *is* more complicated than anything we have worked with thus far. However, just as with anything else, when you tear it down one piece at a time it becomes fairly clear. We just need to work it carefully.

First, we need to understand exactly what the GT does, and at heart it is pretty simple. The GT manages animation, events, and time in a game. It does this by creating *ticks* at predetermined time intervals and sending these out to all the elements in the game. Every tick, the objects that make up the game stop and figure out where they are, what is going on in relation to them and how to deal with anything they need to do (such as die due to being hit by something else or display themselves in a new location). The GT also funnels events to the appropriate components so that they can deal with things such as key input and the like. The GT also handles screen display in a fairly logical way, making sure that all of your game elements are displayed on the screen properly and that they know if they are intersecting another displayed game element (getting hit by something, for example). Games created with the GT have a number of different components, but these components break down into two basic categories: actor stuff and manager stuff.

Actors are the basic unit of the games you will create. *Actors* are the visible, animated units of your game. Bullets, ships, and suchlike things are Actors. Actors are responsible for keeping track of most of their own display information, as well as their status info, such as their x and y position and velocity. You will probably want your Actors to handle much more information than just this, but these are the items included in the GT definition.

Managers are the various objects that are used to keep track of the status of the game. There are managers for keeping track of the Actors, managers to handle the display, managers for scores, and managers to pass off events such as keystrokes.

All of this is coordinated in the top-level object Gamelet. In the *Gamelet,* all of the managers are created and the main timing tick of the game is kept. Keeping track of timing and making sure that all of the elements of the game are coordinated through a single object is really the only purpose of the Gamelet object.

We are going to break down our study of the GT into two parts. First we are going to do a top-level overview of each of the objects in the GT and how they relate to each other; then we will cut apart the code for each object and look in detail at how they work under the hood. So let's take a quick look at all of the parts right now.

Actor

The major default job of the Actor is to keep track of its own image and its position. The Actor will get a graphics object given to it and be expected to draw itself into the graphics object at the right position. The actual screen display functions are going to be handled by the Display-Manager object, which is where the graphics object the Actor works with comes from.

In order to keep track of where they are on the screen, Actors have a number of functions to help them with positioning, including functions for wrapping around the screen and bouncing off of other Actors.

All Actors are registered with the ActorManager object which keeps track of the number of them for other objects that need to deal with the Actors and makes sure that each Actor is passed the tick from Gamelet.

ActorManager

The major function of the *ActorManager* is simply to know how many Actors are running around so that the rest of your objects can run through them all to perform checks, or draw them to the screen, or whatever. When an actor must be nixed, a request for removal is sent to the ActorManager and the next tick that Actor is removed.

The ActorManager also takes care of collision detection and sends notifications to the Actors involved that they have run into each other.

BonusHandler

The *BonusHandler* is simply an interface for those objects that need to deal with bonuses (such as extra men after the completion of a specified level). This interface is totally empty except for the didAchieveBonus method.

DirtyRectSet

DirtyRectSet is a very cool object that helps optimize screen display by taking Actors to be displayed that are close to each other on the screen and mushing them into one image to optimize *blitting* images to the screen. This is used by the DisplayManager object.

DisplayManager

The *DisplayManager* is probably the most critical manager in the GT. This object takes care of making sure that everything is drawn to the screen as rapidly as possible on each tick.

The DisplayManager represents a pretty good display algorithm for any Java game, and you probably want to steal liberally from the techniques used here. Not only are double buffering and update overriding used here, but DirtyRectSet is used to optimize screen blitting and an optimized background display is also provided.

The DisplayManager is initiated by the Gamelet object and uses the ActorManager to run through each Actor object to paint it to the screen.

EventHandler

EventHandler is a simple interface that implements a single method: handleRequestedEvent. These events are passed on from the *EventManager*.

Gamelet

The *Gamelet* is the center of your game applet. The Gamelet has two major jobs. First, it creates the main managers your game is going to need (ActorManager, DisplayManager, ScoreManager and EventManager). Second, it keeps track of time. The Gamelet is where the master tick is generated that will filter down through all of the other objects in your game and make sure that clock cycles are there to create dynamic change in your game.

ImageManager

The *ImageManager* object allows you to load entire groups of images into your game for use at one time and in an automated way. Using the Image-Manager you can implement an automatic image-loading system controlled by an external text file listing the images you want loaded. This makes it much easier to get all your images into the game.

ScoreManager

The *ScoreManager,* pretty self-evidently, handles scoring issues. The Score-Manager keeps track of bonuses and then notifies individual objects when a bonus is achieved.

TiledImage

TiledImage is a very simple class that uses a smaller image to create a larger image that can be used as a background. The DisplayManager takes advantage of the TiledImage class. We will see examples later of using TiledImage to create a star field for a background from a small sample of a star field.

The Coordinated View

The interaction of the classes above creates your working game with the GT. Let's take a moment and look at the coordination of these elements in the abstract and how they link together to create a game.

On the top level you have your Gamelet. The first thing your Gamelet is going to do in the real world is instantiate an ImageManager that will load all of the images used for your game. After you have all of the images loaded, an ActorManager will be created and your individual actors created and added to this manager for cataloging.

Somewhere in here you will instantiate your ScoreManager and tell it what the bonus level is and who to notify if bonus is reached. In most cases you will want the notification to return to the Gamelet to be dealt with.

The Gamelet will also instantiate a DisplayManager and give it the background it should use.

Finally, your Gamelet will instantiate an EventManager and register for the system events it needs to know about in order to make the game work. These will normally be mouseUp, mouseDown, or various key events.

During the course of the game, your Actors will get a tick and any events they are registered for from the ActorManager. By processing their last positions and seeing if any events (such as a command key being depressed) have changed their course, they will recalculate their positions. At the same time, they will change their animation images if appropriate to the next image in their animation sequence.

Then the DisplayManager will go through each Actor (again, by using the ActorManager to request individual Actors) and using DirtyRectSet and other nifty tricks will paint them all to the screen in their proper positions.

This process will essentially continue until the ending conditions of the game have been met. As we will see when we step through a working example of a game created with the GT, there is a lot more to making a working game than this. However, understand that all the GT is doing is roughly what is outlined above: using managers to process events and make sure that display is pulled off correctly.

The Objects

Now with something of a high-level understanding of the GT, let's look at the code for each of the GT's objects and tear them down.

Actor

```
/**
*
* Actor.java
* @author Mark G. Tacchi (mtacchi@next.com)
* @version 0.8
* Feb 23/1996
* Actor is an abstract superclass which defines behavior used in the
Actors the developer creates.
* Actors are responsible for calculating their positions each tick.
They are also handed a <em>g</em> and expected to draw themselves into
it.
*/

package com.next.gt;

import java.util.Date;
import java.awt.Image;
import java.awt.Graphics;
import java.awt.Rectangle;
import java.applet.Applet;
import java.lang.Math;
import com.next.gt.Gamelet;

public abstract class Actor extends java.lang.Object {

  //
  // Image and animation variables.
  //
  protected Image image;
  protected int    numFrames;
  public int       width;
  public int       height;
  public int       currentFrame;
  protected int    hFrames;

  //
  // Position and velocity.
  //
  public double    x, y;
  public double    x_old, y_old;
  public double    velocity_x, velocity_y;

  //
  // The object that owns the Actor.
  //
  public Gamelet   owner;

  //
  // Flag indicating whether Actor should wrap at
  // edgeofscreen.
```

```java
 public boolean wrapAround;

public Actor() {
  currentFrame= 0;
  wrapAround= true;
}
/*Actor()*/

/**
 * Change animation frame, calculate new position, and calculate new
velocity..
 */
public void tick() {
  calculateCurrentFrame();
  calculateNewPosition();
  calculateNewVelocity();
} /*tick*/

/**
 * Set the image used for animation.
 */
protected void setImage (Image theImage,
                         int frameXSize,
                         int frameYSize,
                         int framesHorizontally,
                         int totalFrames)
{
  width= frameXSize;
  height= frameYSize;
  numFrames= totalFrames;
  hFrames= framesHorizontally;
  image= theImage;

} /*setImage(,,,,,)*/

/**
 * Set the image used for animation. Good for an image that has all
frames within it and none empty.
 */
protected void setImage (Image theImage)
{
  int imageHeight;
  int imageWidth;

  do {
    imageHeight= theImage.getHeight (owner);
  } while (imageHeight == -1);
do {
    imageWidth= theImage.getWidth (owner);
  } while (imageWidth == -1);
```

```
  setImage (theImage, imageWidth, imageHeight, 1, 1);
}
/*setImage*/


/**
 * Set the image used for animation. Good for an image that has some
empty frames within it.
 */
protected void setImage (Image theImage,
                         int horizontalFrames,
                         int totalFrames)
{
  int imageHeight;
  int imageWidth;

  do {
    imageHeight= theImage.getHeight (owner);
  } while (imageHeight == -1);
  do {
    imageWidth= theImage.getWidth (owner);
  } while (imageWidth == -1);
  setImage (theImage, imageWidth/horizontalFrames,
            imageHeight / (int)Math.ceil((double)
totalFrames /(double)horizontalFrames),
            horizontalFrames,
              totalFrames
            );
}
/*setImage,,,*/


/**
 * Calculates the new X and Y position based on velocity and time. Also
may check if Actor needs to wrap around at the edges if the
<em>wraparound</em> flag is set.
 */
protected void calculateNewPosition() {

  double   deltaTime= owner.deltaTickTimeMillis()/1000.0;

  //
  // save old position
  //
  x_old= x;
  y_old= y;

  //
  // calculate position based on velocity and time
  //
  x+= velocity_x*deltaTime;
  y+= velocity_y*deltaTime;
```

```
   if (wrapAround) checkForOutOfBounds();
} /*calculateNewPosition*/


/**
 * Override this to provide your own behaviour.
 */
protected void calculateNewVelocity() {
}


/**
 * Calculates the current frame. Behaviour is to flip through frames
sequentially and loop.
 */
protected void calculateCurrentFrame() {
  if (++currentFrame>=numFrames) currentFrame= 0;
} /*calculateCurrentFrame*/


/**
 * Check for out of bounds and wrap if it is.
 */
protected void checkForOutOfBounds() {

  //
  // check for out of bounds and wrap
  //
  if (x > (owner.size().width + width)) {
    x= -width;
  }
  else if (x < -width) {
    x= owner.size().width + width;
  }
  if (y > (owner.size().height + height)) {
    y= -height;

  }
  else if (y < -height) {
    y= owner.size().height + height;
  }


} /*checkForOutOfBounds*/

/**
 * Each Actor is handed a <em>g</em> and is expected to draw itself in
it.
 */
public void draw (Graphics g)
{
  double    offsetx= -(currentFrame%hFrames)*width;
  double    offsety= -Math.floor(currentFrame/hFrames) *
            height;
```

```
  Graphics  g2= g.create ((int)x, (int)y, width, height);
  g2.drawImage(image, (int)offsetx, (int)offsety, owner);
  g2.dispose ();


}
/*draw*/


/**
 * Override this method to handle the case when Actor collides with
another.
 */
protected void collideWithActor (Actor theActor) {
} /*collideWithActor*/


/**
 * Bounce off the specified Actor. Changes it's velocity so that it
appears to bounce off.
 */
public void bounceOff(Actor theActor) {
  double         myCenterX= width/2 + x_old, myCenterY= height/2 +
y_old;
  double         actorCenterX= theActor.width/2 + theActor.x;
  double         actorCenterY= theActor.height/2 + theActor.y;
  double    slope= (myCenterY - actorCenterY)/(myCenterX -
      actorCenterX);
  double         b= myCenterY - slope*myCenterX;

  double         intersectY, intersectX;

  //
  // Check if segments intersect.
  //


  //
  // Check RIGHT side
  //
  if (theActor.x>=myCenterX) {
    intersectY= slope*theActor.x + b;
    if (intersectY>=theActor.y && intersectY <= theActor.y          +
theActor.height) {
      velocity_x= theActor.velocity_x - velocity_x;
      x= x_old;
    } /*endif*/
  }
  //
  // Check LEFT side
  //
  else if (theActor.x+theActor.width<=myCenterX) {
    intersectY= slope*(theActor.x + theActor.width) + b;
    if (intersectY>=theActor.y && intersectY <= theActor.y +
```

```
theActor.height) {
        velocity_x= theActor.velocity_x - velocity_x;
        x= x_old;
    } /*endif*/
 }


    //
    // Check BOTTOM side
    //
    else if (theActor.y>=myCenterY) {
       intersectX= (theActor.y - b)/slope;
       if (intersectX>=theActor.x && intersectX <= theActor.x +
theActor.width) {
          velocity_y= theActor.velocity_y - velocity_y;
          y= y_old;
       } /*endif*/
    }
    //
    // Check TOP side
    //
    else if (theActor.y+theActor.height<=myCenterY) {
       intersectX= (theActor.y + theActor.height - b)/slope;
       if (intersectX>=theActor.x && intersectX <= theActor.x +
theActor.width) {
          velocity_y= theActor.velocity_y - velocity_y;
          y= y_old;
       } /*endif*/
    }

} /*bounceOff*/

} /*BOActor*/
```

The first place real work starts getting done in this code is with the tick method. Here we can see a brief idea of the work we are going to be getting done in Actor. The ticks, originating with the Gamelet object and being distributed to the various code modules through the managers is the heartbeat of the game. With each tick, this object is going to be responsible for finding its current animation frame, calculating its position, and finding out its own velocity.

After this we see three polymorphic definitions for *setImage.* In order to understand what this code is doing, you need to understand how the GT handles animation.

Instead of having a zillion little files to handle all of the animations required for the game, the GT handles animation for Actors as single graphics files with a number of frames inside them butting up against each other. Examine Figure 9.1 to see what an animation file looks like.

You can create this graphic file in any standard paint program by simply pasting the different images side by side so that your images become much easier to work with while coding.

However, obviously, it requires a bit more work to deal with finding and pulling out the frame you want when you are working with images stored in this format. Instead of just telling Java to throw up gif1 then gif2 and so on, you now need to cut the particular frame of animation you need out of the master graphic file. Although this isn't all that onerous a task, it does require a bit more information than just throwing up a full file. You will need to know how big each frame is within your master file in order to be able to cut it out. You will need to know how many frames are stacked horizontally and vertically to see how to pull out a specific image in the sequence. And, of course, you are going to need to know what file to pull all of this out of in the first place.

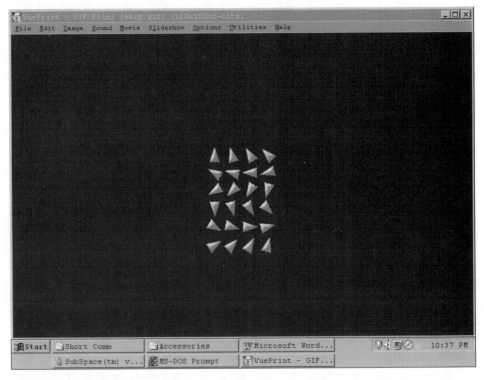

Figure 9.1   Ship animation graphic file.

Getting the file you need is going to be done in the actual code you use that inherits from Actor. You will pull the graphics file, put it in an Image, and then implement it by calling the setImage method with the Image as an argument.

Knowing this, the three setImage methods are pretty straightforward. They are simply methods of setting the proper image to be used for the animations and setting the frame information that is going to be required when actually drawing the image. setImage and draw will be working in conjunction on this.

In general, you will probably find yourself using the setImage(Image) method. For instance, where you don't actually have any animation, but just a single cell in your master graphics file, you will be using the setImage(Image, int, int) method in most other cases, since the latter method quickly calculates your width and height requirements that are going to be needed by the draw method for you.

The *calculateNewPosition* method needs no explanation but it is helpful to know that the *deltaTickTimeMillis* method of the Gamelet class returns the number of milliseconds since the last tick.

calculateNewVelocity is how you determine the movement characteristics for your Actor. You will be creating this from scratch from actor to actor.

calculateCurrentFrame is self-evident; however, you will often be overriding this method in your Actors to prevent the default behavior. A good example we will see before the end of the chapter is with the Ship class used in the Boinkaroids example game. Often we will want to pick our particular frame of animation with great care based on some action the actor is taking at the time. *checkForOutOfBounds* is obvious; however, we should briefly examine the draw method.

draw is the other half of the setImage equation for determining what image to pass on to the rest of the world from our Actor at any given time. The graphics context it is being passed is from the DisplayManager and points to an offscreen buffer Image. The first thing this short method does is to determine the offset to use inside the animation image file to be set to draw the right frame. This is the information it got from setImage. Next we create a new graphics context.

This might seem a little bit confusing if you have forgotten about clipping and how it works from when we covered it back at the tail end of Chapter 6. When you create a new graphics object it acts as a window into the current graphics context you are working in. In this case, we have been passed a graphics context that is drawing to an offscreen buffer Image. So our new g2 Graphics is also drawing to that same image; however, it is only opening up to a window exactly as wide and tall as our Actor and located at the x and y position where our Actor has last reported itself. This smaller window speeds up the amount of time it is going to take to draw our Actor to the Image.

In the actual *drawImage* line we are using the *offsetx* and *offsety* to pick the right frame out of our master animation graphic file to output to our little clipped graphics window. Then we get rid of the g2 once it has served its purpose.

If you are having any problems with tracking what is happening here, go back to the API docs and look over each call and then trace back between this code segment and the DisplayManager to get a firm grasp of what is happening. This use of clipping and drawing to offscreen buffers is a very important thing to have down cold due to Java's inherent sluggishness as an interpreted language and you want to get very familiar with using the optimized display techniques Tacchi is using here in order to make your own games flow as smoothly as possible.

Finally, we have *collideWithActor* and *bounceOff,* methods which simply determine how your Actor will handle collision with other Actors when the two intersect. You will always override collideWithActor to have your own behavior implemented here and will normally use bounceOff as it is. bounceOff is somewhat long, but is just a simple math trick that is easy to trace through.

ActorManager

```
/**
 *
 * ActorManager.java
 * @author Mark G. Tacchi (mtacchi@next.com)
 * @version 0.8
 * Mar 27/1996
 *
 * ActorManager maintains a list of all actors which are participating
 in the game. Actors may be added or removed from this list by
 requesting a change in the list. When it is safe to make changes to the
 list, ActorManager will do so.
 *
 * Collision detection is performed in ActorManager. If Actors
 collide,a message is sent to each Actor indicating which Actor it has
 collided with.
 *
```

```
 * Queries can be made to ActorManager to determine whether an Actor is
in a specific location.
*/


package com.next.gt;

import java.util.Vector;
import java.awt.Rectangle;

public class ActorManager extends java.lang.Object {

  //
  // A reference back to the Gamelet this manager is
  // servicing.
  //
  protected Gamelet owner;


  //
  // The list of actors currently alive.
  //
  public Vector actors= new Vector();


  //
  // The list of actors that will be removed or added when
  // the current heartbeat is over.
  //
  private Vector actorsScheduledForRemoval= new Vector();
  private Vector actorsScheduledForInsertion= new Vector();

  private boolean removeAllActors= false;

public ActorManager(Gamelet theOwner) {
  owner= theOwner;
}


/**
 * The Actor is added to a list of Actors to be added.
 */
public void addActor (Actor theActor)
{
 actorsScheduledForInsertion.addElement (theActor);
}
/*addActor*/

/**
 * The Actor is added to a list of Actors to be removed.
 */
public void removeActor (Actor theActor)
{
 actorsScheduledForRemoval.addElement (theActor);
}
```

```
public void removeActor (Actor theActor)
{
 actorsScheduledForRemoval.addElement (theActor);
}
/*removeActor*/


/**
 * Dump all references to Actors. This is used when a game is
restarted.
 */
public void removeAllActors ()
{
  //
  // give eventManager a chance to clean up
  //
  for (int i= 0; i< actors.size(); i++) {
    owner.eventManager.removeFromNotificationRegistry
      (actors.elementAt (i));
  } /*next_i*/


  //
  // destroy pending lists
  //
  actorsScheduledForRemoval.removeAllElements ();
  actorsScheduledForInsertion.removeAllElements ();


  //
  // destroy all actors
  //
  actors.removeAllElements ();


}
/*removeAllActors*/


/**
 * Test if there is an actor at a specified position.
 */
public boolean isActorAt(double theX, double theY) {
  boolean returnValue= false;

  for (int i= 0; i < actors.size(); i++)
    {
    Actor anActor= (Actor)actors.elementAt(i);

    if (theX >= anActor.x) {
      if ((theX <= (anActor.x + anActor.width)) &&
          (theY >= anActor.y) &&
            (theY <= (anActor.y+anActor.height))) {
        returnValue= true;
      }
```

```
/*endif*/
    }
    else
{
      break;
    }
  }
/*next_i*/


  return returnValue;
} /*isActorAt*/


/**
 * Test if there is an actor within a specified Rectangle.
 */
public boolean isActorIn(Rectangle theRectangle) {
  boolean returnValue= false;
  double maxxj= theRectangle.x + theRectangle.width;

  for (int i= 0; i < actors.size(); i++)
      {
    Actor anActor= (Actor)actors.elementAt(i);

    if (maxxj >= anActor.x)
      {
      if (theRectangle.y <= anActor.y)
          {
        if (theRectangle.y + theRectangle.height > anActor.y)
          returnValue= true;
      }
      else
{
        if (anActor.y + anActor.height > theRectangle.y)
          returnValue= true;
      }
    }
    else
{
      break;
    }
  }
/*next_i*/


  return returnValue;
} /*isActorIn*/
/**
 * Insertion sort is used to prep Actors for collision detection. This
technique is ideal because actors are almost always already sorted.
 */
private final void sortActorsByXCoordinate()
```

```
{
  int i, j;
  int size= actors.size();

  for (j= 1; j < size; j++)
  {
    Actor aj= (Actor)actors.elementAt(j);

    for (i= j-1; i>=0; i--)
    {
      Actor ai= (Actor)actors.elementAt(i);

      if (aj.x < ai.x)
          actors.setElementAt (ai, i+1);
      else
          break;
    }
/*next_i*/

    if (j != i+1)
      actors.setElementAt (aj, i+1);
  }
/*next_j*/
}
/*sortActorsByXCoordinate*/

/*
 * Perform collision detection based on rectangles. Future versions
will detect against circles, and polygons.
 */
private final void detectCollision ()
{
  int i, j;
  int size= actors.size();

  for (j= 0; j+1 < size; j++)
  {
    Actor aj= (Actor)actors.elementAt(j);
    double maxxj= aj.x + aj.width;

    for (i= j+1; i < size; i++)
    {
      Actor ai = (Actor)actors.elementAt(i);

      if (maxxj >= ai.x)
      {
        if (aj.y <= ai.y)
        {
          if (aj.y + aj.height > ai.y)
            handleBBCollision (aj, ai);
        }
```

```
        else
{
          if (ai.y + ai.height > aj.y)
            handleBBCollision (aj, ai);
        }
      }
      else
{ .
        break;
      }


    }
/*next_i*/
  }
/*next_j*/


}
/*detectCollision*/


/**
 * Tell each Actor that they've collided with each other.
 */
protected void handleBBCollision (Actor a1, Actor a2)
{
 a1.collideWithActor (a2);
 a2.collideWithActor (a1);
}
/*handleBBCollision*/


/**
 * Add/delete Actors, send current Actors a tick message, and then perform
   collision detection.
 */
public void tick() {

  //
  // add all actors which were scheduled for addtion
  //
  if (actorsScheduledForInsertion.size() > 0) {
    for (int i= 0; i < actorsScheduledForInsertion.size();
      i++) {
      actors.addElement
          (actorsScheduledForInsertion.elementAt (i));
    } /*next_i*/
    actorsScheduledForInsertion.removeAllElements ();
  } /*endif*/


  //
  // remove all actors which were scheduled for removal
  //
```

```
if (actorsScheduledForRemoval.size() > 0) {
    for (int i= 0; i < actorsScheduledForRemoval.size();
    i++) {
        owner.eventManager.removeFromNotificationRegistry
    (actorsScheduledForRemoval.elementAt (i));
        actors.removeElement
    (actorsScheduledForRemoval.elementAt (i));
    } /*next_i*/
  actorsScheduledForRemoval.removeAllElements ();
} /*endif*/


//
// send a tick to each actor
//
for (int i= 0; i< actors.size (); i++) {
    ((Actor)actors.elementAt(i)).tick();


} /*next_i*/


//
// perform collision detection
//
sortActorsByXCoordinate ();
detectCollision();


} /*tick*/
} /*ActorManager*/
```

The function of the ActorManager is very easy. All it does is pass ticks on from the Gamelet to the Actors, keep track of what Actors currently exist in a vector, add to or remove from the tracking vector as Actors enter or leave the game, and check to see if any actors have bumped into each other and notify them if they did.

The only thing you need to know to trace through this code is that eventManager and NotificationRegistry references deal with the EventManager object we will be seeing in a few pages. This object helps keeps track of which system events (such as keyboard strokes) need to be passed to particular Actors so that they may act on them. Thus, when an Actor is removed from the game, the ActorManager makes sure that the EventManager knows it no longer needs to worry about getting information to the dead Actors.

BonusHandler

```
/**
 * BonusHandler.java
 * @author Mark G. Tacchi (mtacchi@next.com)
 * @version 0.8
 * Mar 15/1996
 *
 * An interface. The object which requires notification for bonuses
should implement this.
 */

package com.next.gt;

public interface BonusHandler {
void didAchieveBonus ();
} /*BonusHandler*/
```

DirtyRectSet and DisplayManager

```
/**
 * DirtyRectSet.java
 * Mar 15/1996
 */

package com.next.gt;

import java.util.Vector;
import java.awt.Rectangle;

public class DirtyRectSet extends java.lang.Object {

    private Vector rects;

    public DirtyRectSet() { rects = new Vector(); }
    public DirtyRectSet(int i) { rects = new Vector(i); }

    public void addRect (Rectangle r)
    {
            int size = rects.size ();

            for (int index = 0; index < size; index++)
            {
                    Rectangle curr = (Rectangle)rects.elementAt
                                (index);

                    if (r.x > curr.x)
                    {
```

```
                              rects.insertElementAt (r, index);
                              return;
                 }
         }

         rects.addElement (r);

}

final int GLUE = 64;

final private boolean closeEnough (Rectangle r1,
                              Rectangle r2)

{
    boolean result;

  r1.width += GLUE;
    r1.height += GLUE;
    r2.width += GLUE;
    r2.height += GLUE;

    result = r1.intersects (r2);

  r1.width -= GLUE;
    r1.height -= GLUE;
    r2.width -= GLUE;
    r2.height -= GLUE;

    return result;
}

private void collapse ()
{
        int index = 0;

        if (rects.size () < 2)
             return;

        Rectangle r1 = (Rectangle)rects.elementAt (index);
        Rectangle r2 = (Rectangle)rects.elementAt
                   (index+1);

        while (true)
        {
             // collapse R1 and R2
             if (closeEnough (r1, r2))
```

```
                     {
                              r1 = r1.union (r2);

                              rects.setElementAt (r1, index);
                              rects.removeElementAt (index+1);

                              if (index+1 < rects.size ())
                                   r2 = (Rectangle)rects.elementAt
                                   (index+1);
                              else
                                   return;
                     }

                     // go to next pair
                     else if (index+2 < rects.size ())
                     {
                              r1 = r2;
                              r2 = (Rectangle)rects.elementAt
                              (index+2);
                              index += 1;
                     }

                     // done
                     else
                     {
                              return;
                     }
              }
       }

       public void drawImage (java.awt.Graphics g,
       java.awt.Image img, java.applet.Applet owner)
       {
              collapse ();

       for (int i= 0; i< rects.size (); i++) {
              Rectangle r =
                     (Rectangle)rects.elementAt(i);
                     java.awt.Graphics      g2    = g.create (r.x,
                                     r.y, r.width, r.height);
                     g2.drawImage(img, -r.x, -r.y, owner);
                     g2.dispose ();

                     // g.drawRect (r.x+1, r.y+1, r.width-2,
                              r.height-2);
       }
       }
} /*DirtyRectSet*/
```

```
/**
 *
 * DisplayManager.java
 * @author Mark G. Tacchi (mtacchi@next.com)
 * @version 0.8
 * Mar 28/1996
 *
 * DisplayManager provides optimized screen display. Images are drawn to
an offscreen buffer and blitted out to the display. If images are close
to one another, they are coalesced and blitted as a single image.
 *
 * A read only cache is kept which represents an untainted background
image. This is used in the optimization algorithm as a source for a
clean background.
 */

package com.next.gt;

import java.awt.Rectangle;
import java.awt.Graphics;
import java.awt.Image;
import java.awt.MediaTracker;
public class DisplayManager extends java.lang.Object {
  private Image            background;
  private Image         offScreenBuffer;
  private DirtyRectSet dirtyRects= new DirtyRectSet();

  /**
   * A reference back to the gamelet this manager is servicing.
   */
  protected Gamelet owner;

public DisplayManager(Gamelet theOwner) {
  owner= theOwner;
} /*DisplayManager()*/

/**
 * Refresh screen.
 */
public void refresh ()
{
  dirtyRects.addRect (new Rectangle (0, 0,
          owner.size().width, owner.size().height));
} /*setBackground*/

/**
 * Set the background image to the specified image.
 */
public void setBackground (Image theImage)
```

```
{
  MediaTracker tracker= new java.awt.MediaTracker(owner);

  tracker.addImage(theImage, 0);
  try
{
      tracker.waitForID(0);
  } catch (InterruptedException e) {
  }

  background= theImage;
  offScreenBuffer= owner.createImage (owner.size().width,
                                owner.size().height);
  offScreenBuffer.getGraphics().drawImage (theImage, 0, 0,
                                  owner);

  dirtyRects.addRect (new Rectangle (0, 0,
          owner.size().width, owner.size().height));

}
/*setBackground*/

/**
 * Tile the background with the specifed tile image.
 */
public void setBackgroundTile (Image theImage)
{
  MediaTracker     tracker= new java.awt.MediaTracker(owner);

  tracker.addImage(theImage, 0);
  try
{
      tracker.waitForID(0);
  } catch (InterruptedException e) {}

  setBackground(TiledImage.createTiledImage(theImage,
      owner.size().width, owner.size().height, owner));
}
/*setBackgroundTile*/

/**
 * Display changed portions of screen.
 */
public void paint(Graphics g) {
  DirtyRectSet flushRects;
  Graphics osb= offScreenBuffer.getGraphics ();

  //
  // clear background behind actors...
```

```
    //
    dirtyRects.drawImage (osb, background, owner);

    flushRects= dirtyRects;
    dirtyRects= new
            DirtyRectSet(owner.actorManager.actors.size ());

    //
    // draw actors
    //
    for (int j= 0; j< owner.actorManager.actors.size (); j++) {
      Actor anActor=
            (Actor)owner.actorManager.actors.elementAt(j);
      Rectangle r= new Rectangle ((int)anActor.x,
        (int)anActor.y, anActor.width, anActor.height);
      dirtyRects.addRect (r);
      flushRects.addRect (r);
      anActor.draw (osb);
    }
/*next_j*/

    flushRects.drawImage (g, offScreenBuffer, owner);

} /*paint*/
} /*DisplayManager*/
```

DisplayManager and the helper class DirtyRectSet are an excellent example of optimized graphics programming in Java. The purpose of Display-Manager is simple: output all of the Actors to the screen each tick in order to create the graphics for our game.

We have already seen optimized display strategies used in the clipping routine that Actor's draw method implements and DisplayManager will call those routines. But the really neat part here is the combination of Display-Manager's use of an offscreen buffer in conjunction with DirtyRectSet to only paint those parts of the image that have changed, and further to coalesce different Actor images that are close to each other to blit them out to the screen as a single image and save time.

To understand what is going on here, we have to look at DisplayManager and DirtyRectSet together. What is going on in most of DisplayManager is pretty obvious, but we do want to concentrate on the core code trick here, which is located in the paint method.

Paint method calls in the overall Applet are going to get passed on down the line to the DisplayManager to handle. Thus, the paint method we are seeing here is going to be the actual display code for the entire game.

First the paint method creates a DirtyRectSet object called *flushRects* and then opens up a Graphics context to the offscreen buffer image initialized earlier in the DisplayManager called—in a burst of originality—*offScreen-Buffer.*

The method then uses the dirtyRects object to paint our background where our Actors were last time. Now the first time this is used we will have called the setBackground method to create and load our background image and dirtyRects will simply fill offScreenBuffer with the background image. But for the majority of the life of the Applet, there is going to be a list of the Actors drawn the previous tick living in the dirtyRects object. To see what this call is going to do, we will need to jump to DirtyRectSet.

If you glance through the code of DirtyRectSet it is pretty easy to trace what the majority of the object is doing. We have a group of methods that allow us to add rectangles to a vector, sorted by their x value. When two rectangles are within a glue value of each other (64 pixels) we can use the collapse method to create one larger rectangle in place of the two smaller ones.

This doesn't seem to have much a point, except for one fact: All of the rectangles we are creating have the precise values of a specific Actor. They are at the same x and y values the Actor is at, and they have the same width and height dimensions. This allows us to use the vector of Rectangles to open clipped drawing windows to blit our actors out to the screen.

This trick is actually accomplished in the drawImage function. Here we hand the DirtyRectSet object a Graphics object and an Image object and it will open clipping windows into Graphics context and draw selected rectangles from the Image into these clipped Graphics contexts.

The only thing in here that might be confusing is the use of the negative values in the g2.drawImage() argument list. What is happening here is that drawImage is working with two images that are as big as the total display area of the game. The first is represented by the graphics context we are handed as an argument to drawImage, the other is the Image we are getting handed. Think of these as two screens of the exact same size. We are opening little windows in the g screen and drawing a selected section of the Image screen into the hole.

The hole we are opening in the g screen is located where we want our picture to be displayed and it is exactly as big as the picture we are going to be moving from our Image screen. If the setting is 0,0 then the upper lefthand corner of our Image screen is going to line up with the upper lefthand corner of the *window* we have cut in the g screen. If this hole is 10 by 10, we would get the first 10 x and 10 y pixels off the Image screen inserted into our g screen where we cut the window.

But what we want to display is much more likely to be a 10 x by 10 y pixel block that falls in the middle of our Image screen. The negative offset has the effect of moving the underlying Image our hole is looking at so that we get the right part of the Image moved to the graphic.

If you are still having problems envisioning this (it took me a while to get comfortable with this) think of cutting a small square out of one piece of paper and putting another piece of paper under it. The paper with the small square cut out of it is the graphic screen we are drawing to and the paper under it is the Image.

Now that we understand what is going on with the DirtyRectSet we can go back to the paint method in DisplayManager and see that the dirty-Rects.drawImage call is going to paint the background over any Actors we defined last tick in the offScreenBuffer.

Then we put all of our Actors into a new DirtyRectSet called flushRects and have them draw themselves to the offscreen buffer. Finally we use the drawImage function of flushRects to paint the sections of our offScreen-Buffer that have changed since the last tick to the display.

This use of rectangle vectors for clipping and displaying offscreen buffers is pretty clever and you will probably want to adapt something like this to your own code when graphics speed is paramount.

EventHandler and EventManager

```
/**
 * EventHandler.java
 * @author Mark G. Tacchi (mtacchi@next.com)
 * @version 0.8
 * Mar 21/1996
 *
 * The objects which require notification for events should implement
this.
 */


package com.next.gt;


import java.awt.Event;
public interface EventHandler {
public boolean handleRequestedEvent(Event theEvent);
} /*EventHandler*/
```

```
/**
 * EventManager.java
 * @author Mark G. Tacchi (mtacchi@next.com)
 * @version 0.8
 * Mar 21/1996
 *
 * EventManager maintains a list of objects that require notification
when a particular Event occurs. Objects register with a specific Event
or a list of Events that it would like notification on.
 *
*/

package com.next.gt;

import java.util.Vector;
import java.awt.Event;

public class EventManager extends java.lang.Object {
  protected Vector                objectsToNotify;

public EventManager() {
  objectsToNotify= new Vector();
} /*EventManager()*/

/**
 * Register for notification of an event with a Vector of events.
 */
public void registerForEventNotification (Object theObject, int[]
theEventVector) {
  int       theEventID;

  for (int i= 0; i < theEventVector.length; i ++) {
    Vector        registerVector= new Vector(2);

    theEventID= theEventVector[i];
      // the object to notify
    registerVector.addElement(theObject);
      // theEventID
    registerVector.addElement(new Integer(theEventID));
    objectsToNotify.addElement(registerVector);

  } /*nexti*/

} /*registerForBonusNotification*/

/**
 * Register for a single notification of an event.
 */
```

```
public void registerForSingleEventNotification (Object
                        theObject, int theEventID) {
  Vector    registerVector= new Vector(2);
  // the object to notify
  registerVector.addElement(theObject);
  // theEventID
  registerVector.addElement(new Integer(theEventID));

  objectsToNotify.addElement(registerVector);
} /*registerForBonusNotification*/

/**
 * Remove object from notification registry.
 */
public void removeFromNotificationRegistry(Object theObject) {
  Vector    anObject;

  for (int i= 0; i<objectsToNotify.size(); i++) {
    anObject= (Vector) objectsToNotify.elementAt(i);
    if (anObject.contains(theObject)) {
        objectsToNotify.removeElementAt(i);
      } /*endif*/

  } /*nexti*/

} /*removeFromNotificationRegistry*/

/**
 * Handle the event by notifying registered objects.
 *
 */
public boolean handleEvent (Event theEvent) {
  Vector    anObject;
  Integer   n1;
  Integer   anInteger;
  boolean   returnValue= false;

  for (int i= 0; i<objectsToNotify.size(); i++) {
    anObject= (Vector) objectsToNotify.elementAt(i);

    n1= (Integer) anObject.elementAt(1);

    if(theEvent.id==n1.intValue()) {
      EventHandler      theEventHandler= (EventHandler)
                                    anObject.elementAt(0);

      returnValue=
          theEventHandler.handleRequestedEvent(theEvent);
      } /*endif*/
```

```
  } /*nexti*/
  return returnValue;

} /*handleEvent*/
} /*EventManager*/
```

Nothing here is all that complicated. Any game element that we wish to handle events should implement the EventHandler interface, which insures the EventManager that any object being passed an event will have a routine for dealing with it.

The EventManager itself just keeps track of what objects want notification of something and what they want notification of. This is accomplished by creating a two-dimensional vector with the object for notification and the event id or ids it is waiting for. When an event is passed to it from Gamelet, the EM runs through the vector searching for the event id and if it finds it, then it notifies the associated object.

Note that events are denoted by integers. Though we use event constants such as KEY_DOWN to mark off our events when we are coding, underneath each event is an integer that denotes what kind of event it is. If you are feeling rusty on event notification you might want to look up the Event object in the API docs and make sure you are pretty strong on events for the simple reason that they are critical to your games. The Event object is one of those things you are going to be using constantly as you program games in Java.

Gamelet

```
/**
 * Gamelet.java
 * @author Mark G. Tacchi (mtacchi@next.com)
 * @version 0.8
 * Mar 27/1996
 *
 * Gamelet contains a thread which is used for distributing ticks to all
manager objects. A tick is basically an instant in time and represents
the time granularity of the game.
 */

package com.next.gt;

import java.util.Date;
import java.util.Vector;
import java.awt.Graphics;
import java.awt.Event;
```

```
abstract public class Gamelet extends java.applet.Applet
                              implements Runnable {

  //
  // This is the main thread, used for ticks.
  //
  public Thread runner= null;
  public Thread runner= null;


  //
  // Gamelet is the master time keeper.
  //
  public long currentTickTimeMillis=
                              System.currentTimeMillis();
  public long lastTickTimeMillis;


  //
  // Gamelet is the manager of the managers.
  //
  public ActorManager actorManager= new ActorManager(this);
  public DisplayManager displayManager= new
                                   DisplayManager(this);
  public ScoreManager scoreManager;
  public EventManager eventManager= new EventManager();


  //
  // Sleep time for the thread.
  //

  public int                    SLEEP_MILLIS= 50;

/**
 * Generate a random double between two doubles.
 */
public static double randBetween(double a, double b)
                                                     {
  double val, scale, tmp;

  if (a > b) {

    tmp= a;  a= b;  b= tmp;
  } /*endif*/

  scale = (b-a);
  val = scale * Math.random();

  return (a + val);

} /*randBetween*/
```

```
/**
 * Initialize.
 */
public void init() {
} /*init*/


/**
 * Start the thread.
 */
public void start() {
  if(runner==null) { //start new thread if it doesn't exist
    runner= new Thread(this);
    runner.start();
      //runner.setPriority (Thread.MAX_PRIORITY);
  } /*endif*/

} /*start*/


/**
 * Stop the thread.
 */
public void stop() {
  if (runner != null)
    runner.stop (); //kill thread when applet is stopped
  runner= null;
} /*stop*/


public long sleepMillis ()
{
  return SLEEP_MILLIS;
}


/**
 * Execution loop. Used to call tick().
 */
public void run() {

  while (runner != null){
      try {
            Thread.sleep (sleepMillis ());
         } catch(InterruptedException e) {} //sleep
    tick();
  }/*endwhile*/

  runner= null;

} /*run*/
```

```
/**
 * Distribute tick to the ActorManager and update display.
 */
public void tick() {

  lastTickTimeMillis= currentTickTimeMillis;

  currentTickTimeMillis= System.currentTimeMillis();

  actorManager.tick();

  repaint();

} /*tick*/

/**
 * Pass the event along to the EventManager for handling.
 */
public boolean handleEvent (Event theEvent) {
  boolean returnValue= false;

  // ignore events which occur before objects are ready for
  // them

  if (eventManager!=null)
    returnValue= eventManager.handleEvent(theEvent);

  return returnValue;
} /*handleEvent*/

/**
 * Calculate the difference between the current tick and the last one.
 */
public double deltaTickTimeMillis() {
  return (double) (currentTickTimeMillis -
                                 lastTickTimeMillis);
} /*deltaTickTimeMillis*/

/**
 * Override update to avoid screen clears.
 */
public void update(Graphics g) {
  paint(g);
} /*update*/

/**
 * Pass the Graphics onto the DisplayManager.
 */
```

```
public void paint(Graphics g) {
  displayManager.paint(g);
} /*paint*/


/**
 * Provide standard Gamelet info.
 */
public String getAppletInfo() {
  return "The Gamelet Toolkit\nVersion 0.8\nWritten by Mark Tacchi,
mtacchi@NeXT.COM\n\nYou are free to use, copy, and modify the source
without restriction. However, it is requested that the author is
mentioned in any pertinent credit sections released with code developed
with the Gamelet Toolkit.";
} /*getAppletInfo*/
} /*Gamelet*/
```

Now that we have seen most of the core code up to this point and have become familiar with the approach used by the GT, the Gamelet object is fairly easy to understand. The first thing we do here is instantiate all of the Managers, which except for the ScoreManager we have already traced through.

Next we have a simple utility routine to help out with random number generation and then we set up our thread and the methods for starting and stopping it. We then distribute a tick to the ActorManager where it spreads out to the various sections of the program as the Actors maintain themselves and set their new positions.

Any events are then passed on to the EventManager for distribution to any registered objects. The deltaTimeTickMillis method we dealt with earlier, and it is used by actors to compute where they should display on the screen. The next two methods simply take care of paint functions by overriding the update and paint methods to pass them to the DisplayManager. Finally, the getAppletInfo method is defined where Mr. Tacchi asks only for credit for the use of his toolkit, which is pretty darned little to ask in my estimation.

ImageManager

```
/**
 * ImageManager.java
 * @author Mark G. Tacchi (mtacchi@next.com)
 * @version 0.8
 * Mar 19/1996
 *
 * ImageManager is used to force-load images at once to avoid taking the
```

```
hit during gameplay and distrupting game flow. Images to be cached are
listed in a cache file located in the <codebase>/images directory. The
default cache file is images/.cache.
 */


package com.next.gt;

import java.net.*;
import java.io.*;
import java.awt.*;
import java.awt.image.*;

public class ImageManager extends java.lang.Object{
  Gamelet   owner;

/**
  Cache those images which are listed in images/.cache.
*/
public ImageManager(Gamelet theOwner) {
  this(theOwner, ".cache");
} /*ImageManager()*/


/**
  Cache those images which are listed in the specified cache file. This
cache file should exist under the images directory.
*/
public ImageManager(Gamelet theOwner, String cacheFile) {
  URL                  myURL= null;
  InputStream          myStream= null;
  DataInputStream data= null;
  String               line;

  Image                theImage;
  Image                offScreenBuffer;
  MediaTracker         tracker;
  int          imageCount= 0;


  owner= theOwner;

  //
  // create the offscreen buffer
  //
  offScreenBuffer= owner.createImage (1, 1);

  //
  // create URL that points to cache file. the cache file
  // lists all images that are to be preloaded.
  //
  try {
    myURL= new URL (owner.getCodeBase().toString()+"/images/" +
```

```
cacheFile);
  }
  catch(MalformedURLException e) {
    System.out.println("GT: ImageManager cannot read "+
                    "cache file; " + e.getMessage());
  }


  //
  // cycle through all images
  //
  try {
    myStream= myURL.openStream();
      data= new DataInputStream(new
                        BufferedInputStream(myStream));
      while ((line= data.readLine())!=null) {
      imageCount++;
        theImage = owner.getImage(owner.getCodeBase(),
                  "images/"+line+".gif");
      tracker= new java.awt.MediaTracker(owner);

      tracker.addImage(theImage, imageCount);
      owner.showStatus ("GT: Caching image: " + line + ".");


      //
      // wait for images to be cached
      //
    try
{
          tracker.waitForID(imageCount);
    }
    catch (InterruptedException e) {
          System.out.println("GT: ImageManager ridiculous"+
                      " image; " + e.getMessage());
    }


    offScreenBuffer.getGraphics ().drawImage (theImage, 0,
                                          0, owner);
    } /*endWhile*/
  }
catch(IOException e ){
    System.out.println("GOOF: ImageManager can't getImage; "
                  + e.getMessage());
  }

} /*ImageManager(,)*/
} /*ImageManager*/
```

ImageManager (IM) is a handy bit of code, providing a standard way to load a group of images for our game up front. The image files to be used are assumed to be in a directory named *images* under the applet code directory. To control the loading process a file is created called .cache and placed in the image directory. This file is composed entirely of the names of the images you want to load, with a return after each name.

The functioning of the IM is, like everything else in the GM once you get the knack of what is going on, pretty easy to see. However, one interesting thing we are seeing here is the use of *external* information files. We have worked so far with external image and sound files, but not with external configuration information files.

In order to open a new file and read lines out of it, we first form a URL object pointing to the file that we want to read from. Then we open a stream, in this case called myStream to that URL. As an experienced C++ programmer, you already know about the use and abuse of streams. However, the reason for the wrapping of the BufferedInputStream in the DataInputStream that occurs in the cycle through images block might not be readily apparent.

Looking in the API docs under the java.io package will familiarize you with the large number of high-level objects Java provides for use in IO, including a number of stream methods. The major input object is *DataInput-Stream.* The methods in this object provide a number of different ways to access data from an external source, including reading in a line at a time as a string, which is what we are using in this example.

The *BufferedInputStream,* however, is more optimized for working with networked information. It brings in data from the source in blocks and then stores it in a local buffer for reading, speeding up the time required to access the information. In order to take advantage of the higher-level methods of DataInputStream but still get the more optimized communications of BufferedInputStream, it is common to wrap a BufferedInputStream in a DataInputStream in order to get the best of both worlds. You want to note this technique, because you will probably be using it frequently in your own programs.

The ImageManager object uses these streams to pull in each line of the cache file and then convert this to a file name, which is then loaded with a MediaTracker object watching the process. Note that we are loading all of these images to an offscreen buffer since all we need to do is get access to them without delay later, and we aren't actually going to be doing anything with this particular loading.

ScoreManager

```java
/**
 * ScoreManager.java
 * @author Mark G. Tacchi (mtacchi@next.com)
 * @version 0.8
 * Mar 15/1996
 *
 * ScoreManager maintains the current score and provides accessor
methods for objects to access/update the score. It also allows
objects to register for notification when a specific point level has been
reached. This is most useful for rewarding player with some sort of bonus.
 */


package com.next.gt;

import java.util.Vector;

public class ScoreManager extends java.lang.Object {
  public    int                 score;
  private   Vector              objectsToNotify;

public ScoreManager() {
  objectsToNotify= new Vector();
} /*ScoreManager()*/

/**
 * Add to the score.
 */
public void addToScore(int theValue) {
  score+= theValue;
  checkForBonus(theValue);
} /*addToScore*/

/**
 * Set the score.
 */
public void setScore(int theValue) {
  score= theValue;
} /*setScore*/

/**
 * Subtract from the score.
 */
public void subtractFromScore(int theValue) {
  score-= theValue;
} /*subtractFromScore*/

/**
 * For every 'bonus' points, notify requestor.
 */
```

```
public void registerForBonusNotification (Object theObject,
                                          int theValue) {

  Vector    registerVector= new Vector(3);
   // the object to notify
  registerVector.addElement(theObject);
   // bonus every
  registerVector.addElement(new Integer(theValue));
   // bonus counter
  registerVector.addElement(new Integer(0));

  objectsToNotify.addElement(registerVector);
} /*registerForBonusNotification*/


/**
 * Check if it's time for a bonus.
 */
private void checkForBonus(int theValue) {
  Vector    theObjectToNotify;
  Integer   n1, n2;
  Integer   anInteger;
 for (int i= 0; i<objectsToNotify.size(); i++) {
    theObjectToNotify= (Vector)
                       objectsToNotify.elementAt(i);

    //
    // increment bonus counter
    //
    anInteger= (Integer) theObjectToNotify.elementAt(2);
    theObjectToNotify.setElementAt(new
          Integer(anInteger.intValue() + theValue), 2);

    //
    // check if bonus counter is greater than the bonus // level
    //
    n2= (Integer) theObjectToNotify.elementAt(2);
    n1= (Integer) theObjectToNotify.elementAt(1);

    if (n2.intValue() >= n1.intValue()) {
      BonusHandler    theBonusHandler= (BonusHandler)
                      theObjectToNotify.elementAt(0);
      theObjectToNotify.setElementAt(new
      Integer(n2.intValue()- n1.intValue()), 2);
        theBonusHandler.didAchieveBonus();
    } /*endif*/
  } /*nexti*/

} /*checkForBonus*/
} /*ScoreManager*/
```

This object has no tricks that we haven't seen already in EventManager. Here we create another two-dimensional vector setup by putting three element registerVectors into our objectsToNotify vector. The three elements of *registerVector* are the object that is going to need notification of bonuses, what score to hit the bonus at, and the number of bonuses that have been awarded.

When another object requests a check for bonuses, then the ScoreManager runs through the *objectsToNotify* vector and sees if any of them have reached their bonus requirements. If one has, then a call is made to that object's *didAchieveBonus* method. Note that the ScoreManager works in conjunction with the BonusManager interface. Any object that can get a bonus notification must implement the BonusManager interface, which insures there will be a didAchieveBonus method to get the ScoreManager call to that object.

There are also miscellaneous methods to increment and deliver scores to any requesting object. These objects that might increment or request the current score don't have to implement the BonusManager interface, only those objects that will need to handle bonus notifications.

The natural reflex is going to be to use this object to create a traditional scoring system where every time you kill an opponent you get more score. However, there is no actual forcing of *what* you are scoring. You could use an implementation of the ScoreManager to keep track of levels, puzzles solved, or anything else as opposed to individual kills.

Tiled Image

```
/**
 * TiledImage.java
 * @author Mark G. Tacchi (mtacchi@next.com)
 * @version 0.8
 * Feb 24/1996
 *
 * TiledImage is a simple class with the sole responsibility of
replicating an image tile to produce a large tiled image. This is
useful for creating a background image.
*/

package com.next.gt;

import java.awt.Graphics;
import java.awt.Image;
```

```
public class TiledImage extends java.lang.Object {
  static Image        tiledImage;

public static Image createTiledImage(Image theImage, int
          width, int height, Gamelet owner) {
  int       i, j;

  tiledImage= owner.createImage(width,height);
  for (i= 0; i< width; i+= theImage.getWidth(null)) {
    for (j= 0; j< height; j+= theImage.getHeight(null)) {
      tiledImage.getGraphics().drawImage(theImage,i,j,owner);
    }
  }
  return tiledImage;
} /*TiledImage(,,,)*/

} /*TiledImage*/
```

This simple class does nothing but use a small sample image to create a complete background image for use by the DisplayManager as a background. It takes the image it is given and tiles it across the entire width and height of the Image it is handed.

A Whopper of an Example

Now that we have a pretty good clue of what, exactly, it is that the GT does, we can now look at how to actually use the GT to create a game.

First we should note that the GT is purposely designed as a fairly generic toolkit that will have application for as wide a range of applet-based games as possible. It would be possible to make a much more detailed rapid game development environment, but such an environment would tend to be more specific to particular solutions. All the GT does is optimize your display functions and take care of some of the more obvious things you must have in order to have a game, such as taking care of scoring.

Therefore, reasonably ambitious games written with the GT still require quite a sizable chunk of coding. However, most of this code is pretty easy to write for the simple reason that the GT removes an entire level of implementation decisions. Most of your general object structure is pretty much decided for you by the implementation of the GT actor/manager structure. So while you still have a good amount of code to write with the GT, the vast majority of what you have to accomplish is going to be quite obvious to actually implement.

The Game

The example we are going to examine is Boinkaroids. *Boinkaroids* is a good example for the simple reason that it uses everything available in the GT. This makes it a pretty large example, but after tracing through it, there isn't much about straight GT implementations left to question. Boinkaroids is pretty much a straight Asteroids clone. For those of you born after the premiere of *Miami Vice* (hey, I still have a closet full of pastel sport jackets I am willing to let go cheap . . .), Asteroids is a simple game in which the player takes on the role of a spaceship that starts at the center of the game screen. Unfortunately for the hapless space pilot in charge of the ship, it has wandered into the middle of a rather robust asteroid field. The goal of the game is to destroy the floating asteroids before any of them hit the ship and destroy it. When an asteroid is hit, it doesn't politely disappear, but instead it breaks into two smaller asteroids and these will break into two still smaller asteroids. It is only these final small asteroids that explode when you hit them. So each of the large asteroids that start on a screen breaks down into four smaller asteroids before you can wipe them out.

The entire play area consists of the screen with wrapping enabled, so when something goes off of one edge it comes back into play from the opposite side.

When a screen is cleared of asteroids, a brief pause is followed by a greater number of asteroids appearing. The end of the game is when the player is finally overcome by too many asteroids to kill.

The player starts out with three ships, and at various bonus points extra ships are awarded.

As if all of this wasn't hard enough, a complication is entered in the form of goobies (the goobies are a deviation from the original game that used offensive ships as the complication). *Goobies* are annoying little self-guiding pellets with an affinity for the player's ship. If they touch the ship they will destroy it. At the start of a level, goobies are protected by a Big Oobie sphere. This sphere takes a number of hits to penetrate. When it pops, two goobies are released that start homing in on the player's ship. In the lower levels you start out with only one Big Oobie, but just like asteroids, as the levels progress more Big Oobies will be present at the start of a level.

That is pretty much it. Boinkaroids (like Asteroids before it) is a simple-action shooting game with a progressive difficulty achieved through multi-plication of threats as the game continues. The hooks are in the form of a running score and the achieving of bonus ships as well as simple level pro-gression. Not the most advanced game in the world, but one that has proved over time to be reasonably compelling for a simple implementation.

Just as we did for the GT, let's take a look at what each of the objects in Boinkaroids does before we launch into the actual code.

Asteroid

The *asteroid object* is an actor that handles the behavior of the asteroids that are the main challenge in this game. The Asteroid takes care of its own display through the selection of one of three different graphics files that repre-sent the graphics for the large, medium, and small asteroids.

When hit by a bullet, the Asteroid also takes care of either creating two new Asteroid objects of the next smaller size or of generating an explosion and removing the Asteroid if it was of the smallest size when it was hit.

The Asteroid also adds to the score when it is hit and takes care of gener-ating an explosion if it plows into a player's ship.

Boinkaroids

The *Boinkaroids class* subclasses Gamelet and is the heart of the game. Boinkaroids takes care of pretty much everything that another object doesn't have responsibility for. It implements the managers, initializes the managers, implements the bonus ships, and actually displays the scores as well as man-aging the tick behaviors that are specific to this game.

Bigoobie

Bigoobie takes care of the bigoobie game element, which is a sphere that holds two goobies and takes a set number of hits before it releases these two goobies out to do their mayhem.

This is an Actor and like any other subclassing of the Actor class, it han-dles its own display and location information. It also handles its own colli-sions with the player ship.

Bullet

Bullets are Actors which take care of the two biggest things you need out of a bullet, displaying itself and reporting when it hits something. Bullets are generated by the Ship class in response to key presses. Bullets take care of making things explode. Bullets time out and disappear on their own after a few ticks.

Explosion

The *Explosion* class gets called by everyone else when they may collide with another Actor and have to make an explosion on the screen.

Goobies

We have already discussed the behavior of *Goobies*. When a Bigoobie pops, it will generate two of these Actors. The main thing that Goobies do is go for ships. Other than the movement algorithm, these units behave much like Asteroids.

Ship

The *Ship* is the main player Actor. It handles keyboard events that cause the Ship to move, collides with Asteroids and Goobies to produce an Explosion object, and shoots Bullet objects in response to key presses.

The Code

Now, with a pretty good idea of what the various elements in the game do, let's step into the actual code.

Asteroid

```
/**
 * Asteroid.java
 * @author Mark G. Tacchi (mtacchi@next.com)
 * @version 0.8
 * Mar 11/1996
 * A generic Asteroid class which handles varying sizes of asteroids.
Images should have filenames with corresponding S, M, L, and G appended
to them (example asteroidM.gif).
 * This Actor collides with Bullets and Ships. It is responsible for
creating an explosion object.
*/

import java.applet.Applet;
import java.lang.Math;

import com.next.gt.*;
```

```
public class Asteroid extends Actor {

  //
  // Size of the Asteroid.
  //
  public static final    int    SMALL_SIZE= 0,
                                 MEDIUM_SIZE= 1,
                                 LARGE_SIZE= 2;
  int                    size;


  //
  // The filename prefix.
  //
  String                 name;

Asteroid(Gamelet theOwner, Asteroid explodee, String
                           theName, int theSize) {

  super();

  String[] theImageName= {"S", "M", "L", "G"};
  java.awt.Image theImage;

  owner= theOwner;
  size= theSize;
  name= theName;

  if (theSize==LARGE_SIZE) {
    x= (Math.random()*512);
    y= (Math.random()*512);
    velocity_x= (double)((int)Gamelet.randBetween(0.5,1.5)*2
      - 1) * Gamelet.randBetween(8.,32.);
    velocity_y= (double)((int)Gamelet.randBetween(0.5,1.5)*2
      - 1) * Gamelet.randBetween(8.,32.);
  }
  else {
    x= explodee.x;
    y= explodee.y;
      velocity_x= explodee.velocity_x *
            Gamelet.randBetween(0.6,1.4);
      velocity_y= explodee.velocity_y *
            Gamelet.randBetween(0.6,1.4);
  }
  theImage = owner.getImage(owner.getCodeBase(), "images/"
     +theName + theImageName[theSize] + ".gif");
  setImage (theImage, 4, 32);

  currentFrame= (int)Gamelet.randBetween(0, numFrames);

} /*Asteroid()*/
```

```java
/**
 * Explode asteroid.
 */
public void explode()
{
  Explosion anExplosion;

  //
  // create explosion if smallest asteroid
  //
  if (size==SMALL_SIZE) {
    anExplosion= new Explosion(owner, this);
    owner.actorManager.addActor(anExplosion);
  }
  else {
    owner.play(owner.getCodeBase(), "sounds/explode1.au");
  }


  //
  // split off into smaller bits
  //
  if (size==LARGE_SIZE) {
    for (int i=0; i<2; i++) {
      owner.actorManager.addActor(new Asteroid(owner, this,
                            name, MEDIUM_SIZE));
      ((Boinkaroids)owner).badGuyCount++;
      } /*next_i*/

  }
  else if (size==MEDIUM_SIZE) {
    for (int i=0; i<2; i++) {
      owner.actorManager.addActor(new Asteroid(owner, this,
                            name, SMALL_SIZE));
      ((Boinkaroids)owner).badGuyCount++;
      } /*next_i*/
  }

  //
  // give credit for hitting me, increase score
  //
  owner.scoreManager.addToScore((2-size) * 200 + 100);

  //
  // i'm dead, i should schedule to be removed
  //
  owner.actorManager.removeActor(this);

  //
  // tell the gamelet that there is one less bad guy
  //
  ((Boinkaroids)owner).badGuyCount--;
```

```
} /*explode*/
/**
 * Handle collision with an actor.
 */
protected void collideWithActor (Actor theActor)
{
  String theActorClassName= theActor.getClass().getName();

  if (theActorClassName.equals("Bullet") ||
      theActorClassName.equals("Ship") ) {
    explode();
  } /*endif*/


} /*collideWithActor*/
} /*Asteroid*/
```

Like everything else we are dealing with in this chapter at this point, it isn't too hard to step through this code. However, we will comment on some of the lines where appropriate. First, note the *super() call* right after the Asteroid constructor. This line will call the default constructor in the Actor class to actually instantiate our Asteroid object.

Next our Asteroid determines if it is the large size. Since only large-sized asteroids are created from somewhere else (all medium and small asteroids are created by the explosion of the next larger size up), these Asteroid objects will have to have a random x and y velocity assigned to them. This is handled in a conditional block. The *else* statement of this conditional is going to be executed if the new Asteroid is the result of an explosion of the next larger size of Asteroid. In that case, we assign the x and y velocities from the exploding Asteroid object with a small variation to our new creation.

What this means in effect is that all new large asteroids that are created at the start of a level have a random movement. However, when you shoot an asteroid and it breaks into two smaller asteroids, these new Asteroids will be moving in roughly the same direction with roughly the same velocity as the asteroid you shot. However, the small random variations will make their paths start to diverge from one another over a few ticks.

Next Asteroid loads up the proper image for our Asteroid Actor by creating the file name based on what size specification the Asteroid object was passed at creation. There are three sizes—small, medium, and large—and each of these has its own graphics.

The next method deals with what happens when an Asteroid is hit by a Ship or Bullet (the only things that can collide with Asteroids). First we check to see if the size of our Asteroid is small, and if so, we create an Explosion object to take care of the pyrotechnics. In order to create the explosion object, we instantiate it with an argument of this object so it will know where it is supposed to be located and then we will register it with the ActorManager so that it will be added to the game next tick.

If the Asteroid is of one of the larger sizes, we play an explosion noise so that there are sounds to go with the hit and we create two of the next smaller Asteroid sizes, registering with the ActorManager again to put these two new objects into play next tick.

Then we update the score and schedule with the ActorManager to remove this object on the next tick, so we don't have a screen filling up with new asteroids but the old ones not going away.

Then we deincrement badGuyCount, a variable used by the Boinkaroids module for internal housekeeping.

The final method in the class simply handles collision notifications to see if the notification argument is a bullet or ship, in which case the Asteroid wants to deal with the collision and calls the Explode method we just traced through.

Boinkaroids

```
/**
 * Boinkaroids.java
 * @author Mark G. Tacchi (mtacchi@next.com)
 * @version 0.8
 * Mar 27/1996
 *
 * Boinkaroids is an Asteroids type game developed for the purpose of
showing off the Gamelet Toolkit. It makes use of all of the features
within the Gamelet Toolkit.
 */

import java.awt.*;
import java.io.*;
import java.net.*;
import java.util.*;

import com.next.gt.*;
public class Boinkaroids extends Gamelet implements
                    BonusHandler, EventHandler{

    //
    // Boinkaroids variables
    //
```

```
public Ship        player;
public int         numShips;
public int         badGuyCount;
public int         level;

//
// Should a player be created?
//
private boolean createNewPlayer;

//
// Score label.
//
private Label      myLabel;

//
// This area that has to be clear for a ship to enter
// level.
//
private int        SAFETY_ZONE_WIDTH= 128;
private int        SAFETY_ZONE_HEIGHT= 128;

/**
 * Initialize.
 */
public void init() {
  //
  // cache images
  //
  new ImageManager(this);

  //
  // initialize the score manager
  //
  scoreManager= new ScoreManager();
  scoreManager.registerForBonusNotification(this, 20000);

  myLabel= new Label("Score: 00000000" + " Ships: " +
numShips + " Level: "+ level);
  add("South",myLabel);

  this.newGame();
  //
  // register for events
  //
  eventManager.
    registerForSingleEventNotification(this,
                      Event.KEY_ACTION_RELEASE);
  //
  // paint background image
```

```
    //
    displayManager.setBackgroundTile (getImage(getCodeBase(),
                        "images/background.gif"));


} /*init*/


/**
 * Set up the new game.
 */
public void newGame() {
  scoreManager.setScore (0);
  numShips= 3;
  badGuyCount= 0;
  level= 0;
  player= null;
  actorManager.removeAllActors();
  this.createActors();
} /*newGame*/


/**
 * Advance levels.
 */
public void newLevel() {
  level++;
  this.createActors();
} /*newLevel*/


/**
 * Create the actors for this scene.
 */
public void createActors() {
  for (int i= 0; i< 2*level; i++) {
    actorManager.addActor (new Asteroid(this, null,
                "gumball", Asteroid.LARGE_SIZE));
      badGuyCount++;
  } /*nexti*/
  for (int i= 0; i< 0.5*level; i++) {
    actorManager.addActor (new Bigoobie(this));
    badGuyCount++;
  } /*next_i*/
  this.createPlayer();
} /*createActors*/


/**
 * Create the player object.
 */
public void createPlayer() {
  if (player!=null) {
    actorManager.removeActor(player);
  } /*endif*/
```

```
  player= new Ship(this);
  actorManager.addActor (player);
} /*createPlayer*/


/**
 * Override tick to test for specific game events.
 */
public void tick() {

super.tick();

 if (badGuyCount <= 0) {
   this.newLevel();
 } /*endif*/
 if (createNewPlayer) {
   Rectangle myRectangle= new Rectangle ((int)this.size().width /2 -
SAFETY_ZONE_WIDTH/2,
      (int)this.size().height/2 - SAFETY_ZONE_HEIGHT/2,
      SAFETY_ZONE_WIDTH,
      SAFETY_ZONE_HEIGHT);
   if (!actorManager.isActorIn(myRectangle)) {
     createNewPlayer= false;
       this.createPlayer();
   } /*endif*/
 } /*endif*/
} /*tick*/


/**
 * Handle keyboard events to restart game.
 */
public boolean handleRequestedEvent (Event theEvent) {
  switch(theEvent.id) {
  case Event.KEY_ACTION_RELEASE:
    switch(theEvent.key) {
       case Event.F1:
       this.newGame();
         return true;
     } /*endSwitch*/
  } /*endSwitch*/
  return false;
} /*handleRequestedEvent8/


/**
 * Override paint to display score bar.
 */
public void paint(Graphics g) {
  super.paint(g);
  myLabel.setText("Score: "+scoreManager.score +" Ships: "
           + numShips + " Level: "+ level );
} /*paint*/
```

```
/**
 * Give bonus ship for getting a certain score.
 */
public void didAchieveBonus() {
  numShips++;
} /*didAchieveBonus*/


/**
 * Player must have died, decrement ship count.
 */
public void decrementShipCount() {
  if (numShips-- > 0) {
    createNewPlayer= true;
      player= null;
  } /*endif*/
} /*decrementShipCount*/
} /*Boinkaroids*/
```

In the *init method* Boinkaroids fires off the ImageManager to load all of the images it finds in the .cache file, then sets up the ScoreManager with a bonus value of 20,000 and bonus notification coming back to this object. Next it uses an AWT label object to display the score and level on the screen. It sets the game variables by calling its own newGame method and then registers with the EventManager object for notification of KEY_ACTION_RELEASE events so that it can catch these in a later method and restart the game if a request is made. Finally, DisplayManager is called upon to set the background to background.gif.

The *newGame method* simply sets the various variables this instance of Boinkaroids is going to be needing during its execution and kills any Actor objects that might be hanging around from a previous game. Finally it calls the *createActors method* that takes care of creating the basic Actors present at the start of a game.

newLevel is pretty self-explanatory, and createActors isn't much more complicated, simply creating a couple of large Asteroid objects, a Bigoobie, and a player by calling the *createPlayer method*. All of these Actors are registered with the ActorManager so they will be displayed on the next tick. Note that we are also passing the filename gumball to the Asteroid objects; this is the base filename of all of the various Asteroid graphics.

The next interesting method is the *overridden method* tick. The first thing we do here is call the tick method from Gamelet in order to make sure that all of the basic functions performed there get done. Next we add our own

behaviors which include checking for the need for a new level by the simple
expedient of checking to see if there are any badguys on the screen. If a new
player is created then we create a rectangle of safety and start checking every
tick to see if anything is in it. When the rectangle is clear, we put the new
ship down on the screen. This is to give you a fighting chance when you pop
up and not put you right in the path of an oncoming Asteroid so close that
you don't have a chance to shoot.

The remainder of the code here is self-evident.

Bigoobie

```java
/**
 * Bigoobie.java
 * @author Mark G. Tacchi (mtacchi@next.com)
 * @version 0.8
 * Mar 18/1996
 * A Bigoobie transparent shell containing two orbiting goobies. They take a
 number of hits and then pop.
 *
 * Bigoobies harm ships and bullets harm Bigoobies.
 */

import java.applet.Applet;
import java.lang.Math;

import com.next.gt.*;

public class Bigoobie extends Actor {
  //
  // This actor has to be hit this many times before dying.
  //
  public int       attackResistance= 3;

Bigoobie(Boinkaroids theOwner) {
  super();

  java.awt.Image            theImage;
  java.awt.MediaTracker     tracker;

  owner= theOwner;

  theImage = owner.getImage(owner.getCodeBase(),
          "images/bigoobie.gif");
  tracker = new java.awt.MediaTracker(theOwner);

  tracker.addImage(theImage, 0);
  try
```

```
{
          tracker.waitForID(0);
  }
  catch (InterruptedException e) {}
  x= (Math.random()*512);
  y= (Math.random()*512);
  velocity_x= (double)((int)Gamelet.randBetween(0.5,1.5)*2 -
      1) * Gamelet.randBetween(16.,48.);
  velocity_y= (double)((int)Gamelet.randBetween(0.5,1.5)*2 -
      1) * Gamelet.randBetween(16.,48.);
  setImage (theImage, 4, 12);

  currentFrame= (int)Gamelet.randBetween(0, numFrames);

} /*Bigoobie()*/

/**
 * Explode goobie.
 */
public void explode()
{
  //
  // free the 2 goobies
  //
  for (int i= 0; i<2; i++) {
    owner.actorManager.addActor(new Goobie(owner, this));
    ((Boinkaroids)owner).badGuyCount++;
  } /*next_i*/

  //
  // play explode sound
  //
  owner.play(owner.getCodeBase(), "sounds/pop.au");

  //
  // give credit for hitting me, increase score
  //
  owner.scoreManager.addToScore(500);

  //
  // I'm dead, I should schedule to be removed
  //
  owner.actorManager.removeActor(this);

  //
  // Tell the gamelet there is one less bad guy.
  //
  ((Boinkaroids)owner).badGuyCount--;

} /*explode*/
```

```
/**
 * Handle collision with an actor.
 */
protected void collideWithActor (Actor theActor)
{
 String theActorClassName= theActor.getClass().getName();

 if (theActorClassName.equals("Bullet") ||
     theActorClassName.equals("Ship") ) {
      if (--attackResistance<0) {
       explode();
      }
      else {
          owner.play(owner.getCodeBase(),
                     "sounds/futility.au");
      }
 } /*endif*/
} /*collideWithActor*/
} /*Bigoobie*/
```

From here on out, with a couple of very minor variations, things get really
stupidly simple and are going to require little or no explanation. This is
because all of the remaining objects are subclasses of the Actor class and by
having already gone through the Asteroid class we have already seen how to
create these kinds of objects. The Bigoobie is functionally exactly the same
as the Asteroid except that it uses different animation and sound files; when
it is hit it doesn't create two smaller Asteroids, but instead creates two
instances of the Goobie class.

Bullet

```
/**
 * Bullet.java
 * @author Mark G. Tacchi (mtacchi@next.com)
 * @version 0.8
 * Mar 12/1996
 * A Bullet is created by the Ship object when it is sent a fire message.
Bullets live for a specified time to live (ttl).
 *
 * This Actor collides with all but Ships and Explosions.
 */

import java.awt.*;
import com.next.gt.*;

public class Bullet extends Actor {
```

```
    //
    // variable used to compare against for auto death
    //
    long startTime;


    //
    // time to live
    //
    long ttl= 1500;


    //
    // the ship object
    //
    Ship      explodee;

Bullet(Gamelet theOwner, Ship theExplodee) {
    super();

    double        explodeeVelocity= theExplodee.getSpeed();
    double        explodeeTheta= theExplodee.getTheta();
    Image         theImage;

    owner= theOwner;
    explodee= theExplodee;

    x= (explodee.x + (explodee.width/2.0));
    y= (explodee.y + (explodee.height/2.0));

    theImage= owner.getImage(owner.getCodeBase(),
            "images/bullet.gif");

    setImage (theImage, 4, 16);

    velocity_x= Math.cos(explodeeTheta)*(explodeeVelocity +
        150.);
    velocity_y= Math.sin(explodeeTheta+Math.PI) *
            (explodeeVelocity + 150.);

    x+= (velocity_x * .1);
    y+= (velocity_y * .1);

    startTime= owner.currentTickTimeMillis;

} /*Bullet()*/

/**
 * Override tick to implement a timed death.
 */
```

```
public void tick()
{
  super.tick();

  if (owner.currentTickTimeMillis - startTime > ttl) {
    if (explodee.numBullets>0)explodee.numBullets--;
      owner.actorManager.removeActor (this);
  } /*endif*/

} /*tick*/

/**
 * Handle collision with an actor.
 */
protected void collideWithActor (Actor theActor)
{
  String theActorClassName= theActor.getClass().getName();

  if (theActorClassName.equals("Asteroid") ||
      theActorClassName.equals("Bigoobie")) {
        if (explodee.numBullets>0)explodee.numBullets--;
    owner.actorManager.removeActor(this);
  } /*endif*/

} /*collideWithActor*/
} /*Bullet*/
```

Again, we are looking at a basic variation on a theme with the Actor class. The only interesting thing here is the use of a time factor as opposed to a distance factor in order to determine the life of the bullet. While we could trace the exact distance flown by the bullet in order to determine its life (read: range) it is a much cheaper trick to simply check to see how long it has been alive and then work with that since it will equal a set distance.

The math strangeness going on with setting the velocity_x and velocity_y is simply to make sure the bullet is speeding out in the right direction, that is, the direction the ship is pointed. The ship actor can have a velocity in one vector and be pointing an entirely different direction (we are using the word vector here in a physics sense, not in a programming sense). Therefore we need to have our bullets going the way the ship is pointing. The *getTheta method* will return from our Ship object a facing direction and then we play the math tricks on it to get the bullets with velocities in each direction appropriate to the ship's current movement vector and facing.

Explosion

```java
/**
 * Explosion.java
 * @author Mark G. Tacchi (mtacchi@next.com)
 * @version 0.8
 * Mar 12/1996
 *
 * A simple explosion Actor.
 */

import java.awt.Graphics;

import com.next.gt.*;

public class Explosion extends Actor {

Explosion(Gamelet theOwner, Actor explodee) {
  super();
  java.awt.Image        theImage;
  java.awt.MediaTracker tracker;

  owner= theOwner;

  //
  // play explosion sound
  //
  owner.play(owner.getCodeBase(), "sounds/explode1.au");

  //
  // load the image
  //
  theImage= owner.getImage(owner.getCodeBase(),
          "images/explosions.gif");

  //
  // set up key variables
  //
  setImage (theImage, 60, 60, 4, 16);
  x= (explodee.x - (width - explodee.width)/2.0);
  y= (explodee.y - (height - explodee.height)/2.0);
  velocity_x= explodee.velocity_x;
  velocity_y= explodee.velocity_y;

} /*Explosion()*/

/**
 * Calculates the current frame. Flip through frames sequentially and
die when completed.
 */
public void calculateCurrentFrame() {
```

```
    if (++currentFrame>=numFrames) {
      owner.actorManager.removeActor(this);
    } /*endif*/
  } /*calculateCurrentFrame*/

} /*Explosion*/
```

The Explosion class takes care of those ubiquitous explosions everyone keeps calling. This is a particularly simple example of the Actor class.

Goobie

```
/**
 * Goobie.java
 * @author Mark G. Tacchi (mtacchi@next.com)
 * @version 0.8
 * Mar 18/1996
 * A goobie is just a little green thing that lives within a transparent shell
until that shell pops.
 *
 * Goobies harm ships and bullets harm Goobies.
 */

import java.applet.Applet;
import java.lang.Math;

import com.next.gt.*;

public class Goobie extends Actor {

  //
  // Gravity strength toward the ship.
  //
  private static double GRAVITATIONAL_PULL= 0.5;

Goobie(Gamelet theOwner, Bigoobie explodee) {
  super();

  java.awt.Image            theImage;
  java.awt.MediaTracker     tracker;
  owner= theOwner;

  theImage = owner.getImage(owner.getCodeBase(),
            "images/goobie.gif");
  tracker = new java.awt.MediaTracker(theOwner);

  tracker.addImage(theImage, 0);
  try
```

```
{
            tracker.waitForID(0);
    }
  catch (InterruptedException e) {}


  x= (int) (explodee.x - (width - explodee.width)/2.0);
  y= (int) (explodee.y - (height - explodee.height)/2.0);
  velocity_x= explodee.velocity_x *
          Gamelet.randBetween(0.2,1.4);
  velocity_y= explodee.velocity_y *
          Gamelet.randBetween(0.2,1.4);


  setImage (theImage);

} /*Goobie()*/


/**
 * Gravitate towards player.
 */
public void calculateNewPosition() {
  super.calculateNewPosition();


  //
  // Is the player alive?
  //
  if (((Boinkaroids)owner).player==null) return;


  //
  // gravitate towards player
  //
  if (x> ((Boinkaroids)owner).player.x) velocity_x-=
      GRAVITATIONAL_PULL;
  else velocity_x+= GRAVITATIONAL_PULL;
  if (y> ((Boinkaroids)owner).player.y) velocity_y-=
      GRAVITATIONAL_PULL;
  else velocity_y+= GRAVITATIONAL_PULL;


} /*calculateNewPosition*/


/**
 * Explode goobie.
 */
public void explode()
{
  //
  // play explode sound
  //
  owner.play(owner.getCodeBase(), "sounds/smack.au");
```

```
//
// give credit for hitting me, increase score
//
owner.scoreManager.addToScore(1000);

//
// I'm dead, I should schedule to be removed
//
owner.actorManager.removeActor(this);

//
// Tell the gamelet that there is one less bad guy
//
((Boinkaroids)owner).badGuyCount--;

} /*explode*/

/**
 * Handle collision with an actor.
 */
protected void collideWithActor (Actor theActor)
{
  String theActorClassName= theActor.getClass().getName();

  if (theActorClassName.equals("Bullet") ||
     theActorClassName.equals("Ship") ) {
        explode();
  } /*endif*/
} /*collideWithActor*/
} /*Goobie*/
```

Again, we are dealing with a simple subclassing of the Actor. However, one neat little thing to remember here is the homing technique that moves the Goobie toward the player's ship. This is simple to implement and a great way to increase difficulty by simply increasing the GRAVITATIONAL_PULL value as the game goes on. While this wasn't done here to increase difficulty, you can imagine how more and more ardent homing capabilities in incoming missiles could make life interesting for a player.

Ship

```
/*
 * Ship.java
 * @author Mark G. Tacchi (mtacchi@next.com)
 * @version 0.8
 * Mar 11/1996
 *
```

```
 * The ship is controlled by the user, it registers for specific keyboard events
to handle control.
 *
 * This Actor collides with Asteroids and Goobies. It is responsible for
creating an explosion object.
 */

import java.applet.Applet;
import java.applet.AudioClip;
import java.lang.Math;
import java.awt.*;

import com.next.gt.*;

public class Ship extends Actor implements EventHandler{

  //
  // Limit number of bullets on the screen at once
  //
  private static int        MAX_NUM_BULLETS= 5;
  public int                  numBullets= 0;


  //
  // Animation. ccw= 1, cw= -1
  //
  public int                    animationDirection= 1;
  public boolean              isAnimating= true;


  //
  // Is thrusting
  //
  public boolean              thrusting= false;

Ship(Gamelet theOwner) {
  super();

  Image                theImage;
  owner= theOwner;

  //
  // play warp-in sound
  //
  owner.play(owner.getCodeBase(), "sounds/warp.au");

  x= (owner.size().width/2.0);
  y= (owner.size().height/2.0);
  velocity_x= 0;
  velocity_y= 0;
  String    theImageName= "images/ship.gif";
```

```
    theImage= owner.getImage(owner.getCodeBase(),
            "images/ship.gif");
    setImage (theImage, 4, 24);

  isAnimating= false;

  int events[]= {   Event.KEY_ACTION,
                        Event.KEY_ACTION_RELEASE,
                        Event.KEY_PRESS,
                        Event.KEY_RELEASE
                    };
    owner.eventManager.registerForEventNotification(this,events);

} /*Ship()*/

/**
 * Handle keyboard events that control ship.
 */
public boolean handleRequestedEvent (Event theEvent) {
  switch(theEvent.id) {
  case Event.KEY_ACTION:
    switch(theEvent.key) {
        case Event.RIGHT:
        this.rotateRight(true);
          return true;
        case Event.LEFT:
        this.rotateLeft(true);
          return true;
        case Event.UP:                      //THRUST ON
        this.thrust(true);
          return true;
      } /*endSwitch*/
      break;
  case Event.KEY_ACTION_RELEASE:
    switch(theEvent.key) {
        case Event.RIGHT:
        this.rotateRight(false);
          return true;
        case Event.LEFT:
        this.rotateLeft(false);
          return true;
        case Event.UP:                      //THRUST OFF
        this.thrust(false);
          return true;
      } /*endSwitch*/
      break;
    case Event.KEY_PRESS:
      switch(theEvent.key) {
          case 32:
            this.fire();
```

```
            return true;
        } /*endSwitch*/
    break;
    case Event.KEY_RELEASE:
      switch(theEvent.key) {
          case 32:
              return true;
        } /*endSwitch*/
    break;
  } /*endSwitch*/

  return false;

} /*handleRequestedEvent*/
/**
 * If ship is thrusting, then velocity is increasing. Use friction if not
thrusting.
 */
public void calculateNewVelocity() {
  if (thrusting) {
    velocity_x+= Math.cos(currentFrame*2*Math.PI/numFrames +
          Math.PI/2)*10;
    velocity_y+= Math.sin(currentFrame*2*Math.PI/numFrames -
          Math.PI/2)*10;
  }
  else {
    velocity_x*= 0.99;
    velocity_y*= 0.99;
  }

} /*calculateNewVelocity*/


/**
 * Animation of the ship is based on theta, display accordingly.
 */
public void calculateCurrentFrame() {
  if (isAnimating) {
    if (animationDirection== -1) {
        if (--currentFrame<=0) currentFrame= numFrames - 1;
      }
      else {
       if (++currentFrame>=numFrames) currentFrame= 0;
      }
    } /*endif*/

} /*calculateCurrentFrame*/


/**
 * Handle left rotation.
 */
```

```
public void rotateLeft (boolean keydown) {
  if (keydown) {
    isAnimating= true;
    animationDirection= 1;
  }
  else {
    isAnimating= false;
  }

} /*rotateLeft*/

/**
 * Handle right rotation.
 */
public void rotateRight (boolean keydown) {
  if (keydown) {
    animationDirection= -1;
    isAnimating= true;
  }
  else {
    isAnimating= false;
  }

} /*rotateRight*/

/**
 * Handle thrust.
 */
public void thrust (boolean keydown) {
  if (keydown) {
    thrusting= true;
  }
  else {
    thrusting= false;
  }
} /*thrust*/

/**
 * Fire bullet.
 */
public void fire() {

  if (numBullets<MAX_NUM_BULLETS) {
    Bullet aBullet;

    numBullets++;
    owner.play(owner.getCodeBase(), "sounds/bullet.au");
    aBullet= new Bullet(owner, this);
    owner.actorManager.addActor(aBullet);
  } /*endif*/
```

```java
} /*fire*/

/**
 * Accessor methods (bullet uses this).
 */

/**
 * Ship's angle.
 */
public double getTheta() {
  return (currentFrame*2*Math.PI/numFrames + Math.PI/2);
} /*getTheta*/

/**
 * Ship's speed.
 */
public double getSpeed() {
  return Math.sqrt(velocity_x*velocity_x +
      velocity_y*velocity_y);
} /*getSpeed*/

/**
 * Handle collision with an actor.
 */
protected void collideWithActor (Actor theActor)
{
  String theActorClassName= theActor.getClass().getName();

  if (theActorClassName.equals("Asteroid") ||
      theActorClassName.equals("Goobie") ||
      theActorClassName.equals("Bigoobie") ) {
    explode();
  } /*endif*/

} /*collideWithActor*/

/**
 * Explode ship.
 */
public void explode()
{
  Explosion anExplosion;

  //
  // Tell the ActorManager that I'm gone, and an Explosion
  // Actor should be added.
  //
  owner.actorManager.removeActor(this);
```

```
    anExplosion= new Explosion(owner, this);
    owner.actorManager.addActor(anExplosion);

    //
    // Lower ship counter.
    //
    ((Boinkaroids)owner).decrementShipCount();

} /*explode*/
} /*Ship*/
```

The Ship Actor is slightly more advanced than the rest of the Actors we have seen so far simply because since it is the representation of the player, a bit more code rests here to take care of things like player keyboard actions. However, none of this really bears much discussion. The events are probably the most interesting part, and they are a simple manner of registering for the events with the EventManager and then catching them with a standard event handler which we have discussed in previous chapters. Note that the case 32 statement which handles fire is the ASCII number for the spacebar.

Also note that the animation sequence being controlled by overriding calculateCurrentFrame is somewhat interesting also simply because what is being done here is actually to stop the animation on specific frames of the master image file. Each frame in this file (ship.gif) represents a different ship facing. The default behavior of calculateCurrentFrame would spool through each of the images in the file sequentially. To the player this would have the effect of producing an endlessly spinning ship on the screen and obviously wouldn't do. Instead the overridden method uses the theta (I would have called this facing to help out the mathematically challenged among us, but then again, I didn't come up with this cool toolkit myself) to figure out which frame to display and frame only changes when the left or right arrow keys are pressed to rotate the ship left or right. (See Figure 9.2.)

What We Have Learned

We could go back over all of the salient points of the GT here, but that would be a tremendous waste of time. The important thing to note about the GT itself is simply that it is nothing more than a set of managers and Actors that control event, time, and display issues in your games. In most games these are

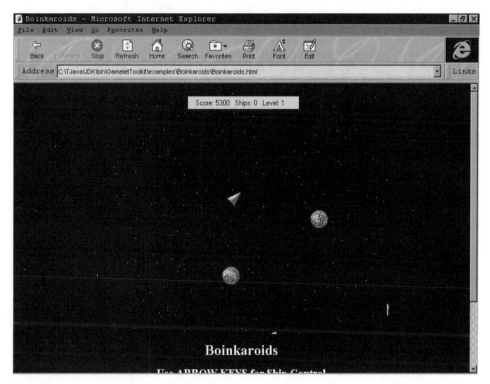

Figure 9.2   Boinkaroids in all its glory.

going to make up the vast majority of all of the tasks you need to worry about.

But we have also learned much more by inference. The GT shows us how reusable objects can link together to form a code body that will help us with our tasks of creating games. The nature of Java makes such library creation natural and easy. We should always be thinking about how to make our code into as many reusable modules as we can in order to save ourselves some coding pain another day.

Another good point of the GT, and any library implementation for games that is well thought out, is that it not only makes things easier for us by giving us a good base of code lines that we aren't going have to retype but also imposes a logical design structure on our later runs at the same basic kinds of tasks that will hopefully save us yet more time.

• • • • • • •
Next Up

In the next chapter we are going to look at that most important frame of your applet: the Webpage. With a few simple techniques, you can spruce up your page and put your brilliant code in a pleasing environment.

CHAPTER 10
· · · · · · ·
WEB PAGE TRICKS

Although the scope of this book has been to look at game programming in Java, the majority of your work is going to be living on the Web. Let's face it—90 percent of Java cool is delivering applets. And your applets don't exist in a vacuum; they live on a Web page.

We aren't going to attempt to teach you the finer points of HTML scripting here. There are plenty of books to do that, as well as a passel of Web-based resources that we have collected on our Web support site. However, we can touch on a few of the cool features you might want to think about incorporating into your HTML pages to spruce things up and provide a better frame for your Java efforts.

Animated GIFs

We have a couple of ways to deal with animation on a Web page. Our first reflex might very well be to code an animation routine in Java to load our individual frames of animation and display them. However, that isn't particularly the best way to do things. For simple static animations, using Java is overkill. We have the overhead of the loading and execution of the Java code itself. Instead of using Java we can just use the tools built into the Graphics Interchange Format (GIF) itself to handle our animation.

Animated GIF technology was developed in 1987, but browser developers have only recently begun to support it. Currently only Netscape 2.0 or later and Microsoft Internet Explorer 3.0 or later support animated GIFs.

Animated GIFs are similar to flip-page animation used by animators to storyboard their work. All that is required is a series of GIFs, like the individual frames of a movie, and a piece of software to put them together. The three most commonly used pieces of GIF animation software are Alchemy Mindworks' GIF Constructions Set for PC, Yves Piguet's GifBuilder for Mac, and Kevin Kadow's WhirlGIF for UNIX.

The software combines multiple images into a single GIF file. Each image can be assigned characteristics such as transparency color, length of time displayed, and whether to loop the image. As with any GIF89a file, animated GIFs may be assigned a transparency color. This is a single color that will be ignored by most browsers. For instance, if an image has a black background and black is chosen as the transparent color it will not show up when viewed through a Web browser. This has the effect of making the image seem to float on the page. The length of time the image is displayed, or the delay, determines how long each individual image will stay on the screen before the next image in the series is loaded. The final setting, whether to loop the image, determines if the series of images will run once or be repeated indefinitely. When creating the individual images for the animation there are a few things which should be kept in mind.

Image size, number of colors, and file size are all important to the final outcome of an animation. If the animation shows changes to the whole scene, all images should be of the same dimension, for instance, 200 pixels wide and 100 pixels high. This ensures that the alignment of each image, when displayed, is correct. If only a small section of the image is to change, such as a letter or word being added, a small image may be used instead. This can be done by assigning an X and Y axis to the image allowing it to be positioned wherever needed.

All images should be created with the same pallet, or number of colors, to prevent distortion. It is also a good idea to have the first image contain the largest number of colors. I have heard reports that color fluctuation can become a problem if a later image uses more colors than the first but have never had this trouble myself. If a transparent background is to be used the color chosen should contrast sharply to the rest of the image. If, for instance, yellow is used in the image it should not be used as the background color. If it is, then all of the yellow in the image will become transparent and part of the image will be lost.

Consider the file size. Large individual images result in a large animated GIF file. Remember that most users are still running 14.4 modems. The best average throughput at 14.4 is about 1.7 kilobytes of data (1.7K = 1700 bytes) per second. This means it will take 36 seconds to download a 60K file, longer considering that the entire Web page is being transferred at the same time and only a portion of the bandwidth is dedicated to the image. The use of fewer colors in the individual image will reduce the file size, but this should be done while creating the images. Reducing the number of colors in an existing image can cause it to look blurred, degrading the image quality. One technique to make the page load faster even with a large image is to use HEIGHT and WIDTH tags when embedding the image into the HTML code like this: <IMG HEIGHT=100 WIDTH=200 SRC= "mycool.gif">. For browsers which support the HEIGHT and WIDTH tags, this tells it how much of the page to set aside for the image. It can then load the rest of the page around this block while the image is still being downloaded.

Finally, remember that not all browsers can display animated GIFs—in fact, most image-viewing software will not display the animation. If the browser cannot display the animation it will only show the first image. Thus the first image of the animation should be able to convey the point. If a company logo were the object of the animation the first frame should clearly show that logo. The subsequent frames could then be used to make it fade, spin, or hop around. If the first frame of the animation is of a tiny image of the logo which is meant to grow in size, a user with a nonanimated GIF-capable browser may see only a tiny speck.

Now that you know how to make an animated GIF, how should you use them? Animated GIFs can be used to highlight parts of the page or simply to entertain. One of the best uses is to draw attention to a particular part of the page. Suppose you have an alphabetized list of articles on a page. If a new article is added it may not be readily apparent to the user. Inserting a flashing new graphic or an arrow that changes size will draw the user's attention to the highlighted article. Animated GIFs can give instruction, showing a user how to accomplish a particular task. Animated GIFs can also be used to display a series of images that have nothing to do with each other, such as a changing billboard.

While animated GIFs are nice and can accomplish many tasks more easily than Java animation, they do have two major drawbacks. First, they are silent. There is no way to include sound in an animated GIF. Sound can be added to the page (and that will be covered later), but it cannot be synchronized with the animation. Second, the entire animation can be hyperlinked to only one file or URL. Java is capable of handling both of these tasks for the same file if needed. The following script produces the examples in Figures 10.1 and 10.2. Note that you will need to download the actual animation from the Web support site in order for this to work. The important thing to note here is that this script is the same as the script you would use to pro-

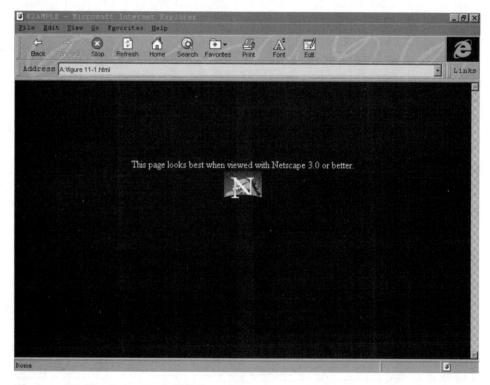

Figure 10.1 Animated GIF first frame in page: Some users will only see this first frame, so make it count.

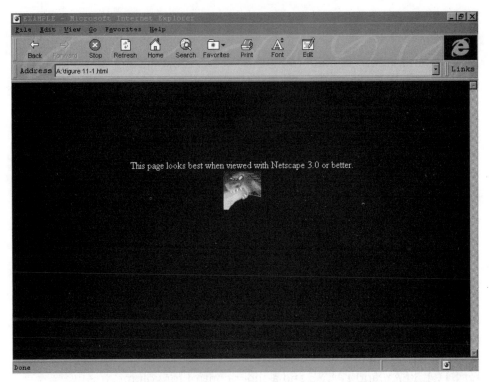

Figure 10.2 A GIF final frame: However, the rest of the world will see a complete sequence; here you see the end frame of our example animation.

duce a static GIF, but produces much different results due to the animated GIF being used.

```
<HTML>
<HEAD><TITLE>EXAMPLE</TITLE>
</HEAD>
<BODY BGCOLOR="#000000" TEXT="#FFFFFF" LINK="#FFFF00" VLINK="#FFFF00"
ALINK="#FFFF00">
</HEAD>
<BR><BR><BR><BR><BR><BR><BR><BR>

<CENTER>
This page looks best when viewed with Netscape 3.0 or better.<BR>
<IMG HEIGHT=64 WIDTH=64 BORDER=0 SRC="mozilla-ani.gif">
</CENTER>
</BODY>
</HTML>
```

• • • • • •
Sound

Short of animation, the one thing the Web is most lacking is sound. There are commercial packages on the market that allow Websmiths to add sound to their pages, but most of them are expensive and require special software on both the server and user ends. An easy way around this is by using the <EMBED SRC> tag which works with Netscape 2.0 or later. This does not work for Internet Explorer. Similar to embedding an image into an HTML document, this allows sound files to be added to a page. The following is an example of embedded sound.

```
<EMBED SRC="coolsound.wav" AUTOSTART=FALSE VOLUME=100 WIDTH=144 HEIGHT=60>
```

The options in this command line are straight forward. AUTOSTART determines whether or not the sound file will begin playing as soon as it is loaded and can be set to true or false. VOLUME determines how loud the file will be played relative to how loud the computer's speakers are set to. The numeric value can be set between 0 and 100, 100 being the loudest. The HEIGHT and WIDTH tags insure that the control panel is fully displayed. When the page loads it will include a small control panel with three buttons for STOP, PLAY, and PAUSE and a slider control for volume.

If the control panel is not wanted on the page, a simple link to the file can be added like this:

```
<A HREF="coolsound.wav">Cool Sound</A>
```

When clicked on, this link will bring up a small window with the control panel in it. Clicking on the play button will then start playing the sound file. This technique also works with Microsoft's Internet Explorer. Explorer will call up Windows' Sound Recorder to control how the sound file is played.

If the sound file is meant to be background music and the control panel is not needed, a small trick can be played with the HEIGHT and WIDTH tags to hide it like this:

```
<EMBED SRC="coolsound.wav" AUTOSTART=TRUE VOLUME=100 WIDTH=1 HEIGHT=2>
```

This will cause the sound file to begin playing as soon as it is loaded. The control panel window will be reduced to a nearly invisible 1 pixel by 2 pixel dot which can be completely hidden by using a dark background for the page. The HEIGHT and WIDTH tags can be set so that either is 2 and the other is 1, but both cannot be set to 1 for this to work. If both HEIGHT and WIDTH are set to 1 the control panel will load full size.

Embedded AVIs

Netscape 2.0 or later supports AVI files embedded into HTML documents using the <EMBED SRC> tag. The following example shows how to load an AVI whose dimensions are 300 × 200.

```
<EMBED SRC="coolflic.avi" HEIGHT=200 WIDTH=300>
```

The HEIGHT and WIDTH tags again set aside a portion of the page for the AVI while the rest of the page loads. In this case they are not optional. This area must be specified in order for the AVI to load. Unlike the HEIGHT and WIDTH tags for normal images, they cannot be used to change the size of the image displayed. If they do not reflect the exact size of the AVI one of two things will happen. If the HEIGHT and WIDTH are set smaller than the actual AVI it will be cropped. If the HEIGHT and WIDTH are set larger, the AVI will have a white border. The AVI is always positioned at the top left of the area designated. Any cropping or bordering will occur along the right and bottom edges of the image.

Unlike embedded sound files, AVIs do not have a control panel. Instead they are controlled by a drop down box accessed by right clicking on the image. Simply playing an AVI can be accomplished by left clicking on it. The drop down box has controls for PLAY, PAUSE, REWIND, FORWARD, FRAME BACK, and FRAME FORWARD and works much like the controls on a VCR. Once the AVI has played through to the end it is ready to start again. No rewinding is necessary.

If you need to link sound with your animations, AVIs are one way to go. Also, if you are working in a corporate environment you might have access to professional tools that easily convert video footage you would want on the Web to AVI files. However, once again, you need to take great care with file sizes. People with big pipes might just love your nifty AVIs but the rest of the world will put you on their *never hit list* if your site is AVI laden.

A good rule of thumb is to give an option for going to an AVI page for those with the pipes to handle it and stay away from AVIs in your general use pages.

• • • • • • • • • • •
Hidden Links

Another interesting thing you can do with Web pages is to include hidden links. Hidden links are clickable links that don't show up on your page. The only way to find them is to run the mouse over them and note the change of the cursor type.

This type of link should only be used for nonessential information as many users will never find them. They are better for giving users bonus information such as tricks and hints for gameplay. One large game company on the Web has used hidden links to parcel out hidden cheat codes in their game just this way.

Older browsers would allow multiple body statements in one document so it was possible to change the color assigned to a single link to match that of the text then change it back for the rest of the links. This is not possible with newer browsers. Instead this trick must now be accomplished with graphics.

The simplest way to do this is to create a link from an unlikely looking graphic. A graphic bar used to divide a page is a good candidate for this trick as is any graphic which appears to be simply window dressing. This method is still a bit more obvious than some.

The HTML script displayed in Figure 10.3 will hide a link in a construction graphic. Again, you will have to download the graphic from our support site if you want this to work with the example written.

```
<HTML>
<HEAD><TITLE>EXAMPLE</TITLE>
</HEAD>
<BODY BGCOLOR="#000000" TEXT="#FFFFFF" LINK="#FFFF00" VLINK="#FFFF00"
ALINK="#FFFF00">
</HEAD>
<BR><BR><BR><BR><BR><BR>
<CENTER>
This is an example of a hidden link graphic. The caution bar below has been
linked to a file called supprise.html. The Border tag has been set to 0 so the
fact that it is a link is hidden.
<BR><BR><BR>
<A HREF="supprise.html">
<IMG HEIGHT=11 WIDTH=560 BORDER=0 SRC="caution.gif">
</A>
<BR><BR><BR>
An image like this is particularly good for a hidden link. Many people use an
image similar to this while the page is being worked on so it does not look like
it would be a link.
```

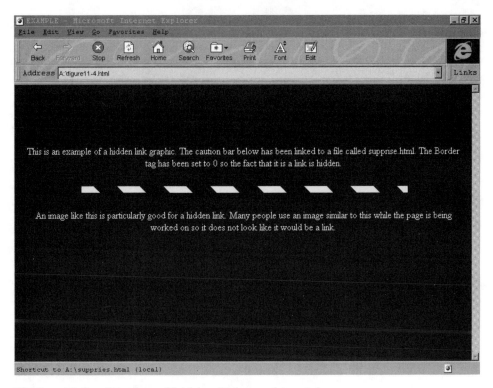

Figure 10.3 Display of hidden link graphic trick.

```
</CENTER>
</BODY>
</HTML>
```

If a truly hidden link is required, the best way to pull it off is to create an invisible graphic. There are two ways to do this. One way is to create an image one pixel in size and the same color as the text. This image may then be placed into the HTML document and used to replace a period. A second way to hide a link is to create a slightly larger image, about 10 pixels square, the same color as the background of the page. This image may then be placed anywhere outside of the text of the page and made a link. It will be invisible to anyone who does not pass a mouse over the image.

Remember to set the image border to 0 so there will be no border around your graphic to give the trick away.

The HTML script shown in Figure 10.4 will produce links hidden in the "periods" of the text.

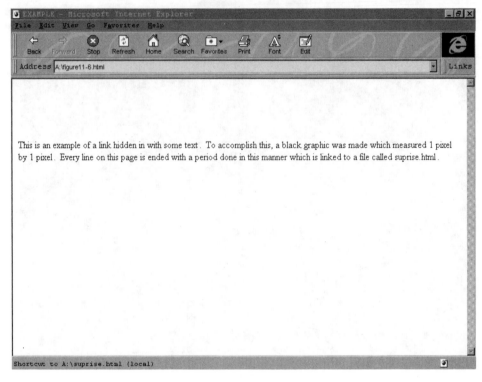

Figure 10.4　Link period in action.

```
<HTML>
<HEAD><TITLE>EXAMPLE</TITLE>
</HEAD>
<BODY BGCOLOR="#FFFFFF" LINK="#0000FF" VLINK="#0000FF" ALINK="#0000FF">
<BR><BR><BR><BR><BR><BR>
This is an example of a link hidden in with some text
<A HREF="suprise.html">
<IMG HEIGHT=1 WIDTH=1 BORDER=0 SRC="onepixel.jpg">
</A>
To accomplish this, a black graphic was made which measured 1 pixel by 1 pixel
<A HREF="suprise.html">
<IMG HEIGHT=1 WIDTH=1 BORDER=0 SRC="onepixel.jpg">
</A>
Every line on this page is ended with a period done in this manner which is
linked to a file called suprise.html
<A HREF="suprise.html">
<IMG HEIGHT=1 WIDTH=1 BORDER=0 SRC="onepixel.jpg">
</A>
</BODY>
</HTML>
```

A Word about Tables

When tables were first introduced into the HTML standard they began to appear like weeds, sprouting up on many sites. They are a very handy way of presenting data such as information from spreadsheets and the like. While the basic functionality of tables is obvious, they have a second and perhaps more important use. Tables are the best way to precisely place information on a page.

Basic HTML code allows for little deviation in the layout of a page. Text is limited to either left justification or centering; graphics have the additional option of being right justified. Of course graphics and text can be placed anywhere horizontally provided they are placed after another object. While this is all well and good for most applications, it doesn't cover all circumstances. Advertising is a major example. Many advertisers wish to duplicate their magazine campaigns on the Web. Another problem is that many companies have their ads designed in-house or by companies that are not familiar with Web design. This can be a major headache for a Websmith. Before tables came into use many layouts were nearly impossible to duplicate. Spacing had to be accomplished by using images that were the same color as the background of the page. Although this technique worked, it worked in only one screen resolution. If the page was designed to be viewed by users with their resolution set to 800×600, another user running 640×480 would see a badly distorted page. For this reason, many ads had to be redesigned.

Tables provide the flexibility to easily position items where they are needed. For example, if a client wanted a series of images positioned on the left and center of the page and a column of text running down the right side, tables would be the only reasonable way to accomplish this. Tables use cells much like a standard spreadsheet program. Each cell can be set to span multiple columns, rows, or both. This gives a designer a lot of flexibility in layout.

We aren't going to go into all of the ins and outs of creating and using tables here. However, you should pay particular attention to the use of tables to help you get the exact layout you desire when you are designing your pages or learning about HTML.

To see the importance of learning as much as you can about tables (and never fear, as for everything else in the text we don't actually cover but talk about, there are tutorials on the subject on our Web support site for you to

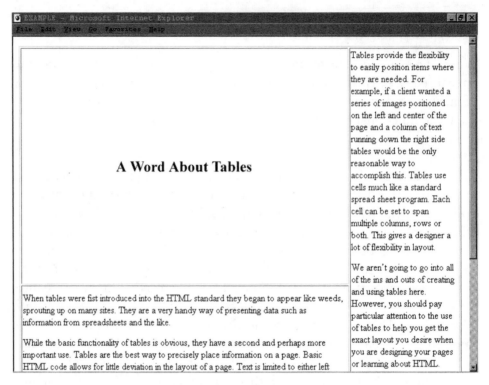

Figure 10.5 An example of using tables for exact positioning.

further study), look at Figure 10.5 to see an example of the layout options you can get from table use.

JavaScript and ActiveX Components

Probably one of the most annoying and enduring problems in teaching people about Java is making sure that they understand that Java and JavaScript have nothing at all in common except names that sound alike. For marketing purposes, Netscape named its advanced scripting language JavaScript to ride the publicity wave on Sun's coattails, but, unfortunately, created a nightmare of nomenclature confusion.

JavaScript has nothing in common with Java. JavaScript is a scripting language that runs on Netscape Navigator browser and allows Web tricks such as getting access to some of the high-end functions of the underlying environment—Windows buttons, for example—into your HTML code. That is not to say that JavaScript isn't useful. First, it is really quick to learn. Second, it is handy for fast stuff such as cool buttons and easy input frames. But it isn't Java so don't get the two confused.

And while we are on the topic of things kind of like Java, we naturally come to ActiveX. In order to compete with the Netscape/Sun/Oracle trio trying to lock MS into an Internet also ran, Microsoft has pulled out some of its old tech, dusted it off, given it a new name, and declared it an open standard.

The technology in question is the Object Linking and Embedding (OLE) technology that Microsoft developed for Windows apps to trade live data. Revamped for the Net, the product was rechristened ActiveX, presumably because it sounds worlds hipper than OLE.

To be fair, ActiveX *is* pretty cool. It allows live data from a wide variety of sources to be served seamlessly though the Net. Wrapping your preexisting code in ActiveX standard calls and support means that you can serve your programs across the Web just like Java, only they aren't Java. They can be C++ or anything else that can wrap itself to MS standard calls.

Most people tend to view ActiveX and Java as an either/or decision. This isn't the case. If you want to get some ActiveX trick that isn't currently in Java, you can wrap Java in ActiveX just as you could any other language. It doesn't go the other way, however. If you are learning Java right now and are worried that somehow ActiveX is going to make Java go away, take heart: Your Java skills won't die if ActiveX mysteriously ends up being perceived as burying Java (a pretty unlikely proposition right now, no matter what a few misguided pundits might think).

At the time of this writing, ActiveX has a few serious drawbacks for Web development. First is that it does its magic tricks by hooking into the Windows Component Object Model (COM). Using the COM is fine for the majority of the world on Wintel boxes. But the UNIX and Mac surfers won't get to see your pretty creations if you are relying on ActiveX wrappers to get your data out. Around 20 percent of your market just went poof. There are plans in the works to create Mac and UNIX extenders for the package, but as of this writing nothing has been shown to the public but a bunch of press releases. And given Microsoft's fame at slipping schedules, there might be three zeros on the end of the year before we actually see these implementations.

What We Have Learned

First, while Java is the point of this book, we still need to take into account that most of our Java work is going to be presented on Web pages. And while HTML isn't exactly meant to be a sexy scripting language, there are still a few cool things you can do within the confines of normal HTML that will add a little zest to your pages.

Animated GIFs

While Java is good for dealing with animation, for simple animations you gain load speed by using simple animated GIF files. There are packages for all the major platforms that allow you to produce these animations. As a side note, your Java applets running in browsers can also make use of animated GIFs.

Sound

Sound files can be linked directly into your page, again without the need for Java programming as an intermediary. Adding sound to your Web page can help set the tone for your page the same way that it helps with the veracity of your games.

AVIs

AVI files are also directly supported by the two major browsers on the market. While most people might not have much use to run movies off of their pages, some PR types could find a real use for this kind of serving. However, AVIs are bandwidth monsters and if you are going to use them you should give your users plenty of warning and only load these huge hits of data upon request from the user.

Hidden Links

Hidden links are a cool little way to get information to your users. There are a few ways to hide a link: You can embed it in a graphic, make it look like a period, or just hide it as a GIF image the exact same color as your background. When users drift over these hidden links you can give them hints or tidbits of data that you think they are going to be interested in.

Tables

Tables are an often overlooked tool for precisely positioning information on your page. HTML is not particularly strong at putting things where you want them, but with tables you can more precisely align information on the page. The biggest use of this on the Web is probably in making Web layouts match print advertising. If you are working for a big company and get caught with the nasty task of putting some of the corporate PR on the Web, you will find tables an invaluable ally to help satisfy PR.

JavaScript and ActiveX

JavaScript is a cheap attempt to steal the marketing thunder of Java and has nothing in common with Java except for the name. JavaScript is a midlevel scripting language (Perl it ain't) allowing your HTML pages to do a bit more to interact with their environment. JavaScript is a cinch to learn and if a large part of your life is creating pages, you might find it to be a valuable tool to add to your arsenal.

ActiveX, on the other hand, is a wrapper and extension technology allowing almost any type of programming content, such as Java applets, to be served over the Web. ActiveX boasts some decent advantages, the most notable of which is that it can be wrapped around almost any programming language base for people who don't have the time or inclination to learn Java. However, although some see it as competing with Java, the fact is that Java can be wrapped in ActiveX as well (in order to steal this functionality set).

At this particular time, unfortunately, ActiveX suffers from a couple of drawbacks, the most notable of which is that it currently excludes a sizable chunk of the wired public due to platform restrictions. However, in the future expect ActiveX to be ported to all the major surfing platforms.

● ● ● ● ● ● ● ● ●
From Here

Hey, from here it's go to it. Pat yourself on the back: You have learned Java and the fundamentals (and some things that aren't so fundamental) of designing and executing games in Java. While there will always be more to learn, you should know enough at this point to execute Web games free of the common beginner mistakes you see constantly on the Web.

I hope you found what you needed in the material here and on the Web support site and that you have had as much fun reading this book as we have had writing it. Good luck on your efforts.

INDEX